HOW SHOULD I READ THESE?
NATIVE WOMEN WRITERS IN CANADA

One of the few books on contemporary Native writing in Canada, Helen Hoy's absorbing and provocative work raises and addresses questions around 'difference' and the locations of cultural insider and outsider in relation to texts by contemporary Native women prose writers in Canada. Drawing on postcolonial, feminist, poststructuralist, and First Nations theory, it explores the problems involved in reading and teaching a variety of works by Native women writers from the perspective of a cultural outsider. In each chapter, Hoy examines a particular author and text in order to address some of the basic theoretical questions of reader location, cultural difference, and cultural appropriation, finally concluding that these Native authors have refused to be confined by identity categories such as 'women' or 'Native' and have themselves provided a critical voice guiding how their texts might be read and taught.

Hoy has written a thoughtful and original work, combining theoretical and textual analysis with insightful and witty personal and pedagogical narratives, as well as poetic and critical epigraphs – the latter of which function as counterpoint to the scholarly argument. The analysis is self-reflective, making issues of difference and power ongoing subjects of investigation that interact with the literary texts themselves and render the readings more clearly local, partial, and accountable. This highly imaginative volume will appeal to Canadianists, feminists, and the growing number of scholars in the field of Native studies.

HELEN HOY is an associate professor at the School of Literatures and Performance Studies in English, University of Guelph.

11064545443

How Should I Read These?

Native Women Writers in Canada

HELEN HOY

UNIVERSITY OF TORONTO PRESS
Toronto Buffalo London

© University of Toronto Press Incorporated 2001
Toronto Buffalo London

Printed in Canada

ISBN 0-8020-3519-1 (cloth)
ISBN 0-8020-8401-X (paper)

Printed on acid-free paper

Canadian Cataloguing in Publication Data

Hoy, Helen, 1949–
How should I read these? : native women writers in Canada

Includes bibliographical references and index.
ISBN 0-8020-3519-1 (bound)   ISBN 0-8020-8401-X (pbk.)

1. Canadian prose literature (English) – Indian authors – History and
criticism.*   2. Canadian Prose literature (English) – Women authors –
History and criticism.*   3. Native peoples in literature.*   4. Canadian prose
literature (English) – 20th century – History and criticism.   I. Title.

PS8089.5.I6H69 2001   C818'.54089'9287   C00-932880-7
PR9188.2.I5H69 2001

University of Toronto Press acknowledges the financial assistance
to its publishing program of the Canada Council for the Arts and the
Ontario Arts Council.

This book has been published with the help of a grant from the Humanities
and Social Sciences Federation of Canada, using funds provided by the Social
Sciences and Humanities Research Council of Canada.

University of Toronto Press acknowledges the financial support for its
publishing activities of the Government of Canada through the
Book Publishing Industry Development Program (BPIDP).

For Thomas, Christian, Benjamin, and Elizabeth,
essential parts of the story

Contents

Acknowledgments

For support of this research, I would like to acknowledge the University of Minnesota Faculty Summer Research Fellowship, the University of Minnesota Graduate School Grant-in-Aid, and the McKnight Summer Fellowship; the American Association of Learned Societies Fellowship; the University of Guelph Research Grant; research assistants Barbara Hodne, Don Moore, Anna Booth, and Tim Pettipiece; Minneapolis–St Paul writing group, Maria Damon, Pamela Fletcher, Valerie Miner, Martha Roth, and Susan Welch; Charlie Sugnet, Erik Peterson, Carol Miller, Greg Staats, Donna Palmateer Pennee, Dorothy Hadfield, Margaret Allen, Frances Mundy, Thomas King; and my graduate and undergraduate students with whom so much of this work occurred.

Portions of this book have been previously published as follows: (with Barbara Hodne) *World Literature Written in English* 32.1 (Spring 1992); *Canadian Literature* 136 (Spring 1993); *Ariel* 25.1 (Jan. 1994); *Essays on Canadian Writing* 60 (Winter 1996); and *Resources for Feminist Research* 25.3/4 (Winter 1997).

Excerpt from 'Distances' reprinted from *The Business of Fancydancing* © 1992 by Sherman Alexie, by permission of Hanging Loose Press. Excerpts from 'Because I Was in New York City Once and Have since Become an Expert,' 'Song,' 'On the Amtrak from Boston to New York City,' and 'All I Wanted to Do Was Dance' reprinted from *First Indian on the Moon* © 1993 by Sherman Alexie, by permission of Hanging Loose Press. Excerpts from 'How to Write the Great American Indian Novel' reprinted from *The Summer of Black Widows* © 1996 by Sherman Alexie, by permission of Hanging Loose Press. Excerpts from 'Red Blues' and 'Introduction to Native American Literature' reprinted from *Old Shirts and New Skins* © 1993 by Sherman Alexie, by permission of Sherman

Alexie. Excerpts from 'Visions,' 'Indian Woman,' and 'World Renewal Song' reprinted from *Breath Tracks* © 1991 by Jeannette Armstrong, by permission of Theytus Books. Excerpts from 'Tricks with Mirrors' reprinted from *Selected Poems 1966–1984* © 1990 by Margaret Atwood, by permission of Oxford University Press Canada. Excerpt from 'How to Make Good Baked Salmon from the River' reprinted from *The Droning Shaman: Poems* © 1988 by Nora Marks Dauenhauer, by permission of Nora Marks Dauenhauer. Excerpts from 'Helen Betty Osborne' and 'Circle the Wagons' reprinted from *A Really Good Brown Girl* © 1996 by Marilyn Dumont, by permission of Brick Books. Excerpt reprinted from *Tracks* by Louise Erdrich, © 1988 by Louise Erdrich, reprinted by permission of Henry Holt & Co., LLC. Excerpts reprinted from *Medicine River* © 1989 and *Green Grass, Running Water* © 1993 by Thomas King, by permission of the author and HarperCollins Canada. Excerpt from '*Ka-Nata*' reprinted from *Bent Box* © 2000 by Lee Maracle, by permission of Lee Maracle. Excerpt from 'For the White Person Who Wants to Know How to Be My Friend' reprinted from *Movement in Black: The Collected Poetry of Pat Parker, 1961–1978* © 1978 by Pat Parker, by permission of Firebrand Books. Excerpts from 'The Bridge Poem' reprinted from *The Black Back-Ups* © 1993 by Kate Rushin, by permission of the author and Firebrand Books. Excerpts from 'On Cultural Expropriation' reprinted from *Poems Selected and New* © 1998 by Heather Spears, by permission of the author and Wolsak and Wynn Publishers.

HOW SHOULD I READ THESE?
NATIVE WOMEN WRITERS IN CANADA

Introduction

The over-riding fear is that cultural, ethnic, and racial differences will be continually commodified and offered up as new dishes to enhance the white palate – that the Other will be eaten, consumed, and forgotten.

(hooks, Black 39)

In 'Queen of the North,' a short story by Haisla-Heiltsuk writer Eden Robinson, Adelaine, a disaffected Haisla teenager, has to contend with the familiarities of a white powwow spectator, hungry for sexual and cultural stimulation. Eyeing her bare legs and arms, subjecting her to a sequence of increasingly personal questions, Arnold slaps down one twenty-dollar bill after another to enforce his desire for bannock, after the booth where Adelaine is volunteering has closed down:

> I handed him the plate and bowed. I expected him to leave then, but he bowed back and said, 'thank you.'
> 'No,' I said. 'Thank you. The money's going to a good cause. It'll – '
> 'How should I eat these?' he interrupted me.
> With your mouth, asshole. (E. Robinson, *Traplines* 208)

Misreading Adelaine's sardonic bow as a traditional formality (and interrupting her attempt to communicate about the Helping Hands Society), Arnold extends his cultural 'sensitivity' to the protocol for eating fry bread.

Although Adelaine's polite spoken response – 'Put some syrup on them' – restores to the realm of the familiar the fry bread that Arnold posits as foreign, her immediate silent riposte is more eloquent. 'With your mouth, asshole' identifies and even more forcefully repudiates Arnold's act of cultural Othering. Adelaine dismisses his effort to make a basic foodstuff esoteric, to place it beyond the pale (so to speak) of recognizable human activity. Simultaneously the scene identifies and repudiates a predilection by members of the dominant group for *cultural* novelty. Decontextualized, commodifiable tokens of difference take the place of shared involvement in processes of social and political change (here fund raising for the Helping Hands Society) and the more pertinent, political cross-cultural communication that this might entail.[1]

Arnold wants to know how to eat fry bread, in proper Indian fashion. He apparently wants to consume Adelaine as well, to fill some undefined need that will show itself more longingly later, when he asks her to let down her hair:

'... Put some syrup on them, or jam, or honey. Anything you want.'
  'Anything?' he said, staring deep into my eyes.
  Oh, barf. 'Whatever.' (208)

The encounter illustrates well how gender inflects race and race inflects gender in the construction and consumption of difference. The particular blend of aggression, cultural curiosity, and yearning that Arnold brings to his preoccupation with Adelaine reflects her position neither simply as Native nor as woman – nor even as each, in turn – but, quite specifically, as Native woman.

Arnold wants to be the one asking the questions:

'Are you Indian then?'
  ... 'Haisla. And you?'
He blinked. 'Is that a tribe?' (207)

What he does not want is to replace this one-sided acquisition and ingestion with a reciprocal exchange that might challenge racial (and sexual) difference as a source of Othering.[2]

––––––––

A message of racial inferiority is now more likely to be coded in the language of culture than biology. (Razack 19)

'What do you do for poison oak?' a student once asked in a large auditorium where Mabel was being interviewed as a native healer. 'Calamine lotion,' Mabel answered. (Sarris 17)

———•——

The episode, discussed above, from Robinson's short-story collection *Traplines* explores creatively a subject that is increasingly a concern of literary-critical theory. Postcolonial theory – perhaps more properly termed 'decolonial theory' – has challenged the reduction of minoritized peoples to the function of 'self-consolidating Other' for the dominant culture (Spivak, 'Three' 273). It has interrogated their restriction, from a hegemonic perspective, to bounded cultures narrower and more visible than the culture allotted to the majority. At a conference for the Association of Canadian College and University Teachers of English in Montreal in 1995, Plains Cree-Métis scholar Emma LaRocque condemned the propensity of non-Natives to employ notions of tradition and cultural difference to explain everything Indian, from birch biting to biography. As an instance of this fascination with cultural difference, she gave the example of the chaplain who asked, 'How do you people die?' To this, she suggested, in a sentiment that anticipates Adelaine's, the obvious answer was, 'We stop breathing' (LaRocque, 'Place').

'How do *you people* die?'
    'We stop breathing, asshole.'

Although potentially part of a radical politics, respect for social specificity and challenges to ethnocentrism can produce, ironically, 'a kind of difference that doesn't make a difference of any kind' (Hall 23). Or, worse, they can introduce new forms of domination. As Eden Robinson illustrates, ostentatious cultural deference ('How should I eat these?') can coexist unabashedly with a superior sense of entitlement to the cultural productions of a people and even to the people themselves. Sherene Razack warns that 'the cultural differences approach reinforces an important epistemological cornerstone of imperialism: the colonized possess a series of knowable characteristics and can be studied, known, and managed accordingly by the colonizers whose own complicity remains masked' (*Looking* 10). Like the power relations it reflects, difference functions asymmetrically.[3]

For Native writers, the 'knowable characteristics' expected to inform their writing have changed somewhat in recent days but still exert disturbing force. Cree-Métis poet Marilyn Dumont describes the pressure on contemporary Native writers: 'If you are old, you are supposed to write legends, that is, stories that were passed down to you from your elders. If you are young, you are expected to relate stories about foster homes, street life and loss of culture and if you are in the middle, you are supposed to write about alcoholism or residential school. And somehow throughout this, you are to infuse everything you write with symbols of the native world view, that is: the circle, mother earth, the number four or the trickster figure.'

What if you are an urban Indian, like herself, she asks ('Popular' 47). Even in the absence of specific expectations or stereotypes, the marked status of minority groups, by contrast with the unmarked status of the normative group, ties identity and authority, for the Native writer, to one overriding signifier.[4]

Whenever she addresses an audience, Muscogee (Creek) poet Joy Harjo observes that she is asked more about Native culture than about writing ('In Love' 58). Lee Maracle, Salish-Métis writer and activist, similarly protests that her Indigenousness, her location quite specifically as 'Native writer,' 'Native woman,' not as 'writer' or 'woman,' is the restrictive grounds of her authority for white readers or white feminists (Sojourner's 60, I Am 20–1).[5] Emma LaRocque echoes Maracle's concern, pointing out that the ghettoizing of disparate writings under the category 'Native' limits public access to relevant material: 'For example, an analysis of the Canadian school system by a Native author is rarely placed under "education" or "sociology" or "social issues"' ('Preface' xviii). Harjo seems to experience the identification as inappropriately broad – requiring her to illuminate entire peoples rather than her area of expertise, her own writing; Maracle and LaRocque as inappropriately narrow – requiring them to restrict their insights only to their own race. All three, however, object to being perceived primarily, and disproportionately, in terms of their race. Referring specifically to the tokenizing of 'Third World women' on panels, at meetings, and in special issues of journals, Trinh T. Minh-ha comments, 'It is as if everywhere we go, we become Someone's private zoo' (Woman 82).

Where do you begin telling someone their world is not the only one? (Maracle, Ravensong 72)

The act of enforcing racelessness in literary discourse is itself a racial act. (Morrison 46)

I hesitated, none the less, to open this book with the *Traplines* episode because the discussion might be read as arguing pluralistically for a common humanity leading to a shared perspective and understanding. 'Why can't we all just get along?' – with its potential obliviousness to the inequitable access to resources and authority that engenders division – is emphatically not my argument. (Of course, as an aspiration, 'Why can't we all just get along?' has very different political implications coming from a Black man brutalized by white Los Angeles police officers and witnessing the interracial violence of disadvantaged groups turning against each other than from a person like me, privileged by race and class.) While resisting being turned into 'otherness machine[s]' (Suleri, *Meatless* 105), writers and theorists of colour have been equally adamant in resisting universalizing gestures that ignore difference and absorb disparate historical and material realities into dominant paradigms. 'Because you sleep / does not mean you see into my dreams,' writes Spokane-Coeur d'Alene poet and novelist Sherman Alexie, in his poem 'Introduction to Native American Literature' (*Old* 4).

Understanding Indians is not an esoteric art ... Anyone and everyone who knows an Indian or who is *interested*, immediately and thoroughly understands them.

You can verify this great truth at your next party. Mention Indians and you will find a person who saw some in a gas station in Utah, or who attended the Gallup ceremonial celebration, or whose Uncle Jim hired one to cut logs in Oregon or whose church had a missionary come to speak last Sunday on the plight of the Indians and the mission of the church. (V. Deloria 5)

Necessarily, we must dismiss those tendencies that encourage the consoling play of recognitions. (Foucault, 'Nietzsche' 153)

Race and gender (among other identity classifications) may well be inventions, constructed categories that signal the deviation of marked races and gender(s) from the norm, but their effects are tangible, producing distinctive racialized and gendered subject positions. The appropriation-of-voice debate in Canada – which flourished in the late 1980s and early 1990s, with Native people challenging non-Native creative writers particularly to stop 'stealing our stories' – invoked this question of difference. Although it pivoted also on questions of Native copyright, racist structures of publication and reception, and arrogation of profits, the challenge insisted on perspectives and knowledges located in the particularities of Native histories, cultural and political experiences, and story-telling traditions. 'There are a lot of non-Indian people out there speaking on our behalf or pretending to speak on our behalf and I resent that very much,' says Okanagan writer and teacher Jeannette Armstrong. 'I don't feel that any non-Indian person could represent our point of view adequately' ('Writing' 56). The focus of the appropriation-of-voice debate has been on the non-Native creative writer who employs a first-person Native perspective or retells stories from the oral tradition. (Lee Maracle, in fact, argues that the incursion should properly be called 'appropriation of story' on the grounds that voice cannot be commandeered ['Coming' 83].) In either case, the writer is seen as both displacing the Native author and subject and presuming – and, in the process, producing – knowledge of realities at some remove from his or her own.

A broader argument is also underway in antiracist and feminist theoretical circles over the 'epistemic privilege' of the socially marginalized, the superior knowledge of their own situation (and, by some accounts, that of the oppressor) available to group insiders. (For differing conclusions on such knowledge claims, see, for example, Uma Narayan, 'Working,' and Bat-Ami Bar On.)[6] The epistemological status of such claims is under dispute, especially in a poststructuralist framework sceptical about transcendent truths and about reality as an unmediated source of verification. Still, members of marginalized groups are pressing to be recognized as socially differentiated subjects whose understandings are distinctive, not simply interchangeable with those of other groups or instantly accessible to outsiders. Addressing non-Native feminist educators and students, Osennontion (Marlyn Kane, Mohawk) is determined to convey the message 'that *we are absolutely different!*,' stressing the necessity for readers to 'twist their minds a little bit (or a lot) to try to get into the same frame of mind as us' (7). In the context of white cultural rapacity, one of Sherman Alexie's fictional characters in *Indian Killer*, John Smith (himself an instance of the theft of Native children for white adoption), in conversation with an Indian wannabe, mounts a grimly ironic defence of at least a minimal entitlement:

'What is it?' Wilson asked. 'What do you want from me?'

'Please,' John whispered. 'Let me, let us have our own pain.' (Alexie, *Indian* 411)

In Canada, and North America more generally, the First Nations face a particular, historically grounded insistence by descendants of European settlers on obliterating difference and claiming connection. Margery Fee points out that a Euro-Canadian desire to naturalize the seizure of Native land and a Romantic hunger for 'community, nature, and a personal sense of the numinous' (represented, in the white imagination, by Native people) have prompted 'an identification and a usurpation' in relation to Indigenous people ('Romantic' 25, 15).[7] (To Fee's two motives, I would add the urgent white-Canadian self-image of non-racist tolerance – often cited in contradistinction to U.S.-American iniquity – with First Nations as the critical Canadian test case.)[8] Fee focuses her discussion of this spurious 'white "literary land claim"' on the creation of Native characters in literature and on suspect literary representations of a 'totem transfer' from Native to newcomer, legitimizing the newcomer's claim to place and nostalgic reconnection ('Romantic' 17, 21). But similar needs can drive the *reader* or critic of literature from cultures and histories other than her own. Too-easy identification by the non-Native reader, ignorance of historical or cultural allusion, obliviousness to the presence or properties of Native genres, and the application of irrelevant aesthetic standards are all means of domesticating difference, assimilating Native narratives into the mainstream. Along the way, they are a means of neutralizing the oppositional potential of that difference.

On a larger scale, the very attentiveness of postcolonial theory to the diversity of world cultures and decolonizing struggles can ironically produce, in Ann duCille's words, a colonizing 'master narrative that contains all difference' ('Postcolonialism' 33). The various stories become a single story, retold by sympathetic Western critics. Similarly, the postmodern crisis of meaning, destabilizing of the subject, and hermeneutics of suspicion (with their own local history and function) risk being universalized, as Kumkum Sangari cautions, to quite other texts and cultures. '[A] Eurocentric perspective ... is brought to bear upon "Third World" cultural products,' Sangari argues; 'a "specialized" skepticism is carried everywhere as cultural paraphernalia and epistemological apparatus, as a way of seeing; and the postmodern problematic becomes the frame through which the cultural products of the rest of the world are seen' (183). My own parenthetical qualification two paragraphs above – 'especially in a poststructuralist framework sceptical about transcendent truths' – is an instance of this automatic application of postmodern interpretive assumptions. The difference that is ostensibly the focus of investigation, this expression of political agency, vanishes in the face of Elizabeth Spelman's 'boomerang perception': 'I look at you and come right back to myself' (*Inessential* 12).

In the summer of 1996, my partner – Cherokee-Greek novelist Thomas King – and I were interviewed by CBC Television for an ambitious cross-country documentary or meditation on the nature of Canada. 'Sense of Country,' hosted by Rex Murphy and broadcast on 3 and 4 September 1996, was visually spectacular (facets of a Newfoundland lighthouse reflector blazing kaleidoscopically) – and socially and politically conservative. The search was for a singular, over-arching Canadian identity; the visuals, however stunning, were predominantly rural and romantic; the tone was uplifting. To the best of my recollection, the only people of colour interviewed, apart from Tom, were an Asian-Canadian couple (possibly), members of an Ontario Black women's gospel choir,[9] and members of the Blood tribe in Alberta.

At one point in the interview, trying to challenge ideas of a fixed, given content for Canadianness, of a Canadian character, I proposed that Canada be thought of as a conversation. Shortly thereafter, the interview shifted away from me temporarily, and I began self-consciously rehearsing what I had already said and worrying at the interview questions. Tom was elaborating one of his observations about Canada when he turned unexpectedly to me: 'You know. What's the word I'm looking for ...?'

With the camera whirring and everyone's attention refocused in my direction, I had to disrupt his argument by confessing sheepishly, 'I'm sorry, I wasn't listening.'

The irony of that juxtaposition didn't make the final cut for the television program, but it might well have provided a salutary corrective to some of its rosier narratives of the nation.

'Canada is a conversation.'
    'I'm sorry, I wasn't listening.'

Or, perhaps, transposed to the context of national rather than individual communications: 'I'm sorry, but thanks to my spot in the social hierarchies, I don't need to listen.'

Can you ever have a valid completion of a work by an audience that is a stranger to the traditions that underpin the work? (Philip 32)

The question 'How should I eat these?' or, in the case of Native literature, 'How should I read these?' can involve, then, for the outsider reader, unfortunate occasions either for absolute, irreducible distance or for presumptuous familiarity. And, of course, reifying difference and erasing it are far from mutually exclusive approaches. Himani Bannerji points this out when she describes white bourgeois feminists as failing to 'position themselves with regard to non-white women – whom they rendered invisible by both ascribing difference *and* by practically and theoretically neglecting that very difference' (*Thinking* 21; emphasis added). These simultaneous wrongs are what Pat Parker has in mind in her poem 'For the White Person Who Wants to Know How to Be My Friend': 'The first thing you do is to forget that i'm Black. / Second, you must never forget that i'm Black' (68).

Difference from whose point of view is, of course, the question. I have framed this introduction to *How Should I Read These? Native Women's Writing in Canada* with a discussion of the dangers of fixating on or ignoring difference, because those are factors in my own responses, as a white woman, to the texts I will be discussing here. Though not, I suspect, entirely absent from consideration, difference would presumably play a much more minor role in the responses of a Blood woman analysing Beverly Hungry Wolf's *Ways of My Grandmothers* or an Okanagan woman reading Jeannette Armstrong's *Slash*. But my intention is not so much to explicate the texts here, to provide normative readings, or to imagine how a cultural insider might read them. Instead, this book sets out to explore the problematics of reading and teaching a variety of prose works by Native women writers in Canada from one particular perspective, my own, that of a specific cultural outsider. As the title suggests, the book proffers a question, or series of questions, rather than an answer. I am less interested in resolving the question of the title than in rehearsing some of its attendant challenges and discoveries. And I am interested in locating those challenges and discoveries in the particularities of my reading and teaching experience, as potentially symptomatic of readings from similar subject locations.

Recently, Tom phoned me long distance from California. Partway through our conversation, the phone line made several weird, clicking noises and its tone became distinctly more hollow sounding.

'Hello!?'

'Hello-o!?' I could hear him, but he apparently could not hear me. He could hear me, but I apparently could not hear him.

'Hello? Can you hear me?'

'Hello? Are you still there?'

'Hello? Can you hear me?'

'I'm here. Hello!?'

Eventually we managed to re-establish conversation with each other. The connection had never been broken. Each of us had heard every word of our two blank monologues.

[W]hat does it mean when primarily white men and women are producing the discourse around Otherness? (hooks, *Yearning* 53)

'We read all this American Indian literature, the folklore and everything, and I don't know what I'm reading. I don't know anything about the Indians. I was hoping to know something after today. Like where to start.'

'You just said it,' Anita said. 'You don't know anything. That's where to start ...'

The woman wrung her hands. 'But then how can we know about Indians or this film? I wanted to learn something.'

... 'Listen,' Anita said looking back to the woman, 'do you know who you are? Why are you interested? Ask yourself that.' (Sarris 74)

At the launch of Cree poet Louise Halfe's *Bear Bones and Feathers* in Toronto in 1994, I found myself in animated conversation with a Native woman from British Columbia, both of us buoyed up by the reading and the celebratory atmosphere. The conversation eventually turned to what I was working on. When I mentioned this book, her face instantly became studiously neutral. Guarded. As mine would, too, if a white woman announced a similar project.

White writers ... must understand how their privilege *as white people*, writing *about* another culture, rather than *out of* it virtually guarantees that their work will, in a racist society, be received more readily than the work of writers coming from that very culture. (Philip, *Frontiers* 284)

Most of the writers discussed in this book have indicated, either in interviews or in the texts themselves, that their primary audience is Native, an exception being Eden Robinson, for her first publication at least. (*The Book of Jessica*, being a collaborative endeavour, may have a slightly different audience than Maria Campbell's other writing.) In *I Am Woman*, Lee Maracle begins by declaring that she does not intend to write for the European in Canada, that intimate conversation with her own people is overdue.[10] Within that very paragraph, though, the third-person pronouns applied to a white readership begin to slide into direct address ('you just don't concern me now'). This slipperiness Maracle tackles directly later in the book: 'It sickens my spirit to have to address your madness, but you stand in front of my people, and to speak to each other, we must first rid ourselves of you' (*I Am* 11, 111).

In the past decade, in particular, the establishment of Native-run presses such as Theytus Books (Penticton), Seventh Generation Books (Toronto), Pemmican Publications (Winnipeg);[11] Native theatre companies such as Native Earth Performing Arts (Toronto),[12] De-Ba-Jeh-Mu-Jig (Wikwemikong), and the Centre for Indigenous Theatre (Toronto); Native-run journals and magazines such as *Akwesasne Notes*, *Gatherings*, *Sweetgrass*, and *Aboriginal Voices*; The Committee to Re-Establish the Trickster (Toronto); Canadian Native Arts Foundation (Toronto); and the En'owkin International School of Writing (Penticton)[13] have all reflected the desire of First Nations people in Canada to control the contexts in which they speak with each other. In the area of literary analysis, recent publications such as *Looking at the Words of Our People: First Nations Analysis of Literature*, edited by Jeannette Armstrong, *Iskwewak – Kah' Ki Yaw Ni Wahkomakanak: Neither Indian Princesses Nor Easy Squaws*, by Janice Acoose/Misko-Kìsikàwihkwè, and the forthcoming *IndigeCrit: Aboriginal Perspectives on Aboriginal Literature and Art*, edited by Greg Young-Ing (Cree) insist on Native perspectives regarding their literature and their representation.

At the same time, Native writing, editing, publishing, performing, reviewing, teaching, and reading necessarily take place, at least partially, in contexts shaped and controlled by the discursive and institutional power of the dominant white culture in Canada. Editorial boards, granting agencies, publishing companies, awards committees, reviewers, audiences and purchasers, university and school curricula, and scholarly theorizing and analysis (of which this book is one instance) assess merit, distribute resources, enact policies of inclusion and exclusion, and produce meanings based on norms extrinsic to, even inimical to Native values and interests. Such effects are neither accidental nor simply idiosyncratic. Himani Bannerji stresses the necessity of recognizing that 'a whole social organization is needed to create each unique experience, and what constitutes someone's power is precisely another's powerlessness' (*Thinking* 74).

So what's a white girl like me doing in a place like this?

My metaphor of Canada as a conversation, for CBC's television documentary, like most figurations of Canada that have gone before – part of a wrongheaded quest for a national mythos – missed the mark. Quite apart from ignoring the problematics of language, both for conversation and for Canada's national narratives, the metaphor of conversation ignores issues of power and access. Whose conversation? Whose favourite topics predominate? Who keeps being interrupted? Whose contributions are heard only when paraphrased by someone else? Who is too strident, beside the point, political, incomprehensible? Who is even permitted to be in the room? Who is bringing the coffee? (And to go back to the question of language, is the conversation in one language? Whose? If not, is simultaneous translation possible, and is it power-neutral?) Does the conversation have any effect, and who implements which conclusions? And, finally, for whom is conversation itself a luxury? I had fallen into what Chandra Mohanty dubs the 'discourse of civility' (201), a pluralist celebration of diversity that reduces structural inequities to personal relationships.[14]

The problem, so tendentiously constructed as 'Why can't whites teach *about* racism?' after all should be phrased as 'Why aren't non-white people teaching at all in the university about racism or anything else?' (Bannerji, *Thinking* 116)

Too often, it seems, the point is to promote the *appearance* of difference within intellectual discourse, a 'celebration' that fails to ask who is sponsoring the party and who is extending the invitations. (hooks, *Yearning* 54)

The current academic fashionableness of issues of race, what Susan Friedman (playing on Barbara Christian's 'race for theory') has called 'the race for race' (4), has changed little in terms of the racial composition of university faculties and administration. Ann duCille has noted the historical amnesia around the contributions of Black women scholars and the professional profit derived in the academy by men and white women, but not Black women, from the upsurge of interest in Black women writers. '[B]lack culture is more easily intellectualized (and colonized),' she concludes, 'when transferred from the danger of lived black experience to the safety of white metaphor, when you can have that "signifying black difference" without the difference of significant blackness' ('Occult' 600). Her observation applies equally to the First Nations presence in the Canadian academy, where Native people are more welcomed as objects of study than as subjects of study.

The number of Native faculty in literature departments in Canada can be counted on one hand. Janice Acoose (Nehiowè-Métis-Ninahkawè) recounts her undergraduate experience of a course in western-Canadian literature at the University of Saskatchewan that described the transformation of the prairies from 'no man's land to everyman's land' and that included no First Nations writers (30). Patricia Monture-Angus (Kanien'kehaka or Mohawk), inquiring about a similar course, was informed that there was no First Nations literary work good enough for a Canadian literature course ('Native' 21). Despite the appearance of entire courses on Native literature, ethnocentric courses like the ones confronting Acoose and Monture-Angus continue to exist. But the inclusion of Native work in syllabi and curricula does not necessarily make the academy more hospitable either to Native students and faculty or to Native ways of seeing.

In her own academic work, Emma LaRocque has discovered that her first-hand knowledge of Native life, which at second hand would constitute field work and evidence, is in her own voice devalued as subjective and hence suspect ('Colonization' 12–13). I have observed, and doubtless contributed to, the frustration of First Nations graduate students whose isolation is compounded by the poor fit between prevailing paradigms of literary studies – meaning as endlessly deferred, identities as provisional and strategic, even the invitation to self-disclosure and self-reflexivity – and their own ways of knowing.[15] ('Poor fit' is somewhat euphemistic; in the hierarchies of graduate school, one can readily speculate which epistemology is expected to yield.) As Carole Leclair reports of her graduate experience, 'I was a long distance away from expecting respect and being able to communicate naturally about my Métis values. Eventually, I learned to speak like a middle-class educated academic, but my writing, my thought processes, still reflect the deep ambivalence that living in two (often incompatible) cultural frameworks can produce' (124). I know of one Métis graduate student in literature, finally able to meet another at a national conference, who asked urgently for reassurance that in time she wouldn't cry every day. A more seasoned student shrewdly envisioned her own wary relationship to those Euro-American academic theories potentially useful to her own work as a kind of raiding expedition, during which she stole some good horses and made her escape.

She wants to be the only guest allowed
in the longhouse, and then to refuse the honour
or not to be allowed
because no guest is allowed.
She wants to obliterate herself
loudly.   (Spears, 'On Cultural Expropriation,' *Poems* 89–90)[16]

it will not save you
or talk you down from the ledge
of a personal building
                    (Alexie, 'Introduction to Native American Literature,' *Old* 3)

Given the imperviousness of the academy to Native presences and paradigms, then, the position of the non-Native scholar studying Native literature – my position – becomes a fraught and suspect one. The position is replete with opportunities for romanticizing, cultural ignorance, colonization – and, ironically, simultaneous professional advancement. Although discussions in white feminist, anthropological, and literary academic spheres have become more self-reflexive and self-examining over the past two decades, that development can produce more sophisticated and insidious versions of the same old offences.

Susan Friedman has examined the scripts about race and ethnicity, 'narratives of denial, accusation, and confession' and of 'relational positionality' (the alternative she endorses) that have recently circulated among white feminists and feminists of colour (7). One form of denial Sherene Razack and Mary Lou Fellows have named 'the race to innocence,' the attempt, by emphasizing one's positions of subordination and not of privilege (as a woman, say), to disclaim responsibility for subordinating others. As they observe, such a denial obscures the necessity, as part of ending one's own marginalization, to end all systems of oppression (Razack 14).

Responses to the accusations of racism by women of colour, responses going beyond denial, can take many forms. As an instance of Friedman's third narrative, of confession, Ann duCille alludes sardoni-

cally to 'I-once-was-blind-but-now-I-see' exposés, by white feminist
critics, of our own former racism/sexism *vis-à-vis* texts by women of
colour ('Occult' 610). Elizabeth Spelman elucidates the limitations of
such enactments of guilt: 'guilt is not an emotion that makes us attend
well to the situation of those whose treatment at our hands we feel
guilty about. We're too anxious trying to keep our moral slate clean'
(*Fruits* 109). Indeed, as Maria Lugones elaborates, white theorists have
seemed to focus on the wrong problem, worrying more intensely about
how race- and class-specific generalizations about 'all women' might
damage feminist theory than about how such distorted conclusions
might harm women of colour or working-class women ('Logic' 41). In
largely white feminist classrooms, too, I have seen the determination to
'get it right,' as a form of personal enlightenment about racism, take
precedence over the determination to take action against oppressive
hierarchies and the unequal distribution of power.

The 'retreat response' is one alternative to stances either of unexamined
authority or static self-recrimination. Deciding not to attempt to speak
beyond one's own experience, Linda Alcoff argues, can be a self-indul-
gent evasion of political effort *or* a principled effort at non-imperialist
engagement (although, in the latter case, with seriously restricted scope)
('Problem' 17). Chapter two in this book uses Maria Campbell and
Linda Griffiths's *The Book of Jessica* to examine this alternative in greater
detail. A related stance is the 'embarrassed privilege' accorded the
'postcolonial Woman,' an ostentatious deference which awards iconic,
metaphoric status to the woman of colour as the representative of 'the
good' (Suleri, 'Woman' 758) and simultaneously avoids engagement
with the particularities of her argument. Sky Lee discusses such a
moment at the 1988 Vancouver 'Telling It' Conference, in which no one
challenged a woman of colour on her apparently homophobic remarks,
for fear of demonstrating cultural insensitivity (183–4). In the classroom, Chandra Mohanty suggests, this can produce 'a comfortable set
of oppositions: people of color as the central voices and the bearers of
all knowledge in class, and white people as "observers," with no responsibility to contribute and/or with nothing valuable to contribute'
(194).

What this simple divide misses, Mohanty suggests, is the necessary
acknowledgment of 'co-implication,' awareness of asymmetrical but
mutually constitutive histories, relationships, and responsibilities (194).
Friedman's advocacy of 'scripts of relational positionality' seems to
build on Mohanty's idea of co-implication. Such scripts dismiss the

absolutes of the white/other binary, conceptualize identities as multiply, fluidly, and relationally defined, and recognize that power can flow in more than one direction within multiple systems of domination and stratification. So, a stance of relational positionality allows for coalition work attentive to the complexities of 'shifting positions of privilege and exclusion' (Friedman 40). Denial, accusation, confession, and retreat are not the only alternatives. In practical terms Uma Narayan, noting that one can be at once insider and outsider in relation to different groups and that analogizing from one position to the other may increase one's conscientiousness, proposes 'methodological humility' and 'methodological caution' as strategies for the outsider. Methodological – or epistemological – humility and caution recognize presumed limitations to the outsider's understanding and the importance of not undermining the insider's perspective, in the process of communicating and learning across difference (Narayan, 'Working' 38).

The objective here is not to have complete knowledge of the text or the self as reader, not to obtain or tell the complete story of one or the other or both, but to establish and report as clearly as possible that dialogue where the particular reader or groups of readers inform and are informed by the text(s). (Sarris 131)

From a position of race privilege, I feel a responsibility to combat structures of power and entitlement. Teaching or writing about texts by Native writers, from my position of privilege, may not do that politically efficacious work; my academic activity is seriously implicated in the very systems of stratification and dominance it critiques.[17] What *How Should I Read These?* does undertake is to keep to the forefront the assumptions, needs, and ignorance that I bring to my readings, the culture-specific positioning from which I engage with the writing. The book makes questions of location – the issues of difference and power rehearsed in this introduction – ongoing subjects of investigation, in interplay with the literary texts themselves.

Self-reflexivity and self-questioning can certainly be forms of luxury and self-indulgence. Those of us with power can afford to dispense with some of its more obvious trappings. My hope, though, is that, by making explicit various sources of my responses, I render the readings more clearly local, partial, and accountable, relinquishing the authority that clings to detached pronouncements. *How Should I Read These?*

locates in my own history inside and outside the classroom both the challenges and the new perspectives that the writings by these First Nations women can produce. What I incorporate into the textual analysis are pedagogical and personal *moments*, not a comprehensive narrative. I suspect that these moments, from classroom discussion and my own story, though not representative (no culture is monolithic, and I am multiply located), may be symptomatic, clues to Euro-Canadian cultural tendencies that bear on the reception of First Nations literatures. Though a narrative of my reception might seem to risk displacing the Native text and the Native author, readings (however detached or unattributed) are always just that, readings, meetings between text and reader. As Greg Sarris (Miwok-Pomo) says about his knowledge of Mabel, a Pomo woman who helped raise him, 'I cannot construct Mabel's world independent of my experience of it ... What I can do is reconstruct my relationship to her world, at least to the extent I understand it at this time' (30).

How do you protest a socially imposed categorization, except by organizing around the category? (Epstein 19)

I'm permanently troubled by identity categories, consider them to be invariable stumbling-blocks, and understand them, even promote them, as sites of necessary trouble. (Butler, 'Imitation' 14)

How Should I Read These? Native Women Writers in Canada. As a formulation of my project, the subtitle itself identifies several fertile sites of trouble: 'Native,' 'Women,' 'Writers,' and 'Canada,' for a start.

'Native.' 'Indian' is a much contested term, often dismissed by Native people as a European misnomer and one that conflates the distinctive cultures of the hundreds of tribes occupying North America at the time of the conquest.[18] *We Get Our Living like Milk from the Land*, edited by Jeannette Armstrong and others, calls the word 'Indian' a 'generic racist term,' which 'implies that "Indians" are one large group without separate rights as Nations or Tribes and therefore are all subject to one policy' (33).[19] 'First Nations' and 'Native,' though currently preferred for their affirmation of Aboriginal sovereignty or indigeneity, perform the same homogenization. (Métis[20] and Inuit people have their own distinct historical and cultural identities, and political organizations, within the larger Native rubric; I will be including writers from the former but not the latter group within this book.) Many Native people insist on a tribal designation only.[21]

My scrupulousness about identifying the specific tribal affiliations of each First Nations writer or critic cited, though, only exacerbates the familiar divide between marked and unmarked racial groups, singling out the Native authors in the process of heeding the specificities of their locations.[22] Temporarily, I was much taken with a plan to identify parenthetically the ethnic/racial identities of all critics and theorists whom I cite. The plan foundered on its belatedness but even more on the absence in the public record of the necessary particulars. Consider, for example, Sherene Razack (Indo-Caribbean-Canadian), Trinh Minh-ha (*Surname Viet, Given Name Nam*), Stuart Hall (Black Caribbean-British), Ann duCille (African-American), Himani Bannerji (South Asian-Canadian), with all the attendant inadequacies of such identifications. But what about Judith Butler, Jane Flax, Margery Fee, Heather Spears, Steven Epstein ...?[23] For all its theoretical allure, race within the academy continues to signify more for some writers than for others. Certainly, a proliferation of 'Caucasian American' designations throughout the book (drawing on Beverly Slapin's *Basic Skills Caucasian Americans Workbook*) would have gratifyingly highlighted the reductiveness and presumption of categories such as 'Native' – and even, perhaps, such as 'Anishinaabe' or 'Métis.'

On a more general level, the very decision to organize a book around the racial identity of the writers raises the question of what Marlene Nourbese Philip, in her objection to the segregating of racial-minority writers into separate, less prestigious events at a writers' congress, has termed 'cultural apartheid' (150). Claire Harris calls it 'marginalization by literary category: Immigrant Literature/Writing by Women of Colour/Feminist Writing/Political Literature/Post Colonial Literature/New Literature in English' (28). The risks are very real: of creating simple Native/non-Native binaries, of using race as explanatory, of reducing these texts to cultural documentation. Much of the discussion about reifying and ignoring difference earlier in this introduction amplifies the tension around this category.

'Native' produces stock responses, increasingly for those at a greater distance from Native life.[24] It has been the site of ongoing disputation, both within and outside Native communities, about how Native identity is to be defined and about who is and is not included under its rubric. It is, Louis Owens (Choctaw-Cherokee) asserts, 'a deeply contested space, where authenticity [which Owens earlier glosses as the capacity to be seen at all] must somehow be forged out of resistance to the "authentic" representation' (*Mixedblood* 13). Yet it remains a site that for most Native people must not be abandoned. The goal of *How Should I Read These?* is not to consolidate meaning under the sign of 'Native' but rather to explore and question such consolidations.

'Women.' As Kate Shanley (Assiniboine) points out, feminist mobilization around the category 'woman' has not always coincided with the priorities of Native women, for whom national/tribal sovereignty can be more pressing than gender politics (214–15).[25] For minoritized groups, internal struggles around gender must often coincide with group solidarity in the face of shared external threats.[26] Several of the writers examined in this book identify themselves in feminist terms, notably Jeannette Armstrong ('What' 8) and Lee Maracle (*I Am* 15–22; 'Infinite' 169), but others do not. Historically, gender has functioned quite differently for different First Nations tribes, not all of whom, like the Ongwehónwe (or Iroquois),[27] exemplify the prototypical matriarchal, matrilineal model valued by early second-wave white feminists. European patriarchal structures, moreover, are pervasive in Native lives in Canada. They are embodied, for example, in the *Indian Act* of 1876 (and the preceding 1869 *Gradual Enfranchisement Act*), which until 1985 denied Indian status to Indian women who 'married out' (that is, married men without Indian status), while bestowing status on the non-Indian wives of Indian men.[28]

Native women in Canada *have* organized around the legacy of enforced residential schooling, around violence within their communities and families, around band council reserve-housing practices,[29] around living conditions on reserves, around changes to subsection 12 (1) (b) of the *Indian Act* (on married women's status), and around protection for Native women's rights in the recent constitutional accords.[30] In so doing they have had to negotiate multiple allegiances. Women such as Jeannette Corbiere Lavell (Ojibwa) and Yvonne Bedard (Iroquois) who challenged the *Indian Act*'s marrying-out provisions in court in the 1970s (in Bedard's case taking action against her own band) faced the opposition of their own communities, which feared, among other things, resource implications and the precedent of amending the Act.[31] Bill C-31,[32] which revised the *Indian Act* in 1985, restoring the rights of women who had married out (and those of their children), involved, less happily, yet another external, governmental interference in tribal affairs and new struggles over bands' autonomy to define their own memberships.[33] Because of limited tribal resources and fear about the cultural effects of long-term absences, women on reserves have sometimes felt their interests pitted against those of reinstated Native women. In 1992, the Native Women's Association of Canada opposed the Charlottetown Accord's proposed changes to the Canadian Constitution, as potentially exempting Native self-government from the Charter of Rights and Freedoms and so depriving Native women of Charter protection.[34] The association found itself publicly at odds with the Assembly of First Nations, a national voice of Native people, acting for *Indian Act* chiefs (predominantly male)[35] and represented at times by its female Cree lawyer, which endorsed the constitutional changes for their recognition of the inherent Native right to self-government.[36]

At the same time, like 'Native' or 'Indian,' 'woman' is a space of contestation over meaning: 'As feminism has learned all too often, what it means to be a "woman" is hardly self-evident, and who is or is not included in the class of "women" is a matter of deeply divided debate' (Elam 22). White feminist and conservative women's groups alike have often implicitly excluded Native women (among others) in their formulations of 'women's' experiences and lives. (Feminism is often the target of such criticism, here and elsewhere, because of the incompatibility of such ethnocentrism with its liberatory ideals. Conservative women's organizations such as REAL Women, though, with their middle-class model of the nuclear family and male-supported household, are at least as culpable of substituting a very narrowly based female reality for the plurality of women's needs and interests.) Kate Shanley argues that Native women are fighting to preserve forms of extended tribal and family organization different from the patriarchal nuclear family that second-wave feminists have critiqued (and, I would add, that white conservative women have defended) (214).[37] As Norma Alarcón suggests, then, 'women' can be defined in opposition to other women, and not only through the familiar gender binary, that is, in opposition to 'men' (360).

More fundamentally, the very existence of gender as an ontological category is in dispute. Poststructuralist feminist readings, especially, identify 'woman' as a fiction and female identity as a strategy.[38] Such fundamental questioning is not always apparent in Native discourse. Native women, 'reversing a pattern of exclusion' (to borrow a phrase from the Royal Commission on Aboriginal Peoples [*Report* 4: 21]) and fighting cultural erasure, threats to human and environmental health, and high levels of community violence, often have recourse to historic matrifocal definitions of women's roles and responsibility. 'Woman has had a traditional role as Centre, maintaining the fire – the fire which is at the centre of our beliefs. She is the Keeper of the Culture,' says Skonaganleh:rá (Sylvia Maracle [Mohawk]), for example (Osennontion and Skonaganleh:rá 12). References to woman as giver, as teacher and transmitter of culture, and as community voice and tribal leader are common. Kim Anderson (Cree-Métis) notes that Native cultural teachings about the differing obligations of women and men make a genderless identity less possible for herself (32). *Affirmations* of women's distinctive role, different from that of men's and with its own power, can function, within Native women's circles, as re/visionary, simultaneously radical and traditional, just as *challenges* to gender roles function within some white feminist contexts. As with 'Native,' 'woman' may continue to serve as necessary ground for Native women, though subject always to an essential problematizing of the uses to which it is put and the effects of its deployment.[39] *How Should I Read These?*, particularly through the texts of Jeannette Armstrong, Beverly Hungry Wolf, Lee Maracle, and Eden Robinson, explores a diversity of significations that refuse to coalesce around a singular understanding of 'woman.'

Within certain male-dominated definitions of 'Native' (see, for example, the opening of Section 12 (1) (b) of the *Indian Act*: 'An Indian is a man who ...') and white-dominated definitions of 'woman,' difference – as female and as Native, respectively – functions to destabilize the categories. Because feminist theory, on the one hand, and decolonial and antiracist theory, on the other, share concerns about reified identities and structures of power – patriarchal and colonial respectively – I have found that they can usefully be brought into dialogue with each other around the narratives of Native women writers. I am mindful, none the less, of Sara Suleri's caution about the dangers of 'the coalition between postcolonial and feminist theories, in which each term serves to reify the potential pietism of the other' and in which each term is used to signify heroic embattlement, without an obligation to historical or cultural specificity ('Woman' 759).

'Writers.' Given the long-standing Native tradition of orature, literature within a print culture obviously represents only one aspect of Native oraliture. Though published texts are the focus of *How Should I Read These?* and are the forms privileged within mainstream Western literary culture, these need to be understood as only one part of that larger Native orature/literature continuum and as deriving meaning from within that tradition. (Complicating this and drawing on the example of the Mayan pictoglyphic codices used in precontact schools, Craig Womack [Muskogee Creek-Cherokee] argues that, in Native history, '[t]he idea ... of books as a valid means of passing on vital cultural information is an ancient one ...' [16].)

Emma LaRocque has criticized the narrow scholarly focus on the same three or four Native women writers in Canada ('Colonization' 16–17). This reflects, within the privileging of print culture, a further privileging of canonical literary genres, and in particular the novel.[40] The authors selected here include novelists, and probably the writers LaRocque had in mind. (Prose texts – fiction and non-fiction – are the specific focus of this study.) They also, though, illustrate a range of prose forms, from the incorporation of oral narratives, traditional and recent, in Beverly Hungry Wolf's *The Ways of My Grandmothers*; to the oratory (story in the service of theory) of Jeannette Armstrong's *Slash* and Lee Maracle's *Ravensong*; to the dialogue and collage of Maria Campbell and Linda Griffiths's *The Book of Jessica*; to the apparently mainstream short-story form of Eden Robinson's *Traplines*.

'Canada': '[T]he forty-ninth parallel is a figment of someone else's imagination,' writes Thomas King, about the significance of North American national boundaries from a Native perspective (Introduction, *Native* 10). Even non-Native regulations such as the 1794 British–U.S. Jay's Treaty – granting ready passage for Native people and their goods across the border and invoked today especially by the St. Regis Mohawks – recognize the arbitrariness of the Canada–U.S. border in the histories and lives of tribes organized geographically and politically quite otherwise. Some authors examined here, such as Lee Maracle, explicitly reject identity as Canadian, asserting a prior and incompatible national allegiance ('Native'). Others, such as Beatrice Culleton, use the claim to Canadianness strategically, to confound attributions of inferior status ('Images' 50).[41] Still others, such as Maria Campbell, wield the national designation ironically, as further evidence of ongoing colonization: 'Then I guess I'm a Canadian, because that's who the conqueror happens to be today' (Campbell and Griffiths 98).

'Native-Canadian,' with its suggestion of a hyphenated identity, has not acquired the currency in Canada that its corresponding term 'Native-American' enjoys in the United States. My subtitle originally read 'Canadian Native Women Writers,' reflecting the more common Canadian usage, but even that phrasing seemed to presume too much about some writers' connection, rather than resistance, to the settler nation. The particularities of Canadian legal, legislative, and social history since the European conquest do produce some common ground for the Nations and authors about whom I write.[42] Métis identity, for instance, has a history with political and juridical implications exclusive to Canada. At the same time, a focus exclusively on writers from Canada does have some arbitrariness about it, and I include, therefore, references to and examples from Native-American novelists and poets, as well as, of course, Native-American theorists.

The work constantly reflects back on itself, and everything written in the book can be said to be equally critical of my own activities as writer and thinker. It is important to remember that if one goes directly to an object, if one tries to seize it, one would always somehow lose it ... (Trinh, 'Undone' 3)

The argument in *How Should I Read These?* is neither categorical nor linear. Each chapter pairs a particular author and text with a theoretical issue or problematics around the reading and teaching of Native women's writing. But the overall argument is cumulative, dialogic, interrogative. It is not fully located in any one passage, but works by accretion. Neither individual chapters nor the reasoning of particular sections of chapters can stand as conclusive. [43] Indeed I was sometimes able to argue with conviction a specific reading of an author (Beatrice Culleton, say, or Eden Robinson) only because I knew that I would be going on within the chapter to disrupt the assumptions sustaining that reading.[44] In other cases, a lingering sense of a complication, an unaccounted-for objection, necessitated further qualifications and reformulations.[45] For this reason, perhaps, chapters get longer and endnotes more numerous as the book progresses.

Rather than proposing conclusions, I am tracing a process, rehearsing areas of contention, proffering analysis that is then often itself challenged, modified, or displaced, and ending with partial and provisional answers that invite further challenge. Figuratively, I see the book's structure as a series of switchbacks on a mountain trail, from which it is possible to view the same tree, the same outcropping, not only first from below and then from above, but also from opposing directions. And so, in a sense, the book offers the opportunity to meet myself again, hiking on in the opposite direction, a little higher up, a little lower down.

The highlighted quotations in my text, too, do not all function in the same way. Sometimes they bolster, sometimes they oppose my argument. Sometimes they echo, sometimes they qualify, and sometimes they contradict each other. I am staging arguments with myself, between myself and others, and among the theorists, critics, and creative authors I am reading. Classroom encounters with the texts and the pedagogical and interpretive quandaries they produce participate in the same larger exchange. And there are gaps, gaps that let the unarticulated, multiple connections between components of the book – the quotations, the critical/theoretical analysis, the personal and pedagogical narratives – speak, gaps that invite the reader also into the creation of an argument.

Because I am tracing an evolution, the evolution over time of my encounters as a cultural outsider with Native women's writing, the cumulative discovery of textual, theoretical, and practical pleasures and complications, I deliberately retain the marks of that process. The writing of this book spans almost ten years. I have not erased from the chapters evidence, such as the changing ages of my son and daughter over the course of the book, of temporal (and, by implication, theoretical) discontinuities. Similarly, although conceptualized as parts of an ongoing project, most chapters began as papers at scholarly conferences. I identify their original dates and contexts, so as to preserve the traces of the material, institutional, and intellectual conditions of their production. I incorporate, too, the traces of the dialogues opened up by audience responses to those preliminary conference drafts.

With the exception of the first chapter (whose original publication as an interleaved collaborative piece necessitated reworking for inclusion here), each chapter continues to represent chronologically the stages of my understanding, with further reflections or complexities incorporated into subsequent chapters rather than provoking extensive, retroactive revisions. (Only parts of some previously published chapters have seen print; two-thirds of this book is unpublished material.) As the book develops, self-disclosure and self-reflexivity become more prominent. I begin to discover the impossibility of maintaining the impersonality of the scholarly voice while doing this work, the necessity to make increasingly visible my own implication in the readings that I advance.

How Should I Read These? studies seven contemporary Native women writers in Canada – specifically, prose writers Jeannette Armstrong (Okanagan), Maria Campbell (Métis-Cree), Ruby Slipperjack (Ojibway),[46]

Beatrice Culleton (Métis), Beverly Hungry Wolf (Blood), Lee Maracle (Salish-Métis), and Eden Robinson (Haisla-Heiltsuk). The book begins, in its first two chapters, through *Slash* and *The Book of Jessica*, to address some of the basic theoretical questions of reader location, cultural difference, and cultural appropriation likely to assail, in particular, non-Native readers first approaching Native texts. As I continue, that larger context gives way to analysis of the very specific ways in which cultural and social positioning intervenes in my responses to individual texts. These subsequent chapters turn, too, to the particular contributions the texts make to understanding the cultural place of silence and voice, testimonial artlessness, self and community, gender and racial allegiances, and the constrictions of identity categories.

Considering Jeannette Armstrong first, I analyse the challenge posed by *Slash* (1985), her novel of the 1960s and 1970s Indian movement and one of the early contemporary Native novels in Canada. In *Slash*, Armstrong uses the anguish of an Okanagan youth, eventually involved with the American Indian Movement and with elders within his community, to survey activist, tribal, and personal alternatives to modern Native loss of direction. The novel invites a 'reading from the inside out' (Cliff 21), attention to its own intrinsic values and aesthetics, because, in terms of verisimilitude, individualized characterization, narrative plotting, and rhetorical aims, it does not readily correspond to Western fictional standards. Chapter one begins with students' discomfiture with, and simultaneously appreciation for, the novel. *Slash* itself, I go on to argue, through the repetitive centrality of the word 'hear,' the definition of hearing as an act beyond listening, and the sequence it creates of asking, listening, and hearing, provides a metafictional commentary on how it might be read. The chapter applies Armstrong's theorizing (and that of others) on the use and value of language, on individualism and social connection, and on literary reticence to aspects of *Slash* that pose difficulties to the aesthetics of a Westernized readership. It confronts white feminist disquiet over the focus on a male protagonist, situating that decision in Armstrong's understanding of female responsibility. And it goes on to reflect on the pedagogical benefits and risks of focusing on the cultural embeddedness and 'difference' of this text.

Taking off from the anxieties surrounding the teaching of *Slash*, I use *The Book of Jessica* (1989) as the occasion for an investigation of issues of cultural appropriation. This collaborative non-fiction by Métis-Cree writer Maria Campbell and Scottish-Canadian actress/playwright Linda

Griffiths dissects the tensions of their earlier collaboration on a script of Campbell's life, an effort that produced the play *Jessica*. The promises and especially the pitfalls of Campbell and Griffiths's cross-cultural endeavour provoke reflection on the implications for a parallel, though less direct, cross-cultural interaction, the teaching and criticism of Native texts by non-Native scholars. A disturbing text particularly in terms of Griffiths's apparent domination of the editorial process, *The Book of Jessica* both analyses and reproduces colonial problems of access, cultural conflict, and imbalances of power, while simultaneously insisting on the urgency of communication across difference. Chapter two advances three possible readings of the text, as textual appropriation (becoming Linda Griffiths's text in its metaphors, its material conditions of production, its proportions), as postcolonial deposition (a deliberate heightening of colonialist practices so as to critique them), and as textual resistance (reflecting in substance and format Maria Campbell's ethos of collaborative self-disclosure). In so doing, the chapter signals possibilities and dangers for the outsider scholar more generally. It plays, too, with the contradictory declarations (particularly by critics of colour) on the necessity for and/or impossibility of cross-cultural knowledge.

Once the larger problematics of the entire project have been invoked and their exploration begun, I focus more, in chapters three through seven, on specific sites for potential cultural and discursive cross-purposes. Silence, for instance. Ruby Slipperjack's *Honour the Sun* (1987) sets down over six years the fictive diary entries of a young Ojibway girl growing into discoveries and difficulties in her isolated northern Ontario community. The laconic responses of Slipperjack's characters find a parallel in the discursive reticence of the novel itself, its withholding of interpretation. As a metafictional injunction, the novel's reiterated precept, 'Listen to the silence,' initially prompts me to seek evidence of resistance. I can read the narrative discontinuities that accelerate over the course of the novel as foregrounding cultural silences, creating a divide between insiders to Slipperjack's cultural community, for whom the gaps may not need decoding, and outsiders. But the silences may also signal an alternative metaphysics at odds with a Western critic's (and the novel's own) valuing of verbal communication. Narrative gaps may represent not only the mute eloquence of suppressed pain but also the self-sufficiency of achieved contemplation. *Honour the Sun* forces me to consider what happens when a text implicitly asks me to talk about it less and internalize it more. Simultaneously, chapter three examines the hazards of invoking ethnographic explanations and cultural givens (such as tribal proscriptions on anger) as shortcuts to understanding. It proposes an interpretive caution to match the novel's own narrative restraint.

Another site: authenticity. As supposedly autobiographical fiction, often mistakenly approached as a 'transparent' window on Métis experience, Beatrice Culleton's *In Search of April Raintree* (1983) necessitates in other ways a confrontation with questions of aesthetic standards and cultural hegemony. This first-person novel uses the divergent stories of the Métis narrator, April Raintree, and her darker-skinned sister, Cheryl, to trace intersecting trajectories of maturation and racial identification in a racist society. Early criticism of Culleton's book, valuing it for its simplicity, honesty, and artlessness, implicitly contrasts testimonial immediacy and artistic craft, allotting the former to marginalized peoples. Unseduced by the lure of authenticity, the text itself, I argue, instead takes for granted the multiplicity of selves and the mediating power of representations (amassing contradictory discourses, especially of Native reality). At the same time, in highlighting Culleton's nuanced depiction of reality, experience, and the self as located in discourse, I risk imposing a poststructuralist master narrative of indeterminacy on the text and obscuring its emotional and political power. Culleton's aesthetic seems to replace the distinctiveness, authorial self-expression, and linguistic originality of high (bourgeois) realism with pragmatic and communal values. Chapter four seeks methods of analysis that recognize the artistry and epistemological complexity of such a text.

With Beverly Hungry Wolf's *The Ways of My Grandmothers* (1980), the issue, for me, is subjectivity. This loose compendium of personal narratives, history, ethnographic information, myths, and practical instruction in household arts from the Blood (Blackfoot) community raises intriguing questions about 'autobiography' and about subjectivities constituted within rather than against communal experience and quotidian commonplaces. Given the Western (literary) tendency to link identity and distinctiveness, a narrative self apparently untroubled by the need to set itself apart offers provocative possibilities for thinking the self. Chapter five examines the temptation to tease a singular, unitary 'Beverly Hungry Wolf' out of the narrative, or, alternatively, to subsume the text under a pan-Indian collectivist ethos, neglecting its tribal specificity, its gender implications, and its particular historical moment. I have to situate *The Ways of My Grandmothers* as the outcome of a plethora of discourses, including Blood tribal tradition, second-wave feminism, nineteenth-century ethnography, the counter-culture of the 1960s and 1970s, contemporary Native activism, and Hungry Wolf's family narratives, to account for its continuities and discontinuities. Subjectivity in the book proves to be complicatedly various.

With Lee Maracle's *Ravensong* (1993), I attend to notions of nation and the exacting effort to balance the claims of various subject positions, as woman, tribal member, and global citizen. Affirmation of tribal or national sovereignty has been a strategy to resist colonization and yet may, for a Native or Third World woman, produce reductive and exclusionary allegiances. Through the story particularly of a young girl crossing between the two worlds, *Ravensong* examines a transitional moment in the life of a fictional west-coast Native village (situated across the river from an indifferent white town) in the 1950s. Maracle seems to reinscribe the divide between whites and Natives, subversively repositioning both white and Native reader, so that, within the framework of the novel at least, Native functions as the norm and white as the anomaly. I therefore examine the quite different effects for insider and outsider reader. But, through gender in particular, Maracle also multiplies the separate, even conflicting, claims of identities within the tribe, and constructs plural subjects whose multiple affiliations resist definition within any one imagined community. Rereading *Ravensong*, too, as 'story in the service of theory' (Maracle's definition of Native oratory) produces different expectations of characterization and plot, allowing me to appreciate better the textual integrity and theoretical power of the work and to get a sense for what Maracle means by the oratory that is central to her project.

The final chapter of the book explores the work of a new voice in Native women's writing in Canada, Eden Robinson's, examining what happens when such a writer seems to turn her attention away from specifically Native material. Robinson's focus is the angst of adolescence, sometimes male, sometimes urban, only occasionally coded explicitly as Indian. Looking at her collection of short fiction, *Traplines* (1996), I examine the violence of her stories as a possible allegory of the violence of Native history and experience, a history and experience that are at most implicit in the stories. Simultaneously, I consider the potential violence such an allegorical reading does to these texts, imposing upon them a racialized reading that they seem to have repudiated – and drawing upon a narrow repertoire of what 'Native' signifies. Is any attempt to recognize the salience of an author's Native background susceptible to Greg Sarris's charge that critics reductively try to 'nail down the Indian in order to nail down the text' (128)? Alternatively, I propose an expansive rather than a constrictive reading of *Traplines*, as the contestation of fixed, given notions of Native history and culture.

The concluding chapter examines how the authors studied here have refused either to be confined by or to abandon identity categories such as 'woman' or 'Native.' It explores, too, how they provide, within their texts, a critical voice guiding how their (and other) texts might be read.

1

'Reading from the Inside Out': Jeannette Armstrong's *Slash*

One way to safeguard that integrity [of the Native American story] is by asserting a critical voice that comes from within that tribal story itself.

(Blaeser 61)

The cultural, political, and social complexity of black people is consistently denied in those strands of feminist and multicultural theory that emphasize 'difference' and use it to mark social, cultural, and political differences as if they were unbridgeable human divisions ... Black texts have been used in the classroom to focus on the complexity of response in the (white) reader/student's construction of self in relation to a (black) perceived 'other' ...

(Carby, 'Multicultural' 12)

The novel *Slash* (1985), by Okanagan writer Jeannette Armstrong, was written to convey the spirit of the 1960s and 1970s Native movement to First Nations readers by tracing the emotional, political, and spiritual turmoil of a young Okanagan man, Tommy Kelasket or Slash.[1] In its assumptions and aesthetics (issues of verisimilitude, of individualized characterization, of narrative structure and plotting, of rhetorical aims and strategies), the novel seems to insist upon its own cultural tradition and to resist quite dramatically the imposition of extraneous literary and critical criteria. Not readily assimilable into a Western literary tradition, the book necessitates a confrontation for non-Native and feminist readers with questions of location and cultural hegemony. Even before we had begun our class discussion of the novel in my graduate–undergraduate Canadian-fiction seminar in winter 1991, for example, I was approached by a graduate student questioning my inclusion of such a 'thin' text after the richness of Margaret Atwood's

Surfacing. It was precisely this problematics that I chose to make the focus of discussion.

Though with considerable misgivings, I invoked the cautionary counter-example of Kay Hill in her misconceived 1963 foreword to *Glooscap and His Magic: Legends of the Wabanaki Indians*: 'Although generally moral in tone, the Legends contained a great deal of religious symbolism, meaningful only to the Indian, as well as some savage and erotic elements. They were inclined to wander down byways in the course of which the characters changed disconcertingly not only from good to evil, but from human to animal. Children today are accustomed to the Aristotelian concept of a unified story with a beginning, middle, and end. It therefore seemed necessary to tighten plots, develop characterization, and invent incidents to explain motivation' (8–9). From a pedagogical standpoint, the quotation is gratifyingly economical, overtly cited as a warning against cultural bias and ignorance, but succinct too in its evocation of an alternative aesthetics and alternative metaphysics central to *Slash*. The usefulness of this quotation in illuminating in reverse some features of a Native cosmology can be seen by a comparison with comments from Leslie Marmon Silko (Laguna Pueblo): 'Life on the high arid plateau became viable when the human beings were able to imagine themselves as sisters and brothers to the badger, antelope, clay, yucca, and sun' or 'The stories often contain disturbing or provocative material, but are nonetheless told in the presence of children and women' (683, 684). The Hill quotation is also pernicious, though, in its invitation – for instructor as much as for student – to posture as enlightened white reader in counterdistinction to benighted one, to enter upon the flourishing game of 'diversity oneupmanship.' (The preceding statement, incidentally, can be seen as a more advanced manoeuvre in the same game.)[2]

———•———

In the reading process genuine discovery is possible in the movement away from what is exotic (therefore delightful) and toward what is unintelligible (therefore frightening). (Vangen 122)

I didn't know a lot about really Indian things ... I had spent a lot of time convincing myself that we were the same as non-Indians in every way, except that we were oppressed and angry. Sometimes there were things, though, that would be said or that would happen that were not quite explainable. (Armstrong, *Slash* 180)

———•———

The novel itself, though, is sufficiently inaccessible for many Western readers as to make glib professions of cross-cultural sensitivity difficult. (Only one student in the three classes where I first taught the novel was a *passionate* defender of the book itself – as opposed to of its right to be heard; the class with the least initial resistance was also the least advanced, an illuminating concrete illustration of that much-theorized issue of the university's function in enforcing the master discourse.) I further attempted to make any smug and retrospectively facile repudiation of ethnocentrism self-reflexive, asking the more difficult question of how we were to read white-feminist discomfiture with Armstrong's creation of a male protagonist and with the apparent erasure of female presence in the book, most notably through the deaths of the two significant women characters, Mardi and Maeg.[3]

The alternative method I proposed for students, both in this regard and in regard to their aesthetic difficulties with the text, was 'the intrinsic approach' called for by Armstrong and Lee Maracle (Lutz, 'Native' 29), what Jamaican novelist and critic Michelle Cliff calls 'reading from the inside out.' As Cliff argues, 'Those pieces [of a work] which do not fit the latest exegesis, do not accommodate the jargon, still matter, no matter what' (21). Lest this be misread as a formalist, New Critical insistence on the autonomy of the text, I paired it with the challenging necessity to develop a critical subject position that, as Trinh T. Minh-ha puts it in *Woman, Native, Other*, speaks 'nearby or together with' rather than 'for and about' women of colour (101), and therefore relies extensively on what Native women themselves have said about their writing and experience.

One limitation of the book [Armstrong's children's book *Neekna and Chemai*] is the general blandness of the narrative: there are no really dramatic events. It would also have been effective to explore the friendship of the title characters a little more. Their personalities are not clearly differentiated. (Almon 83)

What I learned there was that there is a certain elite way of writing that is acceptable, and if you write within that framework you can be heard by the public at large. (Armstrong, 'Writing' 55)

We began, then, with students' initial reactions to the novel, sometimes sparked by a questionnaire, devised by a student presenter in the Canadian-fiction class and then modified for use in a graduate feminist literary-theory class, asking among other things whether the novel was well crafted and whether it delineated a meaningful cultural or political point of view. Individual students complained that the novel seemed aimless, slow-paced, artless, emotionally flat, and tract-like, the protagonist boring and implausible, the language generic; that there was too much jumping around and redundancy in the action; that they were 'infuriated by the elision of the good parts,' how the protagonist felt and what actually went on at the meetings; that characters were undifferentiated mouthpieces for position papers. Given the novel's ostensible goal of historical documentation, they were frustrated at the anonymity of the Anna Mae Aquashes, Leonard Pelletiers, and Nelson Small Legs, the missing dates and identifying details of particular marches, occupations, and negotiations. For a number, the novel 'bogged down' in the middle but picked up in section four, where there was more lyricism, individuality, and emotion.

But it was also the students, in class discussion and in their journals and essays, who welcomed the book's decentring power and, long before I mentioned the unfortunate preface to *Glooscap and His Magic*, questioned the limitations of Western literary standards. One student brought in sections of *The Sacred Hoop* by Paula Gunn Allen (Laguna Pueblo) on the absence of conflict, crisis, and resolution in Native narrative patterns, on repetition and circularity instead (54–66). Another suggested that, in the context of healing ceremonials and storytelling, substance was of greater significance than the clothing of the speaker. Someone asked whether we had lost the idea that literature could be good for us. The student presenter on *Slash* in the Canadian-fiction course, Barbara Hodne, introduced the ironically contrasting complaint, by a reviewer, of Louise Erdrich's *Love Medicine* for precisely the 'narrative complexity and beautifully rendered lyricism that kept pain at a distance' (Owens, 'Acts' 54). She also constructed as an invitation to the reader the passage in *Slash* where Danny fetches the protagonist during a visit from their grandfather Pra-cwa: 'Dad wants us to sit around and listen' (17). Another student, in her detailed questionnaire response, highlighted one of her sentences with capitals, circling, and asterisks: 'How can you listen if you don't know how to hear?' *Slash* itself, we discovered, through the increasing urgency of its use of the word 'hear,' its positing of hearing as an act beyond listening, and the trinity it creates of asking, listening, and hearing, provides a metafictional commentary on the challenge it offers its readers (238, 245, 246, 249).

In the spring of 1990, as I was heading down the hall towards a University of Lethbridge classroom, a disquieted dean waved me into his office to take a phone call from the Royal Canadian Mounted Police. The RCMP were trying to reach me to confirm the identity of a colleague and friend found dishevelled and incoherent on the nearby Blood reserve at Standoff. Although she had taught an off-campus course there the previous semester, I was at a loss to explain her presence at the reserve in the middle of an academic day. As I raced my car down the dusty reserve road to identify and intervene for my friend, trying to stay calm enough not to have an accident myself, my panic and bewilderment about her well-being expressed itself as indignation at the obtuseness of the police. My friend, whom I had expected to join for dinner that evening, was a model of self-possession. Obviously, she had come to some harm that the police had been incapable of recognizing. And while I acknowledged, even in my distress, the well-warranted bitterness and frustration that might drive men on the reserve, I was already angry at whatever violence I imagined they might have inflicted upon my friend. What I was doing, in a moment of fear under that bright prairie sunshine, was reverting to a racist reading of the reserve as a place of risk.

My assumptions about the reserve proved to be completely off the mark. Rather than experiencing danger there, my friend, at a moment of personal crisis, had sought it out as a place of refuge. To explain her arrival, she had in fact chosen words from Jeannette Armstrong's *Slash*, which she was then teaching, the same words Kelasket uses to announce his homecoming after incarceration: 'I've returned' (78). ('I wanted to tell him ... how much I hurt and how bad it had been in prison. Everything I felt seemed to seep into his hands and I knew I didn't need to say anything,' Kelasket continues, about the embrace with his father that follows [79].) In the solicitousness of the unknown women at the Standoff community centre, my friend found a similar kind of acceptance.

It was in this disturbing context, taking over (with other colleagues) the teaching of my friend's class, that I first taught *Slash*. What I find in the novel when I read it carries some of the emotional freight of that context. I am moved, not just intellectually stimulated, by how *Slash*, like the incident of my friend's crisis, forces me to confront my racism and cultural arrogance, teaches me to see and hear something other than what I have been taught to see and hear.

Turning to Native writers who might assist the hearing that Armstrong encourages, the class considered Lee Maracle's sense of Native characterization as based in a subjectivity different from Western individualism, her sense of an empowering as well as constraining obligation to the many grandmothers of the past and grandchildren of the future: 'we are each but one person in a long chain of people' (*I Am* 8). So in discussing Slash's discovery that 'being an Indian, I could never be a person only to myself. I was part of all the rest of the people ... What I was affected everyone around me, both then and far into the future' (202–3), we discussed the cultural implications of the symptomatic placement of the word 'just' in one student's earlier conclusion that Slash is 'not an individual, *just* a link in a chain of generations.'[4] Within a different ethos, being *just* an individual rather than a link in a generational sequence, I suggested, might register as the impoverished condition. In response to students' unhappiness with what many felt to be a lack of affectivity and a scanting of psychological realism in the novel, we had recourse to Armstrong's own aesthetic standards. After praising Atwood's work as not just pretty writing but truth, she adds, 'That to me is what literature is: using words well to convey the deep thinking that's hard to convey in words.' In the same interview, she also discusses political oratory as a wellspring for Native writing, oratory whose poetry 'comes from trying to put words to concepts that don't exist in English' ('Rights' 37).

Reading the novel from the inside out conveyed the same message about literary priorities. Exchanges between characters – 'Seems to me there's something more important I'm missing out on,' 'Slash, I like the way you think, but there are many things that aren't answered,' or 'I guess I'll have to examine my own thinking,' for example (84, 98, 224) – seemed to function more as rhetorical markers, signalling stages in the analytic process, than as realistic dialogue. The example a student raised about the implausible motivation for Slash's separation from his lover, Mardi – he can't hitch on to her and has obligations to the activist movement in Canada, he says, but in fact tags along with some others and engages only in a desultory checking out of the Toronto scene – provided another opportunity to consider the novel's commitment to 'deep thinking' about the history and dilemmas of the Native experience more than to localized verisimilitude. Perhaps narrative plausibility and psychological individuation, we speculated, took second place to thorough probing of the political and psychological alternatives facing Native people.[5]

Even the lyrical passages of, almost always, landscape description (which stand out dramatically by contrast with the 'flat,' unheightened prose of much of the book) seemed to fill a primarily metaphysical or conceptual (as opposed to painterly) function in illuminating Native cosmology. The metaphysical weight of landscape, part of Slash's alternative to angry activism, is explored, for instance, in Armstrong's discussion with Victoria Freeman about the 'real feeling of wholeness that this is me, this is my land, and my land is as much me as my skin is' ('Rights' 38). In fact, as Armstrong's title 'Land Speaking' suggests, for Okanagan people the language of the land articulates and produces the larger reality of which the person (and author) is a part: 'The land as language surrounds us completely ... Within that vast speaking, both externally and internally, we as human beings are an inextricable part – though a minute part – of the land language' ('Land' 178).

Of course, when the class turned to Armstrong's discussion of what language means to her, with words as sacred things whose source is the pool of all creation, notions of flat, generic language (mine as well as the students') confronted their cultural relativity.[6] Armstrong speaks of the damage the misuse of words has done and of her responsibility 'to strive for correctness in my presentation, correctness of purpose and accuracy in my use of words in my attempt to transcend the simple actuality of the things I have seen, to the image of those same things in the context of my entire history and the sacred body of knowledge that we, as a people, have acquired' ('Words' 29). With regard to Kelasket's Uncle Joe, Armstrong has insisted that it is mental power and ability as a medicine man, rather than height and facial features, that constitute the reality of the character ('Jeannette' 16). Her comment that she hadn't intended to write about actual individuals (whose stories they or those close to them could tell) and her research focus on the feelings and transformations of the period, the process of political and spiritual growth, suggest an interest in more general patterns than Western realism often pursues ('Jeannette' 17, 19–21). The reader's desire that literature convey 'the simple actuality of the things I have seen,' the desire for descriptive detail, historical specificity, and psychological realism, came to seem very culturally and generically specific.

Inevitably, at the students' request, we also turned to Native reviews of Slash. Lee Maracle responds to two common student concerns, the first in her defence of the 'sparse' and abbreviated romance of Slash and Mardi as 'beautifully typical' in its emotional reticence and subordination of personal desire to community and convictions. Acknowledging her own 'urbanized impatience' with the novel's pace, she also argues that, unlike European literature, which aims to captivate from beginning to end, but like oral stories, *Slash* provides crucial silences, allowing the hearer to reflect on the truth unfolding ('Fork' 42). With the review by Lenore Keeshig-Tobias (Anishinaabe), I alerted students to the ways the reviewer both affirms some of their reservations – 'this book is full of the meetingist bunch of Indians I have ever come across,' and 'Tom Kelasket becomes another of the world's "youngest elders" full of newly learned teachings and militant rhetoric' – and simultaneously moves in directions antithetical or tangential to their own – 'is *Kelasket* a traditional Okanagan name? If so what is its English translation? ... And what are the words to Uncle Joe's song? I'd like to hear them too and feel their power. As it is, I feel cheated out of a really good story' ('Emergent' 39).

––––––•–––––

I've been called by feminist groups for making the central character male, and I'm saying that's the exact reason I did it. You can spend your life cutting down and putting down men, but what the hell are your [*sic*] doing to change them? What the hell are you doing to teach differently? (Armstrong, 'What' 15)

In addition to all the responsibilities already talked about, perhaps the most daunting for woman, is her responsibility for the men – how they conduct themselves, how they behave, how they treat her. She has to remind them of *their* responsibilities and she has to know when and how to correct them when they stray from those. (Osennontion and Skonaganleh:rá 13)

––––––•–––––

Female students who were willing to question their other expectations of the novel were sometimes adamant about the relative absence of Maeg's, Mardi's, and Slash's mother's stories and voices, and about the disappointingly stereotypic positing of a future in the male child, Little Chief. Despite Slash's claim about women's centrality, they found the representation of female experience weak and thin, and wondered why Native women authors such as Armstrong and Leslie Silko choose male protagonists. On the question of what one student called the sidelining of female characters, we began with Armstrong's desire to provide a strong, positive image for men in her community (quoted in Emberley 148) and her explanation that the young Native male was at the forefront of the movement ('What' 14). While the Anna Mae Aquashes were unique personalities, she observes, 'with the men there were enough of them that I could generalize and do a composite' ('Rights' 36) (in itself, incidentally, a commentary on the Euro-American aim of individualization in characterization).

In one class, Blackfoot student Chrystal Soop pointed out the Native notion of women's 'soft power,' a concept illustrated by the description of Maeg's using her organizational ability 'in such a way nobody could see she was directly responsible' (237).[7] I suggested that female power cannot necessarily be judged by Western standards, where the obfuscatory notion of the power behind the throne is deservedly derided, and cited the matrilineal, matrilocal Ongwehónwe or Iroquois/Six Nations confederacy, where *male* clan leaders are elected by and answerable to the women of the tribe (who do at times remove them as leaders, for the well-being of the community).[8]

Armstrong herself describes Native women as 'controll[ing] and shap[ing] the thinking of all family members to the next generation' and Okanagan women specifically as having voice and influence in the instruments of governance ('Cultural' 22–3). My sense that her creation of Tom Kelasket could be read as itself an exercise of this same restorative soft power found confirmation in Armstrong's words at the 1988 Third International Feminist Book Fair in Montreal: 'I was able to have [Slash] think at the end the way I want our men to be. I had the power to show them that' (quoted in Warland 68). This fundamental understanding of female centrality, of women as 'keepers of the next generation in every sense' (Armstrong, 'Cultural' 22), is only once spelled out in the novel: 'We learned early from our mothers and grandmothers that it is women who are the strength of the people' (153).[9] We discussed how, rather than providing discrete instances from within, the novel itself in its entirety functions as an enactment of this feminist principle and as a quite different model of how to do feminist work through literature.[10]

I remain uncomfortable, though, with the insertion of *Slash* into a white Western feminist agenda, even though the discussion forced a dramatic revisioning of possible modes of enactment of the feminist project, making what Gayatri Chakravorty Spivak calls 'the basically isolationist admiration for the literature of the female subject in Europe and Anglo-America' ('Three' 262) look partial and superficial. So we spent more time on the necessity for a broader agenda, shaped equally by the voices of women of colour and 'Third World' women, as urged, for example, by bell hooks. As in *Slash*, racism may well take precedence over sexism as the central axis of oppression and focus of struggle in such a politics. Attending to what Armstrong does say, precisely because it may not reflect the reader's immediate priorities or expectations, becomes a way of participating in that strength in diversity that *Slash* self-reflexively theorizes in the context of Native constitutional strategizing: '[W]e can all support each other on whatever position each of us takes. It doesn't mean each has to take the same position' (235).

In an undergraduate course I was teaching on North American Native literatures at the University of Guelph in 1998, a Cree student was preparing part of a class presentation on N. Scott Momaday's *The Way to Rainy Mountain*. She undertook some independent research and, not finding much in written sources, decided to phone her 'aunt' in Saskatchewan to ask, 'What can you tell me about the Sun Dance?' Her aunt's immediate and not-unexpected response was, 'Why do you want to know?'

Reflecting back over my pedagogical approaches to *Slash*, I am left with a number of concerns. Revisions in students' assessments were substantial, particularly in how many would, by the end of the discussion, choose to teach the novel. 'The book has gone up thirty degrees and my confidence in my interpretation down,' wrote one in his journal. I am struck, though, by the number whose appreciation of the writing resided primarily in its introduction of important, unfamiliar social-historical information, and who treated it not as art but as raw material in a potentially imperializing project,[11] engaging in what Spivak calls the 'information-retrieval approach to "Third World" literature' ('Three' 262). What concern me are not readings that can imagine an aesthetic in which transmission of information is a central value. In fact, the stories I've read by students in Armstrong's creative writing program at the En'owkin Centre seem marked quite distinctively by precisely this imperative. What concern me are disjunctive readings saying, '*Slash* fails as a novel, but I'm glad I read it because I learned a lot about Native history.'

This is part of a larger concern stemming from the very decision to problematize cultural norms with regard to *Slash*, the inevitable risk of re-inscribing the centre and re-establishing Native literature as Other. To use Houston Baker's phrase, the 'hermeneutics of overthrow' (388) is inevitably complicit with the hegemonic discourse. With this go the dangers of pan-Indian homogenizing, of the romanticizing 'nostalgia for lost origins' (Spivak, 'Three' 273), and of reading the postcolonial text solely 'in terms of its author's ancestor's beliefs and customs' (Miller 299) or solely 'in the context of nationalism and ethnicity' (Spivak, *Other* 246). Fully persuaded with Trinh T. Minh-ha that 'Difference ... should neither be defined by the dominant sex nor by the dominant culture' (*Woman* 159n47), I am disturbed by the extent to which Western cultural standards (reductively formulated, at that) operated as norm here.

In future, I have resolved to foreground much more fully *Slash*'s scrutinizing of Euro-American values to create a more reciprocal cross-interrogation. Centred in Native worlds, *Slash* establishes the otherness of Western values: the alienness, for example, of seeking respect through materialist pursuits and externals of clothing and possessions, through being 'a hog,' for a people 'who have always been respected for how much they gave away to each other' (97–8).[12] Focusing more on such perspectives may contribute to the reordering of values that Armstrong pursues, though the risk remains of framing the discussion in dominant terms.

The problematizing of cultural hegemony, too, can become a form of intellectual navel-gazing, with the voice of the Other just as effectively silenced as by hegemonic dismissal. Although we acknowledged, in class discussion of *Slash*, the rhetorical centrality and cultural rootedness of the semi-formalized exchanges of philosophical-political views between the characters, I notice that we did not dwell at any length on the specifics of these exchanges. *Slash* provides detailed elaboration of the arguments around development projects on the reserve, violence as a form of militancy, adoption or misuse of traditional Native dress and symbols, closing versus commandeering the resources of DIA offices, demands for cut-off reserve land versus broader land claims, negotiation of land claims versus repudiation of that process, radical protest versus revival of traditional ways, and pursuit of constitutional rights versus inherent self-determination. (In the course of these arguments, it challenges non-Native readers politically through blunt talk of land theft, corporate exploitation of reserves, bureaucratic squandering of *Indian Act* monies, job discrimination, substandard Native housing and education, high death rates, and future appropriation of land and resources, tied to shaming social programs.)

The novel also explores the fundamental question of what is missing in Slash's efforts ('something was missing' becomes a leitmotif [84, 160, 180, 185]) and his eventual understanding of his necessary connections and responsibilities to Indian ways and to his people. In Slash's hopeful description near the novel's end of what young Indian people are doing – 'They were rebuilding a worldview that had to work in this century, keeping the values of the old Indian ways' – Armstrong summarizes what *Slash* too undertakes (232).[13] The Native men who've read the book, whom Armstrong describes telling her '"that's where I've come to" or "that's where I need to go to,"' are taking to heart the substance of Slash's story in a way that our class discussion did not always do ('What' 15).

I was important as one person but more important as a part of everything else. (Armstrong, *Slash* 203)

About a month or so after my headlong trip to the reserve at Standoff, I found myself making the same drive under the expansive Alberta sky, up and down coulees, and across the prairies again. This time my friend was a passenger (along with my four-year-old son, Benjamin), and I was driving her to the home of one of the women who had earlier talked with her at the community centre. This elder had made a special trip to Lethbridge to visit my friend in the hospital and had then invited her out to the reserve to have her face painted. As we rattled along the straight, dirt road – late, I'm sure, as usual – my Volkswagen hopped and hopped and slid to a slow stop. I had run out of gas on this deserted and unfrequented back road, with nothing but fields and grasslands in all directions. We were still sitting, flabbergasted by the calculations of distances ahead and behind, when a truck appeared on the road behind us and pulled alongside. Taking helpfulness for granted, the two men from the reserve, one of whom turned out to be a close relative of the woman we were visiting, had us at our destination within minutes.

The face painting – Benjamin and I were also invited to have our faces painted, as we too were facing transitions (adoption of a sister/ daughter and a move) – took place as part of an extended visit. Our host told us about the trip she had made to Europe (though still relatively young, she had suffered a stroke that had incapacitated one arm) and the statue of the Virgin in her living-room that she had brought back from a middle-European shrine. While we were visiting, the men took it upon themselves to drive on to the next town for gas, drive back out the road to my car, fill it up, and fetch it for us. What had threatened to be a serious problem for us had been shifted away, through their hospitality and gift of time and effort. And – as another gift – through our host's instructions about how to dispose of the paint we would wipe from our faces in the morning, I came as close as I have yet come to a reconciliation with personal death. We were not to throw away the paint-covered tissues, she told us, but to return them to the prairie, burying them or putting them down a ground-squirrel hole. Looking out her window at the same land on which countless generations had lived, I had a moment of understanding. Within such an ethic of respect and guardianship, I could for once imagine accepting the end of my own life and body and consciousness if it were a continuation of something larger, part of an enduring place and people and story.[14]

Perhaps our relative neglect, in class discussion, of the details of Armstrong's analysis is what Homi Bhabha means when he describes cultural otherness as functioning as a symbol rather than as a sign: 'What is denied is any knowledge of cultural otherness as a differential *sign*, implicated in specific historical and discursive conditions, requiring construction in different practices or [i.e., of?] reading. The place of otherness is fixed in the west as a subversion of western metaphysics and is finally appropriated by the west as its limit-text, anti-west' ('Other' 73). We were attempting a different reading *practice*, as Bhabha advocates. But class focus on *Slash*'s 'difference,' however receptive, rather than on its signification – Kelasket's discovery of personal connectedness and irreplaceability as a carrier of the great laws, say – may impede the novel's potential to communicate its particular vision. Cultural resistance to dominance can all too readily be suborned so as actually to succour the practices it opposes. The discourse of 'otherness' seems particularly vulnerable to such recuperation at this cultural moment.

Secondly, what destructive presumptuousness, distortion, and ignorance entered into our attempts, mine and the students', to go *beyond* symbolic otherness to read the signs of a different signifying practice? Upon what experience, for example, was I basing my notions of plausible dialogue? Is attempting to 'read from the inside out' a form of what Minnie Bruce Pratt, following Cynthia Ozick, defines as 'cultural impersonation' (40)? Responding at the 1988 'Telling It' conference to a question about learning without appropriating, Armstrong points out that 'we do as Native writers suffer because of the kind of cultural imperialism that's taking place when non-Native people speak about Native ceremony and Native thinking, Native thought, Native life style, Native world view and speak as though they know what they are speaking about. That's appropriation of culture because no one can experience and know what I know and experience or what my grandmother knows or what Lee [Maracle] knows and feels, and she can speak with her own voice and so can I and so can my grandmother' ('Panel' 50–1). In other words, we have the obvious, and unfortunately not so obvious, point that it is not *I* who should be teaching *Slash* – which is a different argument, by the way, from the one that I should *not* be teaching *Slash*. I can't teach it, and I can't not teach it. In the interim, until Native people are properly represented in the full range of disciplines within the academy, the necessary bridges Armstrong advocates – listening and waiting until understanding can be voiced, and confirmed then with the Native speaker ('Panel' 51) – offer no easy connections.

———•·•———

INGREDIENTS
Bar-b-q sticks of alder wood.
In this case the oven will do.
Salmon: River salmon,
current super market cost
$4.99 a pound.
In this case, salmon poached from the river.
Seal oil or hooligan oil.
In this case, butter or Wesson oil,
if available.
(Dauenhauer, 'How to Make Good Baked Salmon from the River,' *Droning* 11)

———•·•———

The concomitant risk is of assuming pure insider and pure outsider locations, of treating the Okanagan world of *Slash* and 'Western' culture as monoliths, and monoliths with no mutual influence or points of contact. If a pure inside did exist, as my colleague Charlie Sugnet commented with reference to my argument here, it would be like a black hole (or, I would add, the Freudian unconscious) – existent in theory but impossible to get information from. Arguing for *Slash* as more syncretic than I allow, Barbara Hodne has pointed out that Armstrong has written '*a* novel *in* English *as a* curriculum *project in a* colonial *context'* (Hodne and Hoy 74). Similarly, Aijaz Ahmad, among others, has challenged a sweeping, dehistoricized use of 'First World' or 'Western' that slips inconsistently between the postmodern moment, longer-standing capitalist formations, and all of Judaeo-Christian culture and history (11). My formulations of Western aesthetics risk generalizing from particular locations, periods, and genres. How would *Slash* compare with the Western novel of ideas, for example, rather than the contemporary realist novel? Are there no sites within the Western world for the communal values and personal connectedness that *Slash* espouses?

A third difficulty arises from my implicit injunction that non-Native students bracket their aesthetic (and political?) judgments and operate on the hypothesis that apparent limitations in the text stem from our own cultural confinement. This, one student protested, can lead to paralysis and to denial that one has a voice. Is everything written by 'Third World' women good? Is it respecting a text, she asked, to exempt it from the same critique for heterosexism, say, applied to other texts? I am reminded of the frustration felt by my East Indian colleague Mrinalini Sinha at the refusal by North American feminists to engage with or challenge her contributions to discussion. When liberal sensitivity to difference produces an unwillingness to speak, then, Hazel Carby argues, it becomes 'indistinguishable from not having to take any political position whatsoever in relation to the culture of the other' ('Politics' 85).

The ironic corollary is that this 'sanctioned ignorance,' as Spivak calls it, can simultaneously be the grounds for intellectual complacency (*Other* 209). Even in the face of a vast ignorance about Native life and culture, acknowledgment of one's racism threatens to become an endpoint, a means to self-satisfaction or even academic advancement rather than the beginning of action to change the material conditions for people (and authors) of colour. 'Don't say it, if you don't do it,' admonishes Maria Lugones (an admonishment that I may well be violating here in order to disseminate). Carby points out the disturbing fact that the increasingly 'diverse' curriculum at universities has not been matched by increased numbers of faculty and students of colour in the classroom ('Multicultural' 10).[15] One of my students quoted fellow student Amitava Kumar writing in the campus *Minnesota Daily*: 'Anticolonialist discourses are carried out with a purpose other than shoring up careers of academics.' With that in mind, I conclude with Jeannette Armstrong's indictment of Western writing – which she associates with the cultural shock of being judged by externals of dress and income in the non-Indian community – and her implicit alternative literary standard: 'Everything that is "acceptable" is written to build up people's masks of themselves, to build up a front for the person as a writer, and not really to speak about the truth and the centre of things' ('Writing' 57). Both the teaching of *Slash* and the writing about that pedagogy implicate themselves in the colonial practice the novel itself exposes. The next sentence of my chapter, informed by the other literary ethos that Armstrong articulates, remains to be written.

2

'When You Admit You're a Thief':
Maria Campbell and Linda Griffiths's
The Book of Jessica

Maria: When you admit you're a thief, then you can be honourable.

(Campbell and Griffiths 112)

A subject much argued in Canadian literary circles is the question of the use of Native materials by non-Native authors. This raises by implication the question of whether non-Native readings of Native texts similarly (necessarily?) do epistemological and cultural violence to them.[1] Is teaching and criticism of these texts by non-Natives another form of cultural appropriation? *The Book of Jessica* (1989), a collaborative effort by Métis-Cree writer Maria Campbell and Scottish-Canadian actress/ playwright Linda Griffiths, provides detailed ground for an investigation of these issues. The book concludes with a script of the play *Jessica*. Preceding that, it uses a framing narrative and transcripts of frank conversation to excavate the two women's earlier collaboration on this improvisational drama of Campbell's life. A vexed and troubling text – from the placement of Griffiths's name first in the attributing of authorship, to the devolution of ultimate editorial responsibility eventually to her – *The Book of Jessica*, in all its ambivalence, can be read as modelling aspects of the white scholar–Native writer relationship. From its material conditions of production to the implications of Campbell's extratextual decision to put her energies into Native politics rather than the book, the text both glosses and itself enacts postcolonial problems of gatekeeping, cultural impasse, and imbalances of power, while simultaneously insisting on the mutual imperative to communicate. Chapter two will pair this concrete enactment of the politics of cross-cultural communication with current postcolonial/

feminist theory on issues of appropriation and what Gayatri Spivak calls 'the epistemic violence' of imperialism (*Other* 209). It will study how the theory illuminates the practice and how the practice illuminates the theory.

That's the abstract for this chapter, an academic take on the project.

Let me try another voice.

At the 1991 Learned Societies conference in Kingston, I delivered a paper on teaching Jeannette Armstrong's *Slash*, for a joint Women's Studies/English panel on Pedagogical Approaches to Minority and Marginal Women's Literature. Although conceived otherwise, the panel consisted entirely of white women. I was acutely sensitive to the charge that the act of teaching *Slash*, the manner of teaching it, but most particularly the presumption and self-aggrandizement of delivering a paper on it were colonizing acts. I had been at two previous feminist conferences in which self-critical, scrupulous – from my perspective – white women scholars had been powerfully challenged by Native women writers.[2] Papers before my own at the Association of Canadian University Teachers of English,[3] by Ashok Mathur, Aruna Srivastava, Terry Goldie, and Asha Varadharajan, continued to probe painfully what had ceased being an academic question for me. By the time of the special session 'Woman, Native, Other,' my cognitive dissonance was almost paralysing. To take notes, as my academic training and research interests dictated, during Lenore Keeshig-Tobias's impassioned account of the place of Anishinaabe story-telling felt grotesque. Even if Native protocol permitted the quoting of such material, to do so was to impress the comments into the service of a very different, even antithetical project. In the account by Marcia Crosby (Haida-Tsimshian) of Haida challenges to writer Robert Bringhurst, I placed myself. Bringhurst had at least been learning the language and working collaboratively for years with Haida sculptor Bill Reid. Surprised by tears as I was thanking Keeshig-Tobias afterwards, I marked my crisis disconcertingly by weeping publicly under a tree by the lecture-hall door. The best I could do at articulation for a solicitous white friend was my conclusion that 'anything we do is a violation.'

———•———

There is a false collapsing here of epistemology and appropriation. To know is not always to violate. (Asha Varadharajan, discussion period, Association of Canadian University Teachers of English, May 1991)

Educate yourself that you won't ever ever understand. (Ethel Gardner [Sto:lo], University of British Columbia First Nations' House of Learning, quoted by Aruna Srivastava, ACUTE, May 1991)

————•·•————

'How the theory illuminates the practice and how the practice illumi-nates the theory.' But is *The Book of Jessica* the practice of cross-cultural interaction? Or is it the theory?

TAKE 1: *THE BOOK OF JESSICA* AS TEXTUAL APPROPRIATION

However well-intentioned, *The Book of Jessica* redeploys the strategies of intellectual colonialism. Originally conceived as a full collaboration, it had by the time of publication fallen back under Linda Griffiths's editorial control. So it replicates the originary Native Informant–Master Discourse model of the play itself. (According to Diane Bessai, early program notes for *Jessica* credited Maria Campbell with the subject matter, Griffiths and director Paul Thompson with the dialogue and structure respectively [104]). Campbell's decision to run for president of the Métis Society of Saskatchewan and withdraw from the collabora-tive project, a decision only tersely acknowledged in the introductory 'History' – and unglossed – speaks loudly in the vacuum created by her editorial absence. As a final refusal/expression of indifference/signal of divided allegiance, an eloquently silent codicil to the text and one that resonates with earlier repudiations, it pushes against the reconcil-iatory drift of the narrative. Congenial post-publication interviews by Campbell (see Steed, for example) may mute the contestatory impact of her defection, in the larger context, but the decision functions as a disruption *textually* at least.[4]

It is Griffiths, then, who provides the framing narrative, tellingly referring to herself three times in the opening line alone: 'I thought it was over. Inside I knew better, but on the surface, I thought it was over' (13). It is Griffiths who selects both her own and Campbell's words, in what nevertheless purports to be a dialogue. Just as the program credits for *Jessica* here shift, between 1981 and 1986, from three *co-authors* to 'Written by: Linda Griffiths, in collaboration with Maria Campbell' (116), so the hierarchy of authorship for *The Book of Jessica* – Griffiths followed by Campbell – gives precedence to the one-time, final, formal setting-down-on-paper, to the value of individually exercised verbal and structural creativity and control. What has happened to Maria's gift of 'her life, her philosophy and entry to her deepest self' (48)? But, in one sense, that arrogation of pre-eminence on the title page speaks true. Given the editorial process, this story can now finally only be read as Griffiths's.

———•———

[The leftist colonist] will slowly realize that the only thing for him to do is to remain silent. (Memmi 43)

Silence can be 'oppressive' too. (Fee, 'Upsetting' 179)

or, something I came upon closer to home:

... silence too – even respectful silence – can become a form of erasure. (Hoy 99)

———•———

Over the course of the conference, I reached my decision. I would not send out my paper on *Slash* for publication. Would I even send a copy to the colleagues who had requested one? I would return to the graduate school my grant-in-aid for further research on Armstrong and other Canadian Native women writers and withdraw my notices of a research assistantship. I would abandon my research plan for a book in the area. Not because such work was fraught with political awkwardness and potential discredit (oh, really?) but because it was imperialist. It rewrote Native stories from the perspective of a cultural outsider. And did so at a time when Native readings of the same texts had much more restricted opportunities for formulation and dissemination. I would find work within my own culture(s) that needed doing – it could still be counterhegemonic work – rather than contribute another layer to the colonialist in(ter)ventions that subsequent generations of Native readers and scholars would have to undo.

———•———

No human culture is inaccessible to someone who makes the effort to understand, to learn, to inhabit another world. (Gates, '"Authenticity"' 30)

[T]he tendency to overvalue work by white scholars, coupled with the suggestion that such work constitutes the only relevant discourse, evades the issue of potential inaccessible locations – spaces white theorists cannot occupy. (hooks, *Yearning* 55)

———•———

Other disturbing evidence of appropriation sprinkles the text of *The Book of Jessica*. Within a few lines of the opening, Griffiths refers to the 'familiar arrowhead point in the pit of my stomach' (13). The image illustrates a facile tendency to adorn oneself with metaphors from the appropriate culture, a kind of intellectual souvenir hunting that bedevils cross-cultural critics.[5] The gesture becomes more serious when Griffiths appropriates the Native ceremony of the give-away, the red cloth Maria has learned so painfully to surrender, as trope for Griffiths's letting go of something she cannot claim ever to have had: 'The clearest give-away I have ever been involved in has been *Jessica* ... It's my red cloth' (111). The deceptively objective third-person 'History' extends this transposition of beneficiary and donor to *The Book of Jessica* itself: 'Linda's contribution to [Campbell's] campaign is the editing and structuring of this book ... the red cloth' (10). Using editorial privilege, Griffiths then author-izes this standpoint by entitling the second section of the book 'The Red Cloth.' The interpretive reversal here connects with the paradoxical inversion involved in her theatrical technique of 'sibyling.' Ostensibly the ultimate gesture of self-abnegation – acting as pure medium, a 'self-effacing vessel' (49), a blank so absolute that Griffiths feels herself absent as an emotional being – sibyling becomes the ultimate gesture of ingestion, an imperialist receptivity: 'I was taught that you could open yourself to anything, anyone, let the energy pour through you, and something would happen. I was *ravenous* for those moments' (14; emphasis added).[6] Campbell herself identifies the stance as one of dangerous greediness (49). Are sibyls supposed to end up with copyright, with right of first refusal, with the position of director, with editorial *carte blanche*, with red cloth to give away?

Griffiths's account, moreover, contains disingenuousness – 'the thing was already out of his [Paul Thompson's] domain. It was on paper now, it had passed over to me or maybe you would say I'd taken it' (59); pernicious misreckoning – the designating of Campbell's hostility and other Native people's as racist (34, 48); evasion of responsibility – 'Out of my paranoia and confusion came a little voice: "Yes," I said, "I wouldn't mind having a first refusal on the part of Jessica ..."' (54); unacknowledged perceptual blinkers – 'Women appeared *from nowhere* and cooked a Métis feast' (52; emphasis added); and interruptions of Campbell at critical moments. Students in a recent women's studies 'Race and Gender' course commented on how Griffiths repeatedly gives herself the last word, or at least the last comment of any sub-stance. It is doubtful whether, under Campbell's editorship, the text would have remained so narrowly focused on the *pas de deux* of Campbell and Griffiths, when, as Campbell reminds us, the play was many people. The insistent personalizing of the conflict as a struggle between two well-meaning individuals obscures, too, the broader social and eco-nomic forces at play. But even granting this emphasis, in the absence of editorial reciprocity, *The Book of Jessica* reproduces the inequitable power relations of the original collaboration.

[I]t is also necessary to overcome the position of the white editor – or the white critic – as cultural gatekeeper. (Goldie, 'Majority' 93)

Endless second guessing about the latent imperialism of intruding upon other cultures only compounded matters, preventing or excusing these theorists from investigating what black, Hispanic, Asian and Native American artists were actually doing. (Robert Storr, quoted in hooks, *Yearning* 26)

Towards the end of the Learned Societies conference, during one of those lamentable lapses in conference planning when the afternoon session ends with no friends in sight, I joined a stranger in the near-deserted cafeteria. She turned out to be Barbara Riley, Anishinaabe elder and coordinator of Native social work at Laurentian University. Over burritos, we talked. We sat until midnight, ignoring the discom-fort of our plastic, institutional chairs. Talking about children and grand-children; about the politics of Columbus quincentennial grants; about balance between the intellectual, physical, emotional, and spiritual; about appropriation of Native culture; about growing up; about sweat lodges at the upcoming 1992 Learneds; about the global crisis; about allegiances to place; about our work. The conversation was personal, not academic. I could feel easy countenancing, even promoting, the intensity and intimacy of our exchange because of the express under-standing with myself that I had withdrawn from scholarship on things Native. More accurately, that resolution solidified further on the spot, out of the conviction that Barbara's own candour was predicated on a trust that I would not exploit it. She had spoken unhappily, for ex-ample, of some nearby white women social scientists based in Nicaragua, had associated herself with the Nicaraguan women, and insisted that the latter could well solve their own problems. Whatever clarifications I was groping towards, then, were for my own life, not for academic articles.

Maria: 'You were invited into that circle to help you understand, not to write a book about it.' (Campbell and Griffiths 27)

TAKE 2: *THE BOOK OF JESSICA* AS POSTCOLONIAL DEPOSITION

With illuminating candour, *The Book of Jessica* self-consciously documents the particularities of one extended cross-cultural endeavour, in all its wrong-headedness as well as accomplishment, precisely so as to scrutinize that practice. Some moments, such as Griffiths's classic defence of the forbidden Sun Dance photograph as preservation of a dying culture, almost feel concocted to provide the full panoply of colonialist assumptions. (Notions of this text as artless spontaneity meet their most obvious hurdle with the intrusion of the Voice from the Middle of the Room – an absent presence, director Paul Thompson – into the transcribed conversation.) Just as the play *Jessica* set out to create 'a woman who was Maria, but not really' (17), so the book about the play intensifies the antithetical personae of white *naïf* – 'Where was the exoticism of the books I'd been reading?' (22) – and streetwise Native – 'What a bunch of garbage ... It just sounds so ... so much like a white professor introducing me at a convention of anthropologists' (18) – to throw into relief the postcolonial perplex. Arguments between Campbell and Griffiths, about the (literal) give-and-take of their collaboration, rehearse systematically the sites and tropes of Euro-American–Native contestation: land, treaties, ownership, concepts of time, religion, and cultural copyright. Making her claim to *Jessica*, for instance, Griffiths voluntarily takes on metaphors as counterproductive as homesteading and sacred treaties. Celebrating the difficult successes of pioneers (while acknowledging the cost for Native peoples), she argues, audaciously, 'I stand on the land that is *Jessica* because I'm the mother that tilled that soil' (92). With similar brashness, she responds to Campbell's positioning her as the white government treaty maker with the affirmation, 'maybe *Jessica* is a treaty. To me, it was a sacred thing' (82). Campbell, in turn, frames her objections in the language of conquest: 'He [Paul Thompson] came in between, the conqueror with his piece of paper, when we were both exhausted' (104). Even in the text's silences and suppressions – Griffiths's need not to know the deal Campbell struck with Paul Thompson (42), for instance, or her repeated spurning of an undelivered, angry letter from Campbell, in one case at the moment of insisting that she wants everything said (62, 112) – *The Book of Jessica* signals us insistently with traces of its evasions. The final destabilizing of peaceful reconciliation – 'Are we going to leave people with the faerie tale of it? Because the truth is, I am wrecked over doing this, I'm still afraid of you, still feel like your servant,' says Griffiths (112) – is yet one more invitation to us to continue the anatomizing.

I am an academic. I work alone. For my research, I work in libraries, with bibliographies, with books, with journals, with archives. Until recently, I had never collaborated on an article. By the time I submit my work to any public scrutiny, it feels finished, and I am not anxious for critiques necessitating extensive revision. Except at conferences, paper stands between me and those I write about, between me and those I write to, between me and those who write about me. Paper stands like the barricade of A grades that Alice Munro's Del Jordan stacks around herself (*Lives* 195). I write for other academics. At least in part, I write because the structures of my job require and reward it. I am comfortable in this world. I enjoy the intellectual autonomy and independence and self-direction. Over this area of my life, I have control. I feel safe. I am an academic.

I am a teacher.

I am a feminist.

I am a parent, and a parent of Native children.

I am a citizen of this badly messed-up world.

———•—

Why are you poking your white imagination into our culture? You will not learn anything new when that happens. (Keeshig-Tobias, 'Woman')

I'm surrounded by people saying silly things like 'I can't teach Black writers.' ... It's called 'education' because you learn. (Giovanni)

———•—

The Book of Jessica gives us – in place of a narrative of liberal self-scrutiny on the one hand or anti-colonial resilience on the other, either constructed in comfortable isolation from the other – the less usual and necessarily more nuanced rendering of *mutual* disputation/negotiation in process. What could be static documentation is repeatedly problematized and transformed, through the dynamic of instant accountability, correction, and challenge.[7] Confronted with an embodied reminder, in Griffiths, of 'a society that takes and takes, a society that changes, rearranges, interprets and interprets some more, until there's nothing left but confusion' (91), Campbell must wrestle with her cultural ethic of generosity, of letting go and giving away. Griffiths must confess her determination to write *Jessica* without Campbell's blessing if necessary, confess her misrepresentations of how far she has gone with that undertaking, not simply to the reader, but, as she says about her sibyling, much more disconcertingly with the 'subject' in the room. *Everything* is in the tension. With the ongoing interaction comes also a greater pressure for mutuality. '[Y]ou have to be able to be honest about yourself too,' insists Campbell. 'You can't lay something out, and then say, "Well, I can't do that because it might hurt some people." ... Why is it okay to lay my guts all over the table, but you can only take some of yours, and by the way, madam, let's make sure they're the pretty ones' (88).

A few years ago, I watched the frustration of a white academic friend of mine as she tried to co-edit a collection of essays about and, in some cases, by Aboriginal women. Editorial discussions were at cross-purposes, members of the collective failed to show up for the meetings or showed up unprepared, other issues edged out discussion of the articles. I was grateful that, for the collection of essays *The Native in Literature* that I edited with Thomas King and Cheryl Calver, my co-editors had been fellow academics and rather like-minded. If these other conference papers were ever to see publication, it seemed to me, those most active needed to take charge, and damn the collective process. I can only guess at the perspective from alternative locations, those of the students, activists, and non-academic Indian women: That publication in itself primarily served the academics. That there were more pressing priorities. That the articles aimed more to fit into a scholarly discourse than to inspire change for Native people. That a collection dominated by non-Native perspectives was worse than no collection at all. That the editorial process was pedantic, intimidating, or misguided. That the power to be heard resided with the white academics ... Or, perhaps, that the editing was proceeding exactly as it should ... I can only guess.

Linda: '... the wolverine in me said ... "I have the power to write that play and it will not be written the way I want unless I do it."'

Maria: 'It's easier to go and do it yourself, and face the conflict after ... the hard words and stuff, but not the actual pain of trying to do it together.' (Campbell and Griffiths 79, 98)

In particular, *The Book of Jessica* re-views the discourse and practice of white scholarship, permitting us to track the disjunctures between what Barbara Smith calls 'the pernicious ideology of professionalism' (26) and quite other cultural imperatives of artistic healing, responsibility to community, and personal balance. Griffiths and Campbell display goodwill, shared goals and assumptions, including the conviction that the circle of grandmothers has no colour, and considerable personal investment and sacrifice. Griffiths suffers incapacitating back trouble and extended physical collapse; Campbell faces estrangement from her community, internal discord, and temporary loss of self. (An entire poststructuralist/feminist/psychoanalytic paper on split and shared and overlapping selves, fluid and transgressed ego boundaries, and transposed subject positions, incidentally, is begging to be written on *The Book of Jessica*.) Nevertheless, the differing structures and demands of the communities to which they are answerable impinge divisively on Campbell and Griffiths's joint work. In Griffiths's case, specifically, we can instructively discern at work the inapposite requirements of career advancement, notions of individual creativity and intellectual property, pressures of a print culture, and the economics and legalities of publication.

In her sense of herself as an interpretive intermediary for Campbell's world – 'Make me understand and I'll make an audience understand' (21) – Griffiths has something in common with the literary critic. In comments about her status as watcher and the unsuitability of her linear mental processes at a Native ceremony, she constructs herself self-deprecatingly in the place of the academic outsider. Simultaneously, in her desire not to be one with the other white people at the Native teachers' graduation, she functions as cultural tourist/scholar aspiring to be an insider. When she describes the loneliness of winning approval from no one, the ignominy of prying into the personal life of a stranger, the debilitating conjunction of audacity and ignorance that her improvisations entail, the poignancy of smuggling spiritual rituals into her life under the guise of research, or her vulnerability to Campbell's veto power, Griffiths's honesty illuminates the pain and risk and presumption of this borderlands position.

———•———

So the motive of friendship remains as both the only appropriate and understandable motive for white/Anglo feminists engaging in [theory jointly with feminists of colour]. If you enter the task out of friendship with us, then you will be moved to attain the appropriate reciprocity of care for your and our well-beings as whole beings, you will have a stake in us and in our world ... (Spelman and Lugones 581)

I am automatically on guard whenever the white man enters 'Indian' country. What does he want this time? I ask. What is he looking for – adventure, danger, material wealth, spiritual wealth (perhaps shamanistic power), a cause, a book, or maybe just a story? (Keeshig-Tobias, 'White' 67)

———•———

As I read about White Buffalo Calf Woman in the play *Jessica*, I found myself wishing I had notes from the Anishinaabe storytelling session where I had recently heard the same story. But I remembered rejecting note taking at the time as clearly inappropriate. I remembered, as I had at the time, the reiterated Native injunction, 'Listen carefully because you may not hear this again' (Keeshig-Tobias, 'Woman'; Armstrong, *Slash* 38). I remembered the middle-aged white woman at the same storytelling session, surreptitiously turning on and off a tape-recorder hidden in a paper bag, then refusing organizers' requests not to record the storytelling, insisting it was simply for her own personal research. I remembered the German scholar scuttling along in a loping crouch beside the feet of a Blackfoot fancy dancer, on another occasion, to record the sound of the ankle bells for his students back home.

———•———

The question to ask is 'Whom does it serve?' (Barbara Riley)

———•———

Griffiths's early hankering to hone the unedited transcripts of the improvisations for *Jessica* reveals 'the contemplative *ego* of the writer' beginning to impose itself on the collective process (43; emphasis added).

In her drive to create (which overrides scruples about consultation), her explicit need for accomplishment as a writer, her pain that she cannot own *Jessica*, her desire not so much not to steal as not to be seen as stealing, her belief that she has single-handedly kept the book project together, and her faith in the worth of her creation, she exposes the double-edged values that also impel/impale academia. At the same time, through Campbell, the text documents a countervailing ethos. Campbell invokes respect and a sense of the sacred in place of sophistry regarding entitlement to cultural material. She challenges the concept of creative ownership of *Jessica*. She questions the wisdom of rushing to subject powerful Native spiritual symbols to the same artistic exposure in the West that has depleted Western ones.

The legal contract and later the privately crafted script become tinderboxes because they so pointedly signal the shift from the personal contract between the collaborators to the world of white professionalism. Mainstream conditions of cultural production and reception, and the economic structures sustaining and rewarding them, reveal themselves as potent though largely offstage agents in this drama. Twenty-Fifth Street House Theatre's financial exigency and suspicion of eastern-Canadian theatrical interests, the precedence accorded autonomous authorship (played out in the overall trajectory of Griffiths's career from its beginnings in collective, improvisational drama), and mainstream assumptions about literary ownership, presumed audience, textual integrity, royalties, film rights, and first-refusal rights play themselves out before us on the bodies and psyches of the two women. When Griffiths accuses Campbell, 'But you're not dedicated in the same way, because you would have let *Jessica* die' (78), she equates, in the presence of a self-proclaimed storyteller, the absence of a printed record with extinction. Cultural cross-purposes find a voice here. The two women are indeed not dedicated *in the same way*, and therein lies the conflict they expose.

As my friend comforted me after the 'Woman, Native, Other' panel at the 1991 conference, I was unhappily reminded of reproaches from Black feminists about how, after confrontations over racism, white feminists rally to hearten their distressed white colleague, neglecting the pain of the woman of colour. The direction of my friend's reassurance was unsettling also, drawing some of its force from downplaying the import of what I had just heard. I have shown a similar solicitude myself afterwards for an unknown conference speaker, confronted during question period. Connecting through our shared location, I could read her, a white, tenured, conference panelist, as beleaguered, in ways I failed to read the Native member of the audience, lone voice of indignation and dissension, hell-raiser in the academic atmosphere of restraint and good manners, where consternation at the breach of decorum could blot out the substance of her objections.

———•———

I am waiting to learn from them [white feminist professors] the path of their resistance, of how it came to be that they were able to surrender the power to act as colonizers. (hooks, *Yearning* 151)

So much attention has been paid to analyses of why dominant feminist discourses have been inattentive to women of color that we have yet to see analyses which include these neglected perspectives. (Uttal 42)

TAKE 3: *THE BOOK OF JESSICA* AS TEXTUAL RESISTANCE

The Book of Jessica is Maria Campbell's book. It is her idea initially. The very substance and format of the book are determined by her ethos of mutual self-disclosure as fundamental to any true collaboration. Provoked by the inconsistency of Griffiths's fascination exclusively with a Native past and ignorance of her own Scottish history of oppression, Campbell argues that she and Griffiths can find a meeting place only in an *exchange* of their ancestral histories. Contending that shared personal matters, such as Griffiths's 'boosting' or shoplifting, give her someone solid to interact with, she ensures that this text both theorizes and models a collaborative process of genuine exchange. Though deletions leave their traces – Griffiths's mother's alcoholism (?) cured through religion, for example – Griffiths exposes herself in ways foreign to sibyls and researchers. The textual format of dialogue and interjections, in place of a monologic or synthesized narrative, develops naturally from this insistence on mutuality. The book's forthrightness too reflects Campbell's motive for persisting with a project this painful, the urgency of providing connections and hope in a period of global devastation.

Furthermore, the most eloquent piece of oratory in the book is Campbell's. In its historic concision and controlled passion, it necessarily infuses any reading of the entire collaboration and the book. The speech I mean is her caustic response to Griffiths's contention that the play *Jessica* lives thanks to Griffiths's authorship but requires Campbell's belated modifications and permission:

Now Wolverine is saying, 'I took it. I gave it birth. I gave it life. It was mine and it would have died without me. I salvaged it. I built temples all over the place. I built high-rises all over the place. I put wheat fields out there. I produced it and if it wasn't for me, you would have let this land die. So I came along and I took what you were wasting and I made something productive out of it, because you weren't doing it, but I need you to tell me that I didn't steal anything, that I didn't take anything from you.' (80)

Campbell inserts the entire narrative so forcibly and repeatedly into history, and into a colonial history, that the reader cannot help but read the collaboration as one moment in a centuries-long struggle.

I have not been entirely honest about my crisis over researching Native literature – nor was I with myself at the time. My tormented sense of the impossibility of such work did not derive entirely from a conviction of an absolute epistemological impasse, an impenetrable barrier between cultural insider and outsider that I could only augment by presuming to breach. Nor from a conviction of the inevitability of a colonizing appropriation. Behind those concerns lurked an appalled glimpse of the momentous personal and methodological changes entailed in counteracting my cultural ignorance and presumption. Hell, I like my library fortress, my scholarly garrison. I don't even go out of my way to interview Alice Munro, when I'm writing on her. The negotiations, the accountability, the loss of control over my time, the necessity of functioning off my own turf, the depressingly poor prospects of avoiding missteps were too daunting. (Yet I had felt dismissive of a colleague who simply dropped the idea of organizing a panel on writers of colour when advised she should aim for diversity among the panelists.) A Native elder spoke to me about being affronted (admittedly during a contentious period) by an inappropriate request from another Native person – inappropriate because tendered publicly rather than privately beforehand – to open a meeting with a prayer. I could envision hundreds of such unwitting violations of protocol, big and small, hundreds of *public* failures of understanding, hundreds of comeuppances. 'Everything we do is a violation,' I might have said, 'and the cost of changing that is too high.'

———•———

Guilt is *not* a feeling. It is an intellectual mask to a feeling. Fear is a feeling – fear of losing one's power, fear of being accused, fear of a loss of status, control, knowledge. Fear is real. Possibly this is the emotional, non-theoretical place from which serious anti-racist work among white feminists can begin. (Moraga and Anzaldúa 62)

A non-imperialist feminism ... requires that you be willing to devote a great part of your life to it and that you be willing to suffer alienation and self-disruption. (Spelman and Lugones 576)

——•——

It is Campbell's contribution, too, in *The Book of Jessica* that advances the much-argued contemporary debate over appropriation of cultural materials beyond the reductive poles of imaginative autonomy on the one hand and retreat on the other. She does so through a deft turn on the trope of artistic theft:

Today, most art is ugly, because it's not responsible to the people it steals from. Real, honest to-God true art steals from the people. It's a thief ... It comes in, and you don't even notice that it's there, and it walks off with all your stuff, but then it gives it back to you and heals you, empowers you, and it's beautiful. Seventy-five percent of the art that's out there steals, but it doesn't give anything back. It doesn't bring you joy. It doesn't heal you. It doesn't make you ask questions ... It takes your stuff and it hangs it up on the wall and it says, 'Look what I've done. Isn't that wonderful. I'm an artist.' (83–4)

By arguing that 'you have to first admit you are a thief' and that thereafter 'if you're an artist and you're not a healer, then you're not an artist' (82, 84), she shifts the focus, for the white writer, from a project of moral self-purification – demonstrating cultural sensitivity or entitlement – to one of political/artistic effectiveness. A presumed position of transgression, as a given, becomes, not grounds for profitless apology, but a responsibility incurred, the springboard for socially accountable art – or scholarship. In addition, Campbell's response to the Native ceremony that Griffiths keeps verging on violating through indiscretion points to a *modus vivendi*. To Griffiths's thwarted cry, 'Alright, I'll cut it all out,' Campbell replies, 'No, not *your* experience. You're an artist, find a way to do it' (28; emphasis added). *The Book of Jessica* models that kind of art.

In my own narrative, I have not named the scholar taping the fancy dancers, the particular conference speakers confronted by Native women, the colleague counteracting Keeshig-Tobias's disturbing impact, the editor of the conference papers on Native women, or the friend forswearing the panel on writers of colour. I have even omitted a revealing instance of neocolonial defensiveness because, respecting the friend involved, I can find more sympathetic ways of explicating the comment and because I don't want to be seen as betraying personal conversations.[8] I *have* named Lenore Keeshig-Tobias and Barbara Riley, and reported my conversation with Riley. The literary critics sit on panels with me, they provide me with citations and readings, they critique my work; they are my colleagues and friends. From my academic aerie I am unlikely to cross paths with Keeshig-Tobias or Riley. Only at the moment of offering to send her a copy of this paper, did I become convinced that naming the elder offended by the invitation to pray would be indiscreet.

The Book of Jessica vindicates Campbell's conviction that the Métis role of interpreter between cultures can be, for her, something other than a betrayal. Through her voice and presence, the book both rebuffs imperialist practices – 'Don't do it,' she warns Griffiths (29) – and affirms alternatives – 'How about that, she finally heard me' (30).

You do not have to be me in order for us to fight alongside each other. (Lorde 142)

We will do it ourselves. In our own way. In our own time. (Barbara Riley)

3

'Listen to the Silence':
Ruby Slipperjack's *Honour the Sun*

The song is very short because we understand so much.

(Chona 51)

Honour the Sun (1987) by Ojibway author Ruby Slipperjack traces in
diary format six years of changes in its young protagonist and her small
northern Ontario community. In the opening dialogue of the novel,
Bobby asks the ten-year-old narrator, Owl, and her friend, his sister
Sarah, 'What are you guys laughing at?'[1] The reply anticipates not only
a recurring mode of response within the Ojibway community depicted,
but also the novel's characteristic narrative stance: 'Sarah giggles and
shakes her head. "Nothing"' (9). 'Nothing': an evasion of direct communication, which makes no effort to obscure the possibility of something to be communicated.

As an introduction to the novel, the initial scene resonates further
because what the girls are laughing over and playing at, and withholding from Bobby's scrutiny, are the particulars of female sexual maturity,
the big belly Sarah has simulated with a rolled-up blanket. (And Bobby,
who with puberty is to become a physical and sexual threat, presumes
inauspiciously to instruct Owl in her role, offering her snuff – 'What's
the matter? You're supposed to be a mother with your baby there. Here,
take some' [9] – with an insistence that becomes bullying.) Sexual
maturation, along with the male aggression that attends it, becomes
one of the occasions for discursive reticence subsequently in the text
and coincides with an increasing narrative fragmentation as the novel
progresses. 'Nothing' is what the novel often seems to reply to a reader's
desire for information or explanation.

In 'Godzilla vs. Post-Colonial,' Thomas King argues that access to an Indian world in *Honour the Sun* is 'remarkably limited,' that Slipperjack appears forthright but refuses to share with us the reasons for alcoholism, violence, and departures, that 'non-Natives may, as readers, come to an association with [this community], but they remain, always, outsiders' (16).

HL: Do you get a lot of feedback from Native readers?
RS: No. You don't do that. (LAUGHS) It is like questioning someone! You don't question people. You don't make comments. That is why the lecture theatres are such a foreign environment in universities, the debates, and the discussions, the panels – those are totally foreign. It is just like pointing a finger at somebody. (LAUGHS) (Slipperjack, 'Ruby' 213)

So I find myself awkwardly positioned, as a white academic and cultural outsider, a professional and literal finger-pointer, presuming to teach and deliver papers on *Honour the Sun*. The compulsion to comment that comes easily to me, by culture, by trade, and by temperament, is at odds, it would seem, with the ethos of the book. Some, though not all, of the personal interactions created in the novel; some, though not all, of the thematic implications and narrative strategies of the novel; some, though not all, of the author's statements of principle give precedence to a communicative style and, implicitly, to a way of reading the book that are directed more inward than outward. They encourage an approach more likely to issue in personal self-sufficiency than in scholarly publications. 'More and more,' says Owl, at age thirteen, 'I spend time sitting by the woodpile, listening to the silence' (185).

If you tell a story properly, you don't have to explain what it means afterwards. (Johnston, 'Basil' 234)

Communication in non-verbal fashion, exemplified most thoroughly in the animated but completely wordless Christmas 1962 visit in the family cabin with a nameless old man, is clearly a value in the novel. Owl's mother, Delia, uses silence quite deliberately, taking a deep breath, then pretending Owl isn't there after Owl has ruined her mother's stockings. A 'strange look' from her sister, Barbara, and one from Delia constitute the entire outward familial reaction to Owl's close call with a train. Owl and her older brother, Wess, counteract the emotional distance created by his absences not with words but with punch-and-wrestle sessions. The boundaries of this horseplay are signalled and acknowledged in silence: 'I wipe the mud off my face. I'm not smiling. Wess stops laughing and disappears around the corner of the cabin' (47). Or is Wess's disappearance censure for Owl's lack of resilience, rather than acquiescence in her reproach? Or is it simply withdrawal from an unpromising situation? How am I to decipher the signals recorded?

Sometimes the narrator provides a tentative, though unconfirmed, reading of the silence, as when Wess has directed her to improve her bannock baking: 'I guess I've passed the test because he doesn't say anything and helps himself to a second piece' (46). Occasionally she is, with us, instructed in its purpose, as when her mother explains a decision not to answer Owl's calls, so as to encourage reliance on other senses, in this case attentiveness to the smell of a tanning fire. Usually, the novel proffers unexplicated actions, some at least carrying quite specific or local cultural freight. '[I]f there is a reader from that area,' Slipperjack comments, 'when I describe something in the book, you know, the child just did this, caught somebody's eye over there, and another person maybe shrugs their shoulders. They will know, they will get the message by just mentioning those things. They just burst out laughing because they have caught the unwritten communication in there' ('Ruby' 213).

When the characters do use language, their approach can be minimalist – or, to similar effect, redundant – even teasingly so at times. Wess proposes to name the new puppy 'Little Dog' and, when it is grown ... 'Big Dog.' Delia conveys Owl's opportunity to string a fishnet of her own through a bald statement of fact, leaving Owl to draw the inference: 'Mom calls me over to her sewing bag and indicates the left over spools of twine from her fishnet. "Look how much was leftover [sic]," she says to me' (53). The verbal repetition here underscores the communicative redundancy. Aunty *indirectly* provides occasion for explanation of Owl's mutilated shoe through her entertainingly understated observation that the shoe looks as though it has been cut. Some ostensible questions, such as Delia's 'What happened to you?' about Jane's injuries, followed up with first-aid care rather than conversation (or at least recorded conversation), function rhetorically more as acknowledgments, markers of notice taken, than as requests for information (65). 'Words are very, very rare,' says Slipperjack about her community ('Ruby' 212). Interestingly, one of her two reasons for sharing portions of her manuscript of *Silent Words* with Hartmut Lutz, her German interviewer, was that she had never before written such lengthy dialogue and was wondering whether simply to delete it ('Ruby' 210).

Responses in *Honour the Sun* are similarly minimalist. 'Yep. It's been cut all right' is Owl's unforthcoming answer to Aunty's comment about her shoe (30). Jane's reply about an anthill that Owl thinks Jane may be avoiding is cryptic and non-committal: 'That's an anthill. Some ants are black and some are small. Some can be quite big too' (22). Not surprisingly – to me, at least – Owl finds herself 'not quite sure about the conversation.' Less characteristically, she articulates and shares that uncertainty with the reader. (Is the narrative comment a concession to cultural outsiders, who may require acknowledgment of an interpretive impasse here?) Laughter is a critical component of both verbal and non-verbal exchanges. Particularly when provoked by someone's misadventure, though, this is 'swallowed laughter' (58), laughter largely concealed and shared only covertly. Even for children and within the family, laughter must often be silent, as Owl demonstrates when Jane does land on the anthill.

That economy of language does not imply poverty of response but indeed its inverse may only need saying from the perspective of cultural outsiders. The function of silence as accomplishment rather than lack is explicated in Slipperjack's second novel, *Silent Words*, where Danny is being consciously initiated into the cultural tradition that Owl takes for granted:

I shrugged hopelessly and she [Mrs Old Indian] smiled and looked away. I just did it! I mean talking not in words but by actions. I remembered my second day here, the old man had looked at the old woman, then at me. The old woman smiled and said, ''e say you talk too much.'

I had looked at the old man and said, 'What? I didn't hear him say anything.'

'No,' she said. 'Use your eyes an feel inside you wat da udder is feelin. Dat way, dere is no need for words. Your ears are for 'earin all da udder tings 'round you.' (60)

In *Honour the Sun*, the containment of laughter clearly contributes to an intensification of emotion. After Owl's dunking in the mud by Wess, her mother's silent observation of her is constructed as an active engagement, by its contrast with the reactions of others in the cabin too busy to ask about Owl's muddiness. Delia's response – 'Mom watches me from the bed but doesn't say anything'(47) – reflects a cultural tendency manifested throughout the novel. Simultaneously, it models a possible reading strategy for the novel, though not, evidently, one I have succeeding in adopting.

———•———

Well, [*Honour the Sun*] says, 'this is how I feel,' 'this is what I am feeling,' 'this is what is happening around me,' and 'this is how I am reacting,' 'this is how I am dealing with this situation.' That is where it stops. I cannot tell you why this and this and that happens, you figure that out yourself. (Slipperjack, 'Ruby' 209)

———•———

I am reminded of a Native woman's story of preparing, as a young girl, to bathe her one-year-old brother.[2] She spent the morning heating buckets of water on the stove and lugging them down to pour into the cold, running stream nearby. Her mother and grandmother, she recalled, observed her all morning without comment. I compare my own loquacious leap into histories, taxonomies, physics lessons, ideological disquisitions, and directives at the first signs of inexperience or curiosity in my seven- or three-year-old.

I am reminded, too, of the difficult visit to the home of my Cree daughter's Native foster parents, when we were adopting her. My belief in the efficacy of immediate verbal interchange and in straightforward inquiry as its most efficient mechanism, my deep conviction that I could parent Elizabeth best by energetically ferreting out information, for myself and her, about her history and temperament – not to mention my feminist faith in female self-assertion – found themselves at loggerheads with what I perceived as incompatible cultural norms of indirectness, reserve, and deliberateness. I had painfully to instruct myself in reticence, force myself into silence. Only later, thinking back over the written *notes* I made afterwards to treasure up for Elizabeth the few details of her story that I gleaned – almost every detail a *quotation* from that circuitous conversation – did I ask myself whether there weren't other details I might have recorded, observations derived through non-linguistic channels. And I ponder whether there might not have been a more reflective manner of absorbing impressions – because, of course, I was still observing furiously, albeit silently. Was there a receptivity less aggressive than this kind of social worker/anthropologist's avidity? Here I hesitate. In positing this communicative dissonance, am I romanticizing cultural otherness? Projecting stereotypes of grave and laconic profundity? Quite possibly. I do know that, even silent, I felt my epistemological stance, my investigative assiduity, and my focus on easily transmissible facts uncomfortably out of keeping with my context. My silence felt disingenuous.

Describing an MLA session where a male scholar was criticizing author Zora Neale Hurston for failing to allow Janie in *Their Eyes Were Watching God* to speak in her own newly found voice, Paul Lauter recounts: 'It was, I think, Alice Walker who responded that while *many* of us find our voice, *some* of us learn when it's better not to use it' (86).

———•·•———

We need liberation not only from the colonial legacy of the proverbial white man, we need liberation from our own untruths. To quote Adrienne Rich, we need to look at our 'lies, secrets, and silence' in ourselves, in our homes, in our communities, in our politics. Only then will we produce great literature. (LaRocque, 'Emma' 202)

I was raised to avoid discussion of female issues or sex in public, or even with close friends. In opening these areas to scrutiny, am I violating my culture? (Chrystos, 'Askenet' 242)

———•·•———

Honour the Sun, with its paradoxically reticent surfeit of particularities, negotiates the territory between telling and not telling. Dee Horne borrows Adam Jaworksi's use of the term 'implicature' to describe this capacity of Slipperjack's writing to communicate indirectly (Horne, 'Listening' 123 and *Contemporary* 54). Chapter twelve, 'The New Door,' typifies the challenge, for the non-Native reader, of reading what is not said. When I first taught the novel in a joint graduate-undergraduate course, the student presenter referred straightforwardly to the 'rape' of Owl's mother in this scene. (M.F. Salat states, too, that 'Slipperjack even hints at an actual rape of Owl's mother' [80], and a review speaks less specifically of the men in the novel who, when drinking, 'smash doors, rape women and kill wantonly' [Grant, Rev. 35]). Members of the class stirred uneasily, but the presenter went on immediately to substantiate her inference with passages from the text. Until then I had, myself, inferred some sort of sexual assault without defining it so categorically. Persuaded by the evidence, I felt relieved that a potentially assailable moment in a strong postcolonial/feminist analysis had been sustained. None of the other students questioned the reading, though some, I suspect, privately either hesitated over the conclusion or reproached themselves for earlier critical myopia. We proceeded to use the term 'rape' unproblematically in the succeeding discussion. I missed the opportunity to use the passage to complicate assumptions about what the novel reveals.

What does the scene disclose? The details are limited and equivocal. There is Delia's screaming after she fails to escape the cabin as the drunk breaks in, her heaving shoulders and hair tangled in her face when the children finally return, the quivering voice with which she curses.[3] Most suggestive for me are her hurried trip to the outhouse and her subsequent pouring of water into a basin to wash. As signifiers, though, these are ambiguous, clearly susceptible of a less dramatic reading. Routine details of daily maintenance, cleaning, food preparation, and sewing, are standard ingredients of the narrative. A student in a class taught by doctoral student Barbara Hodne, at the University of Minnesota, responded to an invitation to characterize the novel, with the succinct synopsis, 'Bannock, Bannock, Bannock.' Owl's own washing up, for instance, is described at least eight times in the first quarter of the novel. In a literary/cultural tradition I was more confident of knowing, I would have less hesitation about the relative weighting of apparently incidental details and the ascription of meaning. As Ronald and Suzanne Scollon suggest about the structural divisions they impute to Athabaskan stories, 'Unfortunately, when working outside our own tradition the true ring of an analysis is dangerously suspect' (*Narrative* 106).

Even if I conclude, though, that what is signified here does correspond to what I would designate as 'rape,' I remain uneasy with such naming. The designation 'rape' feels like a violence done to the scene. Conversant as I am with the literature of (often) white feminism, I find myself in a quandary. In feminist analysis, after all, the possibility of naming 'the problem that has no name' – sexism, homophobia, sexual harassment – is often experienced as a transformative perceptual shift, placing in a larger political context what has been felt as anomalous, self-induced, or even delusory. In part, what I experience as the textual violation of labelling here inheres in the inevitable reduction of both the felt specificities of the scene and the inchoateness of Owl's own understanding of it. Even less ambiguous experiences, such as her schoolteacher's drawing her close between his legs, remain from her perspective indefinable: 'I should tell Mom. Tell Mom what?' (126). But I am trying to pinpoint something beyond the incapacity, say, of clinical labels to convey adequately the subjective richness of the consciousness of a Benjy Compston or the narrators in Atwood's *Surfacing* or Eli Danica's *Don't*. To name the violence enacted against Owl's Mom 'rape' feels like both the removal of the scene from the level of ostensibly 'non-verbal' sensory immediacy and potentially the imposition from outside of an entire, internally coherent but/hence somehow inapposite interpretive grid. The word 'rape' does more than describe actions. As part of an ideological archive, it risks superimposing on Owl's report the Euro-American fetishizing and commodifying of female chastity, the prioritizing of the gender wars over other forms of oppression and struggle, the articulation of transgression in terms of individual autonomy rather than communal well-being, and any number of other mirrors that I mistake for windows. Repudiation of the violation here may be framed more, for instance, in terms of the assault on social harmony, communal survival, and the respect owed women as transmitters of life and culture.

———•———

Mirrors
are the perfect lovers
....
throw me on the bed

reflecting side up,
fall into me,

it will be your own
mouth you hit, firm and glassy,

your own eyes you find you
are up against closed closed   (Atwood, 'Tricks with Mirrors,' *Selected* 147)

———•———

Feminist advocacy of 'breaking the silence' is, moreover, nested in a wider Western therapeutic context alert to the 'return of the repressed' and the merits of the 'talking cure.' The advice to Danny in *Silent Words* over the drowning of his friend, 'Don't think about things you cannot change' (214), like Owl's knowledge that her mother will be angered by tears over dead puppies, signals a cultural divergence over the place of naming or even knowing. That difference is now playing itself out, for example, in the inadequacy of traditional twelve-step group recovery programs to serve Native people.

Mohawk psychiatrist Clare Brant suggests, as one of eight Native philosophical principles, that 'Displays of anger could jeopardize the voluntary co-operation essential to the survival of closely-knit groups. Anger must, therefore, not be shown or *sometimes even felt*' (quoted in Opekokew and Pratt 12; emphasis added).[4] At the McMaster University 'Distinct Voices' symposium in October 1992, Slipperjack alluded, without naming it, to Brant's 'Native Ethics and Rules of Behaviour,' citing the feeding of John Bull without reproach some time after he has shot the family's dog as an instance of the proscription regarding displays of anger. Given the fact of cultural hybridization and the impact of colonialism on Owl's community, I found myself asking whether group cohesion is served by application of such an ethic in the face of overt violence that challenges its first principles. Slipperjack's discursive method – descriptive amplitude, interpretive reticence: 'the only thing I can do is remind you of the person you once were' ('Ruby' 209) – may represent a way to repudiate and challenge the violence from *within* that ethic.

The precept downplaying emotional self-expression extends the possible incongruence between Native and Western suppositions about psychosocial self-construction and about psychotherapeutic archaeology, a difference with implications for the realist narrative. Of course, the violence enacted upon Owl's mother, unlike the drowning of Danny's friend or the sacrifice of the puppies, is neither inevitable nor necessary. Some of the silences within and between entries, however, especially later in the novel, may reflect an ethos in which 'speaking bitterness' is far from a cultural imperative and in which silence, even or particularly about painful experiences, may take on a positive as well as a negative valence.

Even more striking for me than the opacity of the novel's finely textured surface (reminiscent of Slipperjack's photo-realist paintings on her novel covers) is the power of its fissures. Hiatuses, factual and temporal, fracture the last quarter of the novel, hiatuses occasioned by and simultaneously eliding both the colonial context and the violence, often sexual, visited on the women and children of the community. The sketchiness of this part of the book has occasioned criticism from reviewers: 'a forgettable blur ...' complains Gloria Hildebrandt, 'more like raw material than a finished, crafted work' (95). For me the silences registered as the most eloquent and evocative component of the narrative, enacting the damage done to the community, the personal and social ruptures being documented. Casting back an eerie light on earlier scenes of familial and community harmony, they also retroactively destabilized the earlier, deceptively artless narrative exhaustiveness.

Except for Owl's early train trip for medical treatment, we hear nothing about her excursions outside the community. The anticipatory questions about life beyond the grade-six seats, life in town, which she provokes in the reader – 'What's it like where Annie is? ... What will it be like when I go off to Boarding School?' (169) – receive, from a reader's perspective, the same evasion as Bobby's early inquiry. Emma LaRocque has spoken appreciatively of the book as 'one of the first novels that focuses entirely on a Native community ... without reference to white people or white society' ('Emma' 197). So Owl's schooling in town mandates season-long gaps in her account, between summer vacations and Christmas holidays. The refusal, within the entries that remain, to allude to the intervening experiences is conspicuous. At the 'Distinct Voices' symposium, Slipperjack spoke poignantly about her own experience of residential school, where she was stripped even of her clothes and hair, and could recognize nothing but her mother's eyes in her own image in the mirror. Schooling she described as an assault from which she retreated through psychic withdrawal and from which she had to renew herself through her annual return home each summer. Clearly, then, the elision here, rather than an indifference to such material, is a considered strategy.

'You've never gotten out of the habit of running around barefoot, have you?' Barbara asks towards the book's conclusion. Owl sturdily shifts the locus of judgment with her reformulation, 'Let's just say, I never got *into* the habit of wearing shoes' (199; emphasis added). In like fashion, Slipperjack refuses to frame difference as lack or deviation, and so chooses, metaphorically speaking, to exclude the normatizing context of shoes. Gloria Hildebrandt's sense that 'the book lacks a view of the subject from a wider perspective ... It is the place so completely, that no other world is possible' identifies this principle of selection. Her recognition – 'We have no sense of location within a greater world, and no method of viewing the action' – captures the disorienting effect for the non-Native reader but with an unfortunate negative spin (95). More positively, M.F. Salat identifies Slipperjack's exclusion of the white world and disinclination to identify the Native world explicitly as such as political acts, challenging white presumptuousness (76–7). Beyond ensuring a counterhegemonic perspectival stability, though, the lacunae proffer silences where projections may echo or the unvoiced may speak.

On my first reading of *Honour the Sun*, the unanticipated rifts towards the end produced an abrupt sense of the novel's structural control and power. Just as the punctuation of coulees on the expanse of prairie, for me, brings definition and appreciation to what I may otherwise experience as unavoidable and hence burdensome spaciousness (a kind of Saussurian definition by difference), so the fractured ending immediately contextualized and revalued the unfolding of the theretofore undramatic narrative landscape. Rereading, with anticipation of the final structural fragmentation, imbued the early entries with a poignancy beyond the familiar retrospective poignancy of narrative foreknowledge. This was a more seismic shift, turning my rereading into a revisiting of as yet dormant faultlines. The novel fell readily into two parts, with the early structural simplicity, cohesion, and thoroughness both heightened and construed painfully as an imperilled achievement. (This may also derive from a bias on my part towards conscious craft.) Subsequent readings eroded that easy division between pre- and postlapsarian social and narrative structures, with tremors felt increasingly early. Now, though, I find myself asking whether my experience of the caesurae as a structural violence more disturbing even than the social and personal losses depicted doesn't represent a kind of cultural misreading, a premature readiness to diagnose withdrawal into the self and silence as dysfunctional.

In part my conviction of *Honour the Sun*'s structural power may reflect my Western postmodern appreciation of gaps of indeterminacy. I much preferred *Honour the Sun* to the early manuscript version of *Silent Words*, for instance, which was low-key throughout and uninterrupted, lacking the more wrenching conclusion and discontinuous epilogue of its published version.[5] Even with the welcome dislocating effects of the revisions made to the ending of *Silent Words*, my instinctive tendency is to find *Honour the Sun* stronger, a critical stance that prioritizes discontinuity and risks ignoring other values the novels serve. In *Other Destinies: Understanding the American Indian Novel*, Louis Owens, while alert to apparent counter-instances, suggests that 'Ultimately, whereas postmodernism celebrates the fragmentation and chaos of experience, literature by Native American authors tends to seek transcendence of such ephemerality and the recovery of "eternal and immutable" elements represented by a spiritual tradition that escapes historical fixation, that places humanity within a carefully, cyclically ordered cosmos and gives humankind irreducible responsibility for the maintenance of that delicate equilibrium' (20). Like the white school-teacher in *Honour the Sun* who, in his new context, has to be shown how to shake the schoolbell (an instrument whose signification he takes for granted) so as to signal school rather than church, I must be alert for unfamiliar codes in a deceptively familiar medium.

Do the silences replicate for the reader the growing estrangement and bewilderment experienced by the maturing protagonist, or deny the reader access to information? Do they effect a rupture between insiders to Slipperjack's cultural community, for whom the gaps may not need decoding, and outsiders? How do readings of the gaps as a kind of narrative violence cohere with the novel's construction of a different silence, the calming and instructive silence of the natural world? To what degree can the silences, counterparts to Owl's growing personal independence, be read positively?

As far back as I can remember, I belonged to a secret society of Indian women, meeting around a kitchen table in a conspiracy to bring the past into the present ... They heard, and they taught me to hear, the truth in things not said. They listened, and they taught me to listen, in the space between words. (Bell, *Faces* 56–7)

Margery Fee has associated the paucity of explanation and interpretation in *Honour the Sun* with the distinction drawn by Ronald and Suzanne Scollon between what they name (unpropitiously) 'bush consciousness' and 'modern consciousness' (Fee, 'Discourse' 46–7). I find Ronald Scollon's account of Athabascan repudiation of specialized, decontextualized, and segmented knowledge suggestive: 'Each is his own expert and rejects the concept of knowledge or expertise which he needs and does not have ... As a result of the integrative aspect of the bush consciousness, all knowledge and social experience that is felt as foreign or as being introduced by forces from outside the individual is resisted where possible and actively undermined where resistance is impossible' (*Context* 40–1). Slipperjack is not, obviously enough, Athabascan; her very act of authorship sets her outside an ethos of communicative independence; and her positioning necessarily entails a cultural hybridity.[6] Danny in *Silent Words* – and along with him the reader? – is being actively inducted into Ojibway skills and mores. Traces of the ethos that the Scollons describe exist, though, in Slipperjack's comments, 'Who am I to tell you your interpretation is not correct? ... You only see what you can see ... Who am I to come and tell you something? It is there for you to see' ('Ruby' 208–9). Danny, moreover, is being less instructed than offered the opportunity to observe.[7]

The distinction between the 'autonomy and self-containment' of 'bush consciousness,' on the one hand, and individuality within 'modern consciousness,' the 'individuality of the component' dependent on the larger system for survival and self-definition, on the other, might clarify the function of communication in *Honour the Sun* (Scollon and Scollon, *Narrative* 103). It might also modify a reading of the novel's conclusion. I construct myself/ves and my accomplishments (including the presentation of this book) in large part through the reception(s) I receive. So I find disconcerting the apparent emotional self-sufficiency within Owl's world, the characters' capacity to absorb rather than reflect experiences. Echo chamber meets acoustic tile. My sense of difference is intensified by the corresponding narrative technique in the latter part of the novel, where events of considerable import – Owl's reconciliation with her mother: 'Somewhere along the way, we came to understand each other' (202); and her decision to leave the community – are noted with absolute parsimony or swallowed in narrative lacunae. (Cultural explanations beckon, like Clare Brant's identification of 'conservation-withdrawal ... characterized by even slower and quieter behaviour' as an adaptive Native reaction to situations of danger and anxiety [quoted in Opekokew and Pratt 13].) It is not the gaps in themselves that disconcert, not for this postmodern reader, but their matter-of-factness. I am taken aback by the possible implication that the narrator rather than any audience is the ultimate endpoint for her experiences. The power, even, of the final, wider vision to situate the personal and social trauma represented within those gaps (along with the clouds, noise, and impermanent human lives) against the persistence of sun and stillness disconcerts me.

I have to ask myself, too, whether my sense of gaps and absences, of personal and social estrangement reflected in structural hiatuses, isn't compounded by inattentiveness to what is present in the narrative. Have I been too busy listening *for* the silence to listen *to* the silence? Euro-American readers may dismiss as mere setting or as extraneous or tedious minutiae the very abundance of natural detail that is central to the cosmology Slipperjack assumes. Gloria Hildebrandt, for example, reaches the startling conclusion that the novel 'is set so utterly in the nameless, unidentified northern forest and lake country, that it fails to capture the spirit of place' (95). 'How do you listen to the silence when silence doesn't have a noise?' asks Owl. 'Or does it? I sit and listen. I can hear my heart beat, my breathing, a bird chirp from across the bay, Brian breaking branches somewhere, a slight wind overhead above the trees, a train coming, a dull hum in the air, and always my heartbeats' (184). Paula Gunn Allen warns about the tendency of Westerners to employ foreground–background perception and, in so doing, to relegate the earth to background in tribal narratives (*Sacred* 241). A feature of the passage above from *Honour the Sun* is its apparently undifferentiated inclusion of human and non-human, natural and technological, internal and external. 'Knowledge doesn't just come from human experience,' Slipperjack insisted, at the 'Distinct Voices' symposium; 'rocks and trees are also keepers of our tradition.' She speaks elsewhere of ongoing interactions with individual rocks and trees and of how they will witness the cycle of one's life and of one's children's thereafter ('Ruby' 207). In the 'Last Entry' of the novel, just where I'm inclined to read dispersal of community in the scattering of Owl's playfellows, the graves of Jere and Little Tony, Delia's neglect of her late husband's grave, and Owl's decision to move away, the narrator writes, 'I love this community. I know every hill and hollow, stump and tree' (209).

Likewise, the silences where I read the muteness of suppressed pain can also be read as the self-sufficiency of achieved contemplativeness. In an animist cosmology affirming relationships other than exclusively human ones, the persistence of the sun and of place may well counter the disruptions of particular human interactions, including that with the reader. The gaps may open onto other vistas. I may be being invited into a different conversation.

But while these are paths I have reconnoitred in attempting to read the differences that the novel represents, I am troubled by them. I fear that I have slipped into the all-too-popular role of ethnographer, one I want to repudiate. '[E]verybody in this country thinks they know what Indian is,' Paula Gunn Allen has observed ('Paula' 27). In the undergraduate 'minority literature' course I taught recently, it was *Honour the Sun* that was treated most as cultural reliquary, whether as accomplishment or compensation for unmet expectations. Captivated or frustrated by the novel, students were quick to focus on the evidence of material culture and social life that it contained, on the information about food, patterns of relationship, household labour ... The task I set myself here has been more to explicate my dilemma as reader than to explicate this text, or worse yet the culture from which it emanates. As Gerald Vizenor (Chippewa) wryly comments about the anthropological invention of Indians, and about the divide separating anthropology from play, humour, and imagination, 'There's nothing more deadly than to have somebody show up with a notebook in the middle of your game' ('Gerald' 170).

Particularly with cultures romanticized and appropriated, defamiliarization and a recognition of silences and impasses rather than quick cultural keys may be a more useful critical stance. I am taken with James Kincaid's suggestion that the dominant culture must 'get past sympathizing so fully and understanding so readily,' that '[t]he challenge is to honor the integrity and generosity of this [Native literary] subversion by reading more widely and warily ... trying harder to understand less' (1, 24). I am struck too by Allen's comment, which Kincaid quotes, about particular books on Laguna traditions, that they are good precisely 'because they make no sense' ('Paula' 24). In any case, as W.D. Ashcroft has pointed out, 'To seek to go to the culture first in order to understand the text is simply to use the culture itself ... as a meta-text on which we have to perform exactly the same procedures as we use for the text' (12).[8] (Ashcroft argues concomitantly that every fiction is ethnography in its creation of a world in which no reader can ever fully share [6].)

Slipperjack at the 'Distinct Voices' symposium used the metaphor of the river to describe her difficult effort to convey Ojibway realities in English. The river, she said, represents concepts, with the Ojibway original on one bank and the English parallel having to follow along on the other. The river metaphor provides a hopeful model, too, for the relationship of non-Native reader to the text, offering the possibility of constructing an equivalent though not identical meaning, while insisting always on the river of difference – foregrounded by silences and reticences – lying between Ojibway storyteller and English reader.[9]

There is more to a mirror
than you looking at

your full-length body
flawless but reversed,

....

the frame is carved, it is important,

it exists, it does not reflect you,
it does not recede and recede, it has limits

and reflections of its own   (Atwood 148)

Where are my words coming from? What do I listen to? Does the verb 'to honour,' like the verb 'to commune,' only fill me with modern discomfort? My three-year-old daughter interrupted me while I was working on the first draft of this chapter. 'Why you doing that?' she asked. 'I'm going to be talking to some people,' I gestured at my computer screen, 'and I have to figure out what I'm going to say.' She was back a minute later to find me deep in my thesaurus, at the category 'interpretation.' 'What you doing?' she asked.[10]

You don't like these metaphors.
All right:

Perhaps I am not a mirror.
Perhaps I am a pool.

Think about pools.   (Atwood 150)

I began this chapter assuming that the silences in *Honour the Sun* would prove to be moments of resistance – resistance, that Waldo that we postcolonial critics seek so diligently in every postcolonial textual land-scape. But I wonder now whether, even more than indicting by indirec-tion the colonizing structures whose effects are felt so painfully because so inaudibly in the text, Slipperjack isn't concentrating on a more revolutionary[11] displacement. I wonder whether the silences may be not only a withholding before an appropriating white gaze (though they are that in part), but also the enactment of an alternative metaphysics. Is this a text in which the *narrative*, as well as the character, increasingly honours the silence, listens to the sun? I began the chapter intending to use the injunction 'listen to the silence' as a guide to reading strategies. Now I question whether that may not be an evasion of the novel's challenge, a stopping short before its invitation to do more than just to elaborate reading strategies. What is at issue here is not just how I read the text but how it reads me. What happens when a text asks one implicitly to talk about it less and internalize it more?

We live in silences,
little bits of spaces,
slim fitted slivers,
wedged between bunches of sound.   (Armstrong, 'Visions,' *Breath* 19)

4

'Nothing but the Truth': Beatrice Culleton's *In Search of April Raintree*

[T]ext is an event under contest.

(McClintock 204)

In Search of April Raintree (1983), by Métis writer Beatrice Culleton, explores, through a first-person voice, the maturation of two Métis sisters contending with a racist society and its messages. Early critical responses to the novel, situating it in terms of its simplicity, honesty, authenticity, and artlessness, implicitly separate testimonial immediacy and artistic craft, assigning uncrafted testimony to the 'Native informant.'[1] Several reviews paradoxically locate the novel's art precisely in its artlessness: 'an earnest, artless journal-cum-fiction that is all the more powerful for its simplicity' (Moher 50) and 'irritatingly naïve at times, but a more sophisticated style would rob it of its authenticity, which is its greatest asset' (A. Francis 20). Or they inadvertently imply an art ostensibly not contained within traditional aesthetic parameters: 'What the book lacks in literary polish is more than made up for in compassion, understanding and *beautifully controlled* emotion' (Sigurdson 43; emphasis added). At best, the reviewers evince a difficulty in devising an aesthetic language to account for the text's emotional power; at worst, they display condescension and nostalgia for the unmediated authenticity of the speaking 'Other.'

Yet even after Indian literature was 'discovered,' attempts to open the canon to it based themselves – mistakenly, to be sure, yet powerfully, nonetheless – on an appeal to the 'naturalness' of this literature, as though it was not individuals and cultural practices but the very rocks and trees and rivers that had somehow produced the Native poem or story, and somehow spoke directly in them. (Krupat, *Voice* 98)

'Trembling, but honest,' is the Crown attorney's characterization of April Raintree's testimony at the rape trial where she witnesses to the assault upon herself. 'Not once did she waver between truth and fiction,' he avers (184).[2] (The inherent destabilizing irony of this assertion, and of the disjunction on which it depends, in the context of a novel, where 'truth' might occasionally be expected to coincide with fiction, is heightened by the publisher's curious placement of the supplemental notes. Appended to a rather anxious differentiation between the story and Culleton's own biography, the conventional disclaimer [that legal fiction, 'any resemblance to people living or dead ...'] is printed on the last page of the story itself, hard upon April's discovery of a sense of purpose and an identification with her people.)[3] In a novel in which the telling of untruths and half-truths proliferates both socially and personally, in which 'lies, secrets, and silence' are inflicted upon April and her sister, Cheryl, by foster parents, social workers, and history books, and prove to be destructive components of their own interactions ('I lie to protect her and she lies to protect me, and we both lose out' [205]), 'honesty' and 'truth' seem to function as talismans.

Certainly they function as talismans for reviewers. Ray Torgrud, selected to promote the novel on the back cover, refers to Gertrude Stein's maxim 'Write the truest sentence that you know' and, describing the book as autobiographical fiction, notes its 'unflinching honesty.' The perceived simplicity of *In Search of April Raintree* is aligned with its presumed honesty: reviewer Rob Ferguson speaks in one breath of 'an unapologetic honesty and a simplicity in writing style' (42).[4] The immediacy of her truth telling becomes Culleton's guarantor of literary power. Judith Russell, speculating that Culleton has 'invented the odd experience,' concludes that, 'in those cases, the story loses impact through distance' (193).[5]

'Honesty.' Under the *Concise Oxford Dictionary*'s definition of 'honesty,' right after 'honesty is the best policy,' I came across what I read as another maxim, this one unfamiliar to me: 'plant with purple flowers and translucent pods.' Taking 'plant' to be the imperative of the verb ('il faut cultiver son jardin,' and all that), I was struck at once not only by the beauty of this long-ago metaphor (although the full significance of the purple flowers eluded me initially) but also by the applicability of the aphorism to perceptions of Culleton's writing. The translucent pod of her story, its near-transparent honesty, had apparently allowed its intense (even over-wrought, 'purple') emotion and bold flowerings to appeal directly to her reviewers. Simple candour might somehow adequately contain literary brashness, as in Penny Petrone's description of the novel as 'elevated from melodramatic cliché by its daring honesty and its energy' (140).[6] Advice on how to live and how to write: 'Plant with purple flowers and translucent pods.'

It's true; that's how I read the *Oxford* entry. Honestly.

And what, after all, can be more unequivocal and straightforward than a dictionary entry?

In a graduate course I taught in the mid-1990s, explicitly directed to Canadian literatures 'on the margins,' it was *In Search of April Raintree* (along with Jovette Marchessault's *Lesbian Triptych*, for quite different reasons) that sparked the most heated discussion about issues of literary merit and literary élitism, about the politics of guilt and the status of the truth claim, about visceral responses and intellectual ones, about literary author-ity and literary audience(s). As far as one student was concerned, the book – so simplistic and poorly written that he wouldn't have chosen to finish reading it – was on the course only because it was written by a Métis writer. This same dedicated student failed, for the first time, to appear for the subsequent class on Culleton and, later, to the Freudian quips of fellow students, confessed somewhat wryly to having lost his copy of the text. By contrast, another student, attributing reader discomfiture to the book's 'naked,' 'unembellished' visceral appeal, described being distraught and off-kilter for twenty-four hours after reading it, without for some time being able to pinpoint the source of her distress. A third proposed the analogy of the car that, despite its ramshackle condition, still provides reliable transportation, wondering whether the book was 'a beater that just won't die.'

The flashpoint in what had hitherto in the term been a decorous class came in reaction to a student suggestion that the novel served to provide Métis readers with a recognizable reality. Why, then, someone shot back, as disconcerting in his abrupt anger as in the rawness of his formulation, did Culleton not simply distribute the book to her friends in local bars. Other students rose to this at once, equally passionately, with countercharges of literary snobbery (though not, interestingly enough, of racism). Clearly even to students versed in notions of hege-mony and counterdiscursive production, the presence of a book such as *In Search of April Raintree* on the syllabus was fraught and disquieting. As with reviewers, subsequent discussion that day tended to eddy around the idea that Culleton had said what she meant and meant what she said (one student's phrase), and the question of whether, from a literary standpoint, such Horton-like faithfulness sufficed. In a later paper, one student, Carter Meland, defended Culleton's aesthetic and a catholic critical reading, arguing that 'The modernist aesthetic and the sentimental sensibility are only separated by a cultural manicheism which privileges the "artful" over the "artless."'

'Translucent' can be, and often is, interchanged with 'transparent.' And, botanically speaking, a translucent pod, by comparison with legumi-nous seed-vessels of a more guarded nature, is relatively forthcoming about its contents. 'Translucent,' though, falling as it does between 'transparent' and 'opaque,' means transmitting light but not without diffusion, seen through but not seen through simply. April, it might be noted, resists the condescension in her attorney's formulation of her-self, refusing his fashioning of her as tormented, honest *naïf*.

Transmitting light but not without diffusion. A second meaning of 'to diffuse,' less well known than the first ('to pour out so as to spread in all directions'), is 'to perplex.'

[A]uthenticity is implicitly a polemical concept, fulfilling its nature by dealing aggressively with received and habitual opinion, aesthetic opinion in the first instance, social and political opinion in the next. (Trilling 94)

Interplaited with the notion of authenticity in *In Search of April Raintree* is the question of identity, both authorial and fictive.[7] Culleton has characterized the novel, initially about alcoholism in her conception, as ultimately about identity ('Beatrice' 99). April and Cheryl come into maturity as Métis women in the face of racist–sexist affronts to that identity, most blatantly represented by the 'native girl' [*sic*] syndrome' detailed by their social worker (66–7). The story of that process is sustained, for most reviewers, by Culleton's own identity as a Métis woman. 'Beatrice Culleton set out to tell a story – her own story – in the plainest available language. Nothing else is needed,' says Judith Russell

(192).[8] Just as Culleton's writing can be read as the straightforward documentation of eclipsed facts of social reality, with her personal experience of racism, foster care, poverty, alcoholism, and sibling suicide warranting the truth status of the novel's representations,[9] so the characters' struggle with identity can be read as a quest for the true self. In particular, April's story can be taken as a dis-covery of an intrinsic selfhood persistently denigrated by others, a sloughing off of false personae ('Only at the end does April realize her mistake of trying to become a white person' [Holman 11]), and a final embracing of an authentic self ('The real April Raintree, the April Raintree she tucked away for safe-keeping, begins to emerge' [Keeshig-Tobias, Rev. 58]). Paul Wilson, who also treats the issue of April's identity as transparent – 'April determines at last to embrace her real heritage' – does admittedly go on at least to nuance that heritage, proposing that April's initial pursuit of a white identity is 'as faithful to a part of her heritage' as Cheryl's identification with their Native background (30).[10]

Such readings, of the author's and characters' breaking through to a reality and a given identity that have been obscured – historically and personally – by inaccurate representations, are the literary equivalents of certain recent directions in history. The tendency in history is one that Joan Scott identifies (and subsequently goes on to interrogate): 'The challenge to normative history has been described ... as an enlargement of the picture, a correction to oversights resulting from inaccurate or incomplete vision, and it has rested its claim to legitimacy on the authority of experience,' with experiential evidence perceived referentially as simply 'a reflection of the real' (776). Such readings treat the novel's medium as transparent, identity as immanent, experience as self-evident, and Culleton as the trembling but honest truth teller.

[A] mixed-blood must waver in the blood and it's difficult to waver [on?] the page. You have to find some meaning not in the sides but in the seam in between and that's obviously where a mixed-blood, an earthdiver, a trickster, must try and find all meaning, imaginative meaning ... We're trouble, and I'd rather be trouble than an image. (Vizenor, 'Gerald' 174)

In Search of April Raintree is not a seamless, unitary narrative. At the simplest level, it contains two voices, April as narrator and the interpolated voice of her sister, Cheryl. The latter voice is represented in a variety of discourses: the stumbling (and unlikely) letters of a pre-schooler; subsequent letters; academic speeches and essays on Métis history; oratory written for a university newspaper but in the end delivered orally and privately to her sister at a powwow; dialogue, most centrally; and, posthumously, diary entries. In addition, the novel either represents or addresses a range of other discourses, including social work and foster-care tutelage, classroom history lessons, Native-produced history, ecclesiastical infallibility, the rhetoric of misogynist/racist violence, legal testimony and courtroom summation, the romance of home-and-fashion magazines, the eloquence of the literary Indian, and the visual/tactile communication of a Native elder. What the characters 'experience' is a series of representations, and, especially in the first half of the novel, conflicting and incompatible representations, and outright falsehoods, sufficient to induce in them a certain exegetical wariness. What the characters impart is likewise a series of contingent, partial (in the sense both of incomplete and of partisan),[11] and discordant renderings, conducive to the same kind of caution in the reader.

Subjects are constituted discursively and experience is a linguistic event. (Scott 793)

In one of Cheryl's letters to April, mourning JFK's assassination, Cheryl concludes, after a brief tribute to the Kennedys' youth and energy, not with the man himself or his political and legislative accomplishments. Instead she gestures towards his speeches and, curiouser yet, towards his speechwriters, expressing the hope that Robert Kennedy will keep the same writers. In preparing to teach *In Search of April Raintree*, I was struck most forcibly by this passage, as a key to reading the novel. The president is dead; long live his discourse. Admittedly, in part the passage represents a narrative nod towards Cheryl's developing literary and oratorical interests, merely a stroke of characterization. But I was startled by the nonchalance of the acknowledgment, the affirmation even, of crafted (and stirring, politically effective) speech that stands in place of the person himself, does not require the authenticating impress of immediate inner emotion, is not necessarily the outer manifestation of an intrinsic self. (Contrast this with the welling up and pouring forth of cathartic torrents attributed to Culleton, by comparison [Sigurdson 43].)

Impervious to the romance of authenticity, Culleton takes for granted the notion of performance (in the delegated, and eventually bequeathed, voice, are there hints of a disseminated, endlessly deferred self?) and our dependence on representations. And this from the point of view of a child, presumably more susceptible to naïve notions of spontaneous self-expression; in the context of a political administration sustained more than many by personal charisma and so by imperatives of sincerity and authenticity; and regarding an earlier period somewhat less proficient in and cynical about manipulation of the political image than the present. Of course, to contemporary readers with the advantage of time and to the author herself – 'At that age, you don't know all the back-room stuff and you just see the image presented,' she comments about her own early admiration for Kennedy (Garrod 88) – the dismantling of the Kennedy myth, the underside of Camelot, adds another, ironic, layer to the passage's recognition of the *making* of a president.

'Accuracy' in history is a genre. (McClintock 226)

Regarding the text's interest in representation, Margery Fee concludes, 'Both [*In Search of April Raintree* and Jeannette Armstrong's *Slash*] show how the dominant discourse functions so clearly that some readers may find the demonstration too "obvious" or explicit to be aesthetically pleasing' ('Upsetting' 177). Certainly, the novel's attention to the hegemonic construction of Native reality is relentless. Cheryl's teacher's vapid assertion 'They're not lies; this is history' marks but one of the narrative's many moments of irony and confutation (57). But its examination of what Michel Foucault calls the 'political economy' of truth (*Power/Knowledge* 131) and our embeddedness in systems of meaning making is more far-ranging than that. In the opening pages of the novel, five-year-old April's capacity to apprehend her circumstances is complicated both by apparent mystifications – the word 'medicine' for alcohol – and by the constraints of her own experience – her perception of a masturbating man as 'peeing' or her mother's childbearing as a hospitalization brought on by obesity. The text is an intricate choreography of (mis)representations, the relationship of the two sisters being no less fraught with the complications of self-construction (and self-invention) than are the versions of themselves and their history that they are fed by a racist society. Mrs Dion's simple instruction that telling the truth is always easier and better than lying, which early on seems a touchstone against which the adult hypocrisies surrounding the children can be measured, becomes less compelling over the course of the book. The entire plot of the novel turns on the considerable impediments to truth telling. The merit of truth telling remains more imponderable. Most unsettling, though, truth itself becomes less self-evident. Is Cheryl's final, bitter, and self-destroying conviction that she is confronting 'the true picture of my father' (217) any less misleading than April's similar callow conclusion as a youngster that 'I knew the truth about them [my parents]' (52)?

During the conversation in which April acknowledges her Métis identity to him, Roger deceives her about his having an adopted Ojibway brother, Joe, to imply a shared experience. I find the lie offensive, especially coming directly after April's dismissal of whites' half-baked claims to know what being Native is like. But it seems to serve a purpose ultimately in creating a playful intimacy between the two suitors, with April shifting to pretended anger and friendly physical contact when Roger is found out. The novel's apparent endorsement of Roger's lie may function to disrupt the moral economy in the novel of wholesome truths and pernicious lies. It confounds not only simplistic judgments but also (given the existence of Roger's Ojibway *friend*, Joe) the ostensible binarism of truth and falsehood itself, being neither simply one nor the other. More radically, since April goes on to note her own bewilderment over Cheryl's drinking, the endorsement could be read as helping to disrupt any singular, totalizing, privileged access, through the authority of experience or otherwise, to 'what it's like being a native person' (157).

'There are no truths, Coyote,' I says. 'Only stories.' (King, *Green* 326)

The acuity and persistence with which the novel registers how the effects of truth are produced render suspect those readings that present the text as a straightforward, corrective telling-it-like-it-is. In fact, Culleton illustrates many poststructuralist conclusions about reality as constituted rather than given.[12] In April's inability to take back dishonest words making her an orphan and in Cheryl's suggestion that April's pretence of not caring seems to be turning into reality, Culleton records the power and autonomy of even second-order discursive constructions. In Mrs DeRosier's precluding of her husband's corroboration of April's mistreatment, poisoning the well with lies about a flirtation, the text documents control of the discursive means of production. Mrs Semple's dismissive 'Don't try to tell me that you walked all that way' (65) and Cheryl's wry surmise that her very resentment at the prejudicial paradigm of the Native Girls' Syndrome marks her as a likely instance of the syndrome both display the catch-22 scope of pre-emptive discourses. In Mrs Semple's presumption that the DeRosier mother and daughter 'have no reason to lie about who did what' (66), we have the familiar 'objectivity' of the hegemonic position and supposed 'interestedness' of counter-discourse. The situatedness of knowledge is given quite literal illustration in April's discovery, regarding an otherwise familiar conversation with her sister about their Native background, that 'sitting there in our tent, surrounded by proud Indians, everything seemed different' (168). April's capacity to draw contrary conclusions from Cheryl's inspirational pieces on Riel – 'Knowing the other side, the Métis side ... just reinforced my belief that if I could assimilate myself into white society, I wouldn't have to live like this for the rest of my life' (85) and 'White superiority had conquered in the end' (95) – like her capacity to see watery eyes and leathery skin where Cheryl sees quiet beauty, conveys the multivalence, the indeterminacy of the text they are both reading.

But here I catch myself saying 'registers,' 'records,' 'illustrates,' 'conveys,' and 'documents,' using the language of, and so reinstating, the very epistemological (and critical) model that I (along with Culleton, I suggest) wish to contest. I am speaking as if the truth, reality – in this case about knowledge and the operations of discourse – were a prediscursive absolute to be brought to view through the window of Culleton's narrative rather than a contested and provisional system of signification in whose workings the text implicates itself.

––––––––

Experience is at once always already an interpretation *and* something that needs to be interpreted. (Scott 797)

––––––––

Culleton has spoken of using *In Search of April Raintree* to rewrite circumstances, using the characters to do what she wishes she had done ('Images' 51). The example she gives is of inventing the Indian and Métis books that hearten Cheryl, resources whose existence in the

1950s she doubts and for which her own novel provides illustration after the fact. Characters, too, rewrite their scripts. In the immediate aftermath of her rape, April uses her scripted role of helplessness and victimization strategically, feigning vomiting to secure the rapists' licence-plate number and, ultimately, their arrest and conviction.[13] (The latter elements may, like Cheryl's Native pride and activism, entail affirmative biographical re-vision on Culleton's part.)[14] At the rape trial itself, the inhibiting instructions about legal evidence and the constraints on inference – 'One could testify to what was directly known,' April has been cautioned beforehand (164) – are shown to discredit and deflate her testimony:

'Now would you say the defendant was intoxicated?'
  'I don't know.'
  'Didn't you state that you smelled liquor on his breath?' (179)

Warned against drawing conclusions, April is then sandbagged for her circumspection. Besides again highlighting disparities in entitlement to (self)representation, the passage provides ironic (and metafictional) commentary on narrow, disempowering definitions of what constitutes experience,[15] on the simple testimonial's vulnerability to appropriation, and on the suspect division of labour between informant (transparent channel for authentic 'raw' data) and specialist (responsible for interpretive elaborations and artistic transformations). Just as April tells a fuller story than her legal role allows, the novel resists the confinement of the witness box.

Transparency. Transparency can be tricky, too. I have become accustomed to using 'transparent' as trope for lucidity, ingenuousness, clarity, or artlessness. In the Toronto apartment we rented for a year, the skylight above my desk imploded. The sonic boom it simulated sent us running out into the street, seeking more distant explanations. Fragments of skylight showered the (mercifully empty) room, from one doorway to the other, splattering around corners, flying into alcoves. Splinters of glass impaled themselves in the desktop, in the baseboard and mouldings. The paperback books on my desk were inscribed in Braille. Once the glass had been swept up, I would survey a patch of rug, reassure myself that it was clear, shift my position several degrees, and catch another sparkle. I would bend to pick up a shard, place my hand on its location, and the glass would have shifted as I stooped. When I switched on the ceiling fan, bits of crystal ambushed me from its blades. I located pieces of transparency at night, with my bare feet.

We knocked out the tracery of filaments, the glass filigree, surrounding the central jagged emptiness, but whenever the skylight had to be opened or closed, a glass rain fell. I placed a bedsheet over my desk and floor for the repeated visits of tradespeople come to measure and note down serial numbers that they could not find. Only a half-dozen shards gleamed against the white, hardly worth the effort. But when I gathered up the sheet, the tinkling colloquy told of a multitude. And I discovered opaque granules I had not seen before. I folded the sheet away, triumphant. But I had neglected to shut the skylight.

Transparency has its secrets. Ah, you say, but I am speaking to the special case, the transparent in fragments. (A single glass chip plops to the floor.) Then this is the pent-up story of transparency, its unspoken promise. (From my bowl of trophies, I would toss a piece up to capture the sound of its encounter with the rug, for this narrative; it would vault against my foot and vanish under the desk. I would find several new fragments instead.) Even whole and intact, transparency is crafty. With the aid of only two Barbadian rum punches, I have walked headlong into a glass door. I have immersed my face disconcertingly in a stream whose surface was closer than I had anticipated. I have watched darkness convert a window to a mirror, sunlight do the same for a lake. I have been instructed by the concluding image of Margaret Laurence's *Diviners*, as the writer-protagonist prepares to set down her final, fictional words: 'Only slightly further out, the water deepened and kept its life from sight' (370).

With my focal point fixed on the Métis experience of Culleton's text, do I risk running face-first into the self-reflexive medium wherein she tells the story of how that experience comes into meaning? In any case, is *In Search of April Raintree* unfractured, monologic, cohesive, a single pane of language? Or is it a scattering of stories, glittering into self-consciousness one moment, craftily effacing the act of storytelling the next, positioning itself here, then with a shift of perspective turning up over there?

Q: What is more elusive than something you cannot see because you see through it?
A: Many pieces of the same thing.

'What is the proper word for people like you?' (Culleton, *Search* 116)

Identity. Shape shifting. Vigilant against being named into Otherness, Cheryl multiplies identities:

'But you're not exactly Indians are you? What is the proper word for people like you?' one asked.
  'Women,' Cheryl replied instantly.
  'No, no, I mean nationality?'
  'Oh, I'm sorry. We're Canadians.' (116)

'Apple' to her little sister, 'Ape' to her vindictive foster sister, April Raintree/Raintry/Radcliff, too, eludes definition, with various selves glinting into and out of sight. Locating herself inconsistently, she can fantasize about 'passing,' about living 'just like a *real* white person' at one point, yet later puzzle over racial slurs wielded by her rapists, surprised she should be '*mistaken* as a native person' (49, 161; emphases mine). With one identity unreal and its alternative mistaken,[16] she challenges assumptions of a fundamental self, a true north against which other positions are measured as self-betraying defections. By acceding to neither designation, locating herself nowhere, she disrupts the binarism that naturalizes such identities.

When Cheryl assures April that at the Roseau powwow she'll finally meet 'real Indians,' April cannot determine whether her sister is being enthusiastic or sarcastic.[17] The novel is similarly equivocal on such matters. Cheryl notes ruefully that her poetic turns of phrase derive from Indian books, that 'most Indians today don't talk like that at all' (175). At the same time, she is reinvesting this rhetorical tradition with significance, having appropriated it from the discursive archive out of which she fashions herself. Where does authenticity lie, when a self-defined Native, in the very course of describing her white-identified sibling as a sister in blood but not in vision, is estranged from her own example, acknowledges herself as unnatural? Suggestively, the space that is opened in the novel for a revelation about Native existence remains emblematically empty, a stubborn lacuna, as the two white men issuing the invitation pre-empt Cheryl's voice and substitute their own convictions.[18] Given that April comes to Métis identity at the moment that Cheryl abandons it and that the itinerary of April's Nativeness is the inverse of her sister's, can the narrative be said to posit any fundamental Métis reality? Can the search for April Raintree be said to end with the book's conclusion?

The doubling of protagonists further confounds the question of identity. Polar opposites, the two sisters are illustrations of antipathetic extremes – of gratification in and repudiation of their Native heritage. Simultaneously, they are said to be, except for skin-colouring, alike enough to be identical twins, so much so that April characterizes her praise for Cheryl's beauty as oblique self-admiration. In place of the bounded and unitary self, *In Search of April Raintree* creates permeable and melded selves. The narrative voice is fluid and inclusive, neither hermetically singular nor neatly bifurcated. (In early third-person drafts, Culleton felt the necessity to represent Cheryl's perspective more equally ['This' 45; Garrod 90]). Rather, April's narrative voice is deflected and expanded by, required to make room for, aspects of Cheryl's vision. The framework of the novel is chiastic (the double helix provides an apt model), with the dual storylines intersecting and reversing direction, protagonists exchanging roles. Structurally, the critical moment of crossover is the rape scene, with the interchange between protagonists enacted physically, as it will thereafter be enacted psychologically and politically. April takes on Cheryl's body, is raped as Cheryl, and thereafter, in narrative time if not chronological time, the sisters trade places regarding Métis pride, Cheryl taking on April's shame, her secretiveness, and her superior knowledge of their parents; April, Cheryl's resilience, her allegiance to community, and, finally, her son.

Julia Emberley argues that, unhappily, the ending marks a reclaiming of '"identity" over difference ... a new synthesis of the split narratives of subjectivity constituted in Cheryl and April ... a new order of unification and reconciliation in which the "Indian-ness" of Cheryl is absorbed into the "whiteness" of April' (162). By contrast with reviewers, Emberley protests what she sees as a reinstating of authenticity in the figure of the Métis. But the narrative has been one of unstable (and even exchanged) subject positions, positions repeatedly renegotiated in response to social and discursive practices. The troubled history of Cheryl's Métis affiliation forestalls conclusiveness in April's move onto the same ground. The self constructed in the novel is multiple, provisional, discontinuous, and shared. To the demand for a 'proper word' to identify people like Cheryl and like April, *In Search of April Raintree* withholds an answer.

––––––––•–•––––––––

'I' is, itself, *infinite layers*. (Trinh, *Woman* 94)

––––––––•–•––––––––

The undermining of unitary and essentialist discourses of identity in the novel countermands notions of the author's own originary identity and the authenticating imprint of her experience.[19] *Which* of these various stories is Culleton's 'own'? *Who* is Culleton? If 'Métis' has been revealed as the product of divers(e), sometimes competing discourses, then the search for Beatrice Culleton becomes more vexed. And Métis, in all its multiplicity, is only one set among a multitude of subject positions, not always commensurable, that Culleton occupies. It does happen to be the exegetical configuration fixed on single-mindedly by most reviewers. Margaret Clarke, by contrast, emphasizing a feminist reading of the novel, suggests that for Culleton the experiences of female identity and Métis identity are inseparable (141). And these are but two of the 'matrices of intelligibility' (Judith Butler's term, *Gender* 17) within which biographical experience might come into meaning. 'Canadian,' for example, is another such matrix, as Cheryl's self-naming and Culleton's pained comments on the exclusion of Native people from Canadian identity suggest ('Images' 50).

The 'author' of the revised edition, as constituted through textual apparatus, moreover, is less simply the subject of life experiences similar to those in the novel than is the 'author' of the original edition. In the revised edition, she is constituted instead as more of a successful professional with speaking engagements in the schools, involvement in Native organizations, and a developing writing career (*April* iv, 185). This is even truer of the 1999 critical edition, where the biography stresses new juvenile fiction, the author's role as playwright in residence, and her work with the Royal Commission on Aboriginal Peoples. The fact that Culleton now goes by and writes under her birth name, Mosionier, simply problematizes again, at the level of the signature, the notion of a singular, unified, and intrinsic identity.

[W]e imagine ourselves, we create ourselves, we touch ourselves into being with words. (Vizenor, 'Gerald' 158)

A reading of the novel as spontaneous, cathartic truth telling, the laying bare of shocking but revealing realities, is complicated, too, by the publication, one year after the initial text, of an expurgated/adapted version, entitled *April Raintree*.[20] Culleton produced this school edition, attenuating or deleting obscene language and the explicit details relating to sexuality in particular, at the behest of the Native Education Branch of Manitoba Education.[21] With the presence of this sister text, Culleton's 'truth' immediately becomes double, duplicitous. The revision acts as a reminder, at the level of dissemination, of precisely the social, economic, and institutional (specifically educational) constraints on what can be said and heard, on how it can be said, that Culleton conveys within the novel. We can observe 'specific effects of power,' which Foucault describes as working to certify 'truth,' being bestowed on one version of the story in preference to another (*Power/Knowledge* 132). Culleton, though, has also demonstrated her commitment to getting Native materials into the schools, to transforming the discourse of Nativeness in practical ways ('Images' 48–51; 'This' 49). To the extent that her cooperation with Manitoba Education is more than a coerced concession to necessity,[22] the textual twinning marks a recognition of the plurality and particularities of places of discursive practice. Oral storytelling, to use another instance, is not fixed but varies with occasion, season, audience, function, and time.

April Raintree, furthermore, is not just a bowdlerized, diminished version of the original. In addition to meeting the requirements of Manitoba Education, Culleton has extensively reworked other aspects of the text. She has corrected matters of fact, such as the name of a Winnipeg bridge.[23] She has improved verisimilitude, making Cheryl's preschool spelling more phonetic and more plausible, for example.[24] She has added explanatory detail, on how April remains ignorant of her fiancé's resources or how she comes to overhear her mother-in-law and her husband's lover. She has toned down potential melodrama, making the assault on Cheryl by a disgruntled aspiring customer less deliberate and prolonged, and eliminating April's revelation to the indignant witness of Cheryl's suicide, 'She was my sister, mister' (*Search* 209; *April* 169). She has revised wording to reflect the participant's rather than an observer's perspective.[25] She has made scenes less static. Cheryl's report of her confrontation with school authorities is contextualized within dialogue with April and a friend, Jennifer. April's solitary readings of Cheryl's letters are dramatized as communications with the dog Rebel, Rebel's inattentiveness permitting more irony and indirection than April's original, temporary enthusiasm. With rare exceptions, Culleton has revised in the direction of reducing rather than increasing editorializing, letting scenes speak for themselves.[26] She has replaced statement with illustration and dialogue.[27] In particular, she has expanded scenes between April and Roger, eliminating his sometimes-ponderous condemnations of 'game-playing,' reducing his knowing comments on Cheryl,[28] and providing engaging, playful banter instead. In these scenes and elsewhere, she invests April with added traces of strength and initiative.[29] Whether in particulars of paragraphing and diction or larger matters of tone and characterization, almost every page of *April Raintree* attests to the existence of an/other version of Culleton's story, and one that has been crafted so.[30]

Neither edition, therefore, can stand as the definitive text of this narrative, each offering details and exhibiting merits that the other lacks. By their divergent existences – with the full story, the 'true' story, flickering into view now in one text, now in the other – *In Search of April Raintree* and *April Raintree* testify against the presumption of artless, raw honesty. Taken as a single, internally discrepant document, *(In Search of) April Raintree* conveys the simultaneity, the layered heterogeneity of the ways the fictions of experience, self, and truth can be composed. Its own boundaries become permeable, its identity elusive, multiple, palimpsestic.

Perhaps the image of the translucent pod, however diffuse its transmission of light, is the wrong metaphor, implying as it does some kernel of reality, of truth, seen through a glass darkly. Perhaps the trope of transparency, however evasive and crafty the transparency, risks reinscribing the divide between seeing and seeing through, between experience and its discursive transmission. Consider instead, then, the secondary definition of transparency, as entity rather than as attribute. Consider *the* transparency – the photographic slide or, better yet, the colour separations used to produce book and magazine illustrations. The representation inheres within rather than existing beyond the transparency itself. Indeed, in the case of colour separations, the representation is constituted entirely in the layering of the medium itself, residing as a totality nowhere. Monochromatic transparencies in combination, through careful registration or alignment, produce a cumulative impression, one readily transformed by simple substitution – of a blue transparency for a yellow one, say – as the versions of the same picture in photography magazines, now in shades of orange, now of purple, can testify. Or, using a bank of projectors, one can create an indefinite series of differing images simply by superimposing projections from carousels of transparencies, in predetermined or random combinations.

The effect, the image, has no single origin, no true original. Like discourse, in Foucault's definition, the transparencies produce the realities they convey (*Archaeology* 49).

In 1991, I gave a paper on Jeannette Armstrong's *Slash* (an early version of chapter one), raising issues I felt needed to be attended to by those of us who found the novel outside the familiar literary parameters of our Western, non-Native cultural experience. After the presentation, a white woman in the audience stood up and presented her dilemma. She wanted to include Native writing in her syllabi but found Armstrong's and Culleton's writing thus far inadequate, although they might mature as writers in the future. It was my first experience with something women of colour describe repeatedly, in their encounters with white feminist audiences, the experience of having been edited out, of not having been heard at all. Not that I thought I had made an irrefutable case. In fact, I was anticipating the argument that, even given my premises, Armstrong's novel did not entirely succeed. But my questioner was so oblivious to the considerations I had put forward and the ways in which they were implicated in her dilemma that, for some time, I was convinced she had arrived only after the panel's conclusion. Her impervious goodwill was a revelation, to me, of what marginalized texts are up against, the incapacity of discursive systems even to register information that lies too far outside their paradigms. My abbreviated and stymied response – what could a thirty-second problematizing of aesthetic absolutes accomplish that a thirty-minute attempt had not? – was to suggest that more harm than good came from teaching works one was convinced were inferior and to recommend other titles by Native authors that she might contemplate using.

Catch-22: It is better to refrain from teaching works (from other cultures) that one considers inferior.

Time for a confession: although I am committed to teaching it, I have, until recently, found *In Search of April Raintree* embarrassing to teach. I have tended to place it on the syllabi of lower-division courses, and, in those instances, of Women's Studies courses where the focus is less on the literary/aesthetic dimension of the text and where students' disciplinary diversity makes them less literarily exigent. In the case of the graduate course I have described earlier, I selected it deliberately as an instance of the problematics of reception, genre, audience, and aesthetic standards. Even there, wary of student unreceptiveness, I scheduled it late in the course, after issues of reception and normativeness had been problematized, to ensure that it received a hearing. Gratified at evidence of literary 'sophistication,' such as the wry allusion to the Battle of Seven Oaks in the naming of the racist social worker, Mrs Semple, I find myself wanting, but largely failing, to vindicate the text in the conventional terms of the academic and literary milieu into which I have introduced it.

My graduate student was not far off in insisting that the text would not have been on the course were it not by a Métis writer. But is that necessarily an insupportable decision? If I hadn't been teaching *In Search of April Raintree*, I wouldn't have had to pay close attention to the text. I wouldn't have been struck by the discrepancy between the novel's attentiveness to signifying practices and the reviewers' uncritical, representationalist appeals to mimetic reflection and authorial experience. I wouldn't have made discoveries from and about the novel.

————•————

the contradiction of reading literary criticism which uses Derridean post-structural theory, for example, in order to abstract indigenous knowledges of interpretation into a First Worldist discursive consumption. (Emberley 164)

————•————

But what is going on here? In reading Culleton as resisting the naturalization of reality, experience, and self, am I co-opting *In Search of April Raintree* into the contemporary crisis of epistemological legitimation? Insisting on applying to the text the 'linguistic turn' in critical theory? Imposing a postmodern/poststructuralist master narrative of polyvocality, instability, and indeterminacy on a (relatively) coherent, realist narrative? Am I simply substituting for authenticity a new value, the capacity for sophisticated discursive critique, to compensate, like the reviewers, for perceived inadequacies of craft? Resuming the trope of transparency, have I, as critic, been putting my fingerprints all over the glass or celluloid of the text and then, in the guise of illuminating the novel, merely studying the intricacies of their whorls?

More importantly, am I in danger of depoliticizing the novel by reducing it to yet another self-reflexive postmodern discourse about discourse? Are the potentially decolonizing effects of the text neutralized by a hermeneutics of indeterminacy? What happens to Cheryl's revising of Métis history or April's final commitment to the future of her people in a reading sceptical of ultimate certainties? Does my problematizing of identity in the novel undermine the politics of identity it may serve, the authority of self-representation the novel claims, the characters' hard-won achievement of an autonomous coherent subjectivity? (Such a subjectivity is, as Fee points out, however illusory its self-determination, both compensatory and subversive within a culture hostile to such subjects ['Upsetting' 172]). Amid calls that room be made for Native voices, have I just erased the Native author behind the text?

Certainly, *In Search of April Raintree* provides a number of passages seeming to resist my reading and to warrant treating the novel as an empiricist reflection of reality. Cheryl expresses a schoolgirl conviction that 'history should be an unbiased representation of the facts. And if they show one side, they ought to show the other side equally' (84). She resolves to transform the Native image so as to give April pride. April's Christmas essay both articulates and implements her wishes for someone to listen to and hear her. As an adult, she hopes that someday she may be able to explain to others why Native people kill themselves. In such moments, one can read self-referential glosses on the novel's positivist undertaking, emphasizing the necessity for *different* representations rather than for the *problematizing* of representation.[31] Speaking of Pemmican Publications' educational mandate and of the wrong ideas about Native people held by many teachers ('This' 49), Culleton (but which Culleton[s]?) seems persuaded of the possibility of replacing a 'clouded' vision with a 'clear' one, to use Cheryl's formulation (175). April's closing words, that it has taken her sister's death to 'bring me to accept my identity' (228), seem to affirm identity as immanent, as does Culleton's concurrence with interviewer Andrew Garrod's suggestion that April earlier isn't being true to herself (85). Is the novel, ultimately, as Penny Petrone claims of Canadian Native writing generally, in a discussion immediately preceding her analysis of Culleton, 'attempting to distinguish once and for all right from wrong, truth from fiction – to set the record straight' (139)?

'Seriousness' has become the justification for our enterprises of academic literary criticism and literary pedagogy and is the source of their tension with the general public. Once-popular books are plumbed in literature courses for their serious content, not for the sources of the enjoyment that drew people to them. (Baym 24–5)

––––•••––––

Then, too, what about the pleasures of narrative, of storytelling? Does my approach evade or even obscure the origins of the novel's appeal to numerous readers, interjecting intellectual complexity into a text I am incapable of appreciating on its own terms because the intellectual is the only (academic) way I know to approach stories? The classes of Native students who, by report, identify most strongly with this novel as a powerful confirmation of their experiences[32] are presumably not identifying primarily with the way the text implicates itself in the deconstruction of discursive singularity or the way it establishes April's newly achieved identity as provisional. What about the nine-year-olds Culleton mentions who helped inspire her rewriting of the book, children who have never read before but who are reading *In Search of April Raintree* (Cahill 62)? What about my women's studies students who describe crying several times while reading the novel?[33] The book is on my syllabi, after all, in part because of my desire to learn more from and about writing that moves and speaks to many, that serves needs that may differ from my own or the academy's.

––––•••––––

The deconstruction of identity is not the deconstruction of politics; rather, it establishes as political the very terms through which identity is articulated. (Butler, *Gender* 148)

––––•••––––

To argue that Culleton is attentive to the politics of representation, though, may not necessarily be to co-opt her writing into a chic critical movement. Native traditions are notable for their respect for the power of language and their sensitivity to the dangers of its misuse. To cite only one example, Douglas Cardinal (Métis) speaks of the human potential to shape reality through language, in ways reminiscent of contemporary Western theory but deriving from an entirely different cultural tradition: 'The essence of creativity in all things is what makes the universe shift. It is to cause something to become from nothing. The word in that way is powerful. When we speak a word we declare something. We create it and then it can be' (Cardinal and Armstrong 89).

Culleton, whose upbringing was largely outside Métis communities, may not be shaped in obvious ways by this discourse. But her own interpellation as 'Native' subject (in itself a self-contradictory formulation from some, colonial, perspectives) into a variety of incompatible and antipathetic signifying systems inevitably produces a parallel awareness. Several of her essays – 'What a Shame' and 'Images of Native People and Their Effects,' in particular – surveying her fraught and painful negotiation of the constructions of Nativeness, suggest that epistemological wariness arises readily from such a position and need not wait on the trends of academic theory. Such wariness lends itself naturally to the highly political question of who gets to tell the stories, but does not preclude the proposing of more plausible stories, however provisional all must be considered to be. Cheryl's final undoing, for instance, can be read as deriving alternatively from a risky reliance on undependable narratives, such as the edited story of her parents' merit,[34] or from the exclusion from public discourse of positive narratives of the Native present, such as the one hinted at in the story of her friend Nancy.

That is how identity politics may be fruitfully understood now: as sites of struggle, rather than as sites of 'identity.' (Chicago Cultural Studies Group 548)

To argue that self and racial identity are constructed, moreover, is not to argue that they have no reality, where that reality is constituted precisely through their effects (Butler, *Gender* 32). To cite a familiar, rueful quip, knowing that race is constructed does nothing to help a Black academic hail a cab in New York during rush hour. Nor does the recognition of self/ves and racial identity/ies as constructs preclude agency. Neither acquiescing in the hegemonic 'felicitous self-naturalization' (Butler's term, *Gender* 33) of constructs such as race[35] nor removing herself to some impossible position outside discourses, April ultimately treats identity as verb not noun, as action not condition, as performative not inherent – and as communal not individual. Her final claim to have accepted her identity has less to do with some essence she discovers in herself (or other Métis or Native people) than with her mobilization of the relations, historic and present, in which she finds herself. She begins to deploy positively connections she has hitherto resisted. Her speaking of the words 'MY PEOPLE, OUR

PEOPLE' (228) enacts a political affiliation, an involvement with others in the hopeful shaping of the future.

[A critic] requests us to read the poems thoughtfully, not because they are good poems, but because we owe a debt to the Aborigines which cannot be redeemed by any Budget allocations ... but what about the quality of the verse? (Narogin 85)

With some other Native texts, such as Jeannette Armstrong's *Slash*, I sense that I am ignorant of the cultural traditions out of which they are written and so I refrain from premature judgment. With *In Search of April Raintree*, part of the problem with my aesthetic appreciation of the text may arise because I assume that I am familiar with its genre, the realist novel, and with the book's limitations according to the standards of that genre. So I fail to consider the uses to which the book is being put. My concerns about formulaic characterization and plotting, wooden dialogue, flat, recapitulative narration, sensationalizing, and stylistic blandness (in most of which I echo the reviewers I have critiqued) draw on the norms of high (bourgeois) realism, with its focus on the individualizing of experience, refinements of self-understanding, aptness of detail, and originality of language. I am requiring the satisfactions of subtlety, indirection, and complexity, values that creep into my summary of the revisions to Culleton's second edition. Yet quite other genres – romance, for example[36] – and quite other pleasures are possible. What about the satisfactions of clarity – moral and otherwise – narrative familiarity, emotional heightening, rapport with a commonplace narrator,[37] pathos?

Wendy Rose (Hopi-Miwok) differentiates the values subtending Native art and Euro-American art, describing the latter as 'special, élite (much of it requires formal training in "appreciation"), non-utilitarian, self-expressive, solitary, ego-identified, self-validating, innovative ("to make it new"), unique, and – in its highest forms – without rules' ('Just' 18–19). While noting the limitations of pan-Indian generalizations, she stresses the place, in Native art, of the ordinary, community-oriented, useful, familiar, cooperatively produced, and communally integrated. Functionality and beauty in this art, she argues, are interdependent.

Culleton has spoken of being influenced by 'what they call the trash books' (note her implicit reservation about the dismissive label) and by movies and television shows, all popular genres (Garrod 87, 95; 'Beatrice'

104).[38] She has expressed surprise at finding her book taught in university classes when she had directed it towards the general reader ('This' 47).[39] The rhetorical conventions that her plain-speaking, expository narrative voice invokes are less those of fiction or even of dramatized storytelling than of family history or the everyday recounting of personal experience, aligning her rhetorically with thousands of unofficial, daily chroniclers. Like the Native art that Rose describes and like the proletarian U.S.-American novels of the Depression era (where the formulaic or generic was also taken to gainsay literary merit), Culleton's writing fuses pragmatic and artistic ends and grows out of the consciousness of a community.[40] Like the proletarian novels also, her book writes beyond the ending of the classic domestic novel or the romance quest, opening up beyond individual self-development into a vision of collective action (see Rabinowitz 77, 70). If novelty, authorial self-expression, and originality of execution give way in Culleton's aesthetic credo to instrumental and communal values, then her writing may require different methods of evaluation that recognize these also as artistic achievements.

—————•—————

Transparent: 4.a Readily understood; clear. b Easily detected; perfectly evident. c Guileless; free from pretense. (*Webster's Dictionary*)

—————•—————

Within a modernist Western criticism, writing such as Culleton's that does not 'distinguish' itself and by extension its author (as different, as superior), writing that speaks with the voice of everyday, has its craft rendered invisible.[41] 'Honest' and 'earnest' are, after all, rather odd recommendations for a fiction. Such writing becomes artless, art-less. Transparent. With the author function, the dimension of discursive production, erased from the text, the writer is restored ironically, not as author but as anthropological site, source of authentic life experience, that which is being viewed. Such a critical stance lends itself further to an epistemology in which not only the text but the reality it purportedly transmits so directly, a reality that can somehow be separated from its textual rendering, is no longer a matter of discursive consensus but remains unmediated, singular, unproblematic. Clarity of language and form threatens to generalize to other critical perceptions, so that first other dimensions of the text and eventually experience itself are understood as equally simple, manifest, and unequivocal.

With its rhetoric of the commonplace, its democracy of manner, *In*

Search of April Raintree does admittedly allow an eliding of its status as artefact for a focus on the experiences it reveals. That illusion of transparency is one of its accomplishments. But only one of its accomplishments. My concern has been to restore some of the density, the craft-iness, of that transparency, the density and craft-iness both of the medium and of the experiences that are constituted within it. *In Search of April Raintree* is a duplicitous (a multiplicitous?) book. In terms of author as well as character, it both invites *and* disrupts notions of the real and of the self, of authenticity and of identity, of truth.

5

'And Use the Words That Were Hers': Beverly Hungry Wolf's *The Ways of My Grandmothers*

I, myself, shall tell you what I have heard my grandmother tell and I shall try to speak in the way she did and use the words that were hers.

(Broker 7)

One of the photographs in *The Ways of My Grandmothers* (1980) shows Beverly Hungry Wolf turned away from the camera, her overexposed facial features barely discernible against the washed-out sky. She displays a carefully beaded cradleboard on her back, in which she is carrying a child. 'Me and my son Okan in his cradleboard' the caption begins; it moves away from Hungry Wolf, however, for the next three sentences, to explain the ways in which earlier tribal women employed cradleboards (97). The photograph is representative of the book in that it focuses on something other than Hungry Wolf herself. What is uncharacteristic about the picture is the relative prominence it gives Hungry Wolf's presence, however obscured. Of the forty-seven photographs in *The Ways of My Grandmothers*, she appears in only seven (and partially, in the background, of an eighth), and never alone. Only two pictures – of Hungry Wolf and husband, Adolf, with four of their children, and another of Hungry Wolf with mother and grandmother – fit the rubric of the classic Western autobiographical or biographical illustration with its personal signifying. Almost half depict scenes and individuals with no direct connection to the author, and many others are of distant relations (at least in Euro-American terms). The transpersonal and inclusive nature of the text is captured by the choice of cover illustration, a turn-of-the-century photograph of a Crow woman,

Helen Goes Ahead, who is not from Hungry Wolf's (Blood) people[1] but rather, as she notes, from among her ancestors' respected enemies.

––––—•·—––––

The autobiography of a Pueblo Indian is about as personal as the life story of an automobile tire. (White 327)

[W]herever a knowledge speaks, an 'I' is spoken. (P. Smith 100)

––––—•·—––––

Although listed in various bibliographies of Native autobiography (Allen, *Studies* 64, 98; Bataille and Sands 160; Brumble 235), *The Ways of My Grandmothers* is far from a straightforward life story. A loosely organized compendium of personal narratives, ethnographic and historical information, myths, recipes, and other practical instruction in household arts – and, as I've indicated, historical and contemporary photographs – the work is replete with the stories and first-person voices of women other than the narrator. Speakers include Ruth Little Bear, Hungry Wolf's mother; AnadaAki, her grandmother; Mary One Spot, her 'aunt'; Mrs Rides-at-the-Door, the Blood holy woman she knows best; Brown Woman (Mrs Annie Wadsworth), an elder married at the age of seven; Rosie Davis, the oldest living Blood woman; Paula Weasel Head, an important wise woman in Hungry Wolf's life; and Annie Red Crow, Weasel Head's sister.

The narrative of Beverly Hungry Wolf's own life is developed primarily, and cursorily, in the two-page introduction. There the first paragraph detailing her birth, upbringing, education, and early adult life and work compresses the material for a classic realist autobiography into a few sentences. That she is not seeking to provide personal revelation is made explicit in her acknowledgments, when she indicates that many of her mother's and grandmother's stories, with the family history they contain, are of use mainly to family members. (Her *Daughters of the Buffalo Women* [1996], a subsequent compilation of tribal and personal narratives, contains more of the latter stories.) *The Ways of My Grandmothers* encompasses a wider range of stories, Hungry Wolf notes in the acknowledgments, because with it she is speaking to a broader audience. In one of those apologias familiar to students of women's writing, but with the added valence produced by the history of ethnographic profiteering from tribal informants (and the possible influence of traditional modesty), she protests in her introduction that she is claiming no expertise in tribal culture and seeking no profit herself. Instead, Hungry Wolf is offering a tribute to her grandmothers, filling a vacancy in the historical record.

But we do not find such [preliterate] Indians telling stories in such a way as to suggest just how it was that they came to be just the men or women they were ... their tales are not designed to work together to convey a unified idea of the narrator as an *individual* ... (Brumble 135–6)

One Native American poet was cautioned against writing her autobiography by a member of her tribe and could not, finally, produce an autobiographical text for us, asserting the traditional sense of Indian peoples that not the individual as personal self but, rather, the person as transmitter of the traditional culture was what most deeply counted for her. (Swann and Krupat, *I Tell* xii)

Like the life stories by Athapaskan-Tlingit elders in *Life Lived like a Story*,[2] which begin with genealogies of parents and husbands (and which answer questions about the narrators' own histories by recounting traditional stories), Hungry Wolf's narrative is introduced through the ancestral matrix in which she takes her place. 'Who My Grandmothers Are,' the opening and longest section of the book, begins with her own grandmother and great-grandmother, but expands not only to the oldest women of the tribe (with memories of treaty signings, enemy raids, a Riot Sun Dance, child marriage, boarding school, traditional diet, and medicine-bundle responsibilities) and nineteenth-century accounts (including reports of two women warriors), but also beyond, to women from the mythic past.

Intriguingly, although 'Myths and Legends of My Grandmothers' has its own separate section, 'Who My Grandmothers Are' includes two mythic narratives on the origins of the holy women's Natoas or Sun Dance headdress. The legends immediately follow stories of Mrs Rides-at-the-Door and a historic predecessor, Catches-Two-Horses, both of whom sponsored a number of Sun Dances, as though the 'who' of these women cannot be separated from the understandings contained in the legends. Or maybe the women of the old stories – the woman who married the morning star, for instance, and returned to earth with a turnip-digging stick for the Natoas bundle – are not to be distanced from contemporary ones. Perhaps the new stories, themselves old stories in the making, are not to be seen as qualitatively different from the old in their capacity to carry tribal meaning. As Hungry Wolf says later, 'Even in my own lifetime I have watched such incidents turn into legends' (137–8).

Stories of an elk transformed to a man who brings gifts to the people, or of a captured wife reclaimed through the power of medicine, commingle casually with accounts of returning from Montana for the 1877 treaty enrolments, instructions for making sweet-pine perfume, stories of accidentally sitting in a mess of eggs, and reflections on the disrespectfulness of modern youth. As Hertha Wong says about the mixing of tribal myths, community narratives, and individual life stories in Leslie Marmon Silko's *Storyteller*, 'No one story is more important than another; no one narrative is insignificant. Each story, like each individual, is made whole through connection to shared remembering and telling' (189).

Although working admittedly in an entirely different genre, Edith Josie in *Here Are the News*, a collection of her *Whitehorse Star* newspaper reports from the Loucheux (or Gwich'in) Yukon village of Old Crow, reveals something of the narrative place of the individual within tribal communities. Her entry for 19 August 1963, sandwiched between entries on Sarah Kay's hospitalization and on Peter Lord and Daniel Frost's successful hunt, begins 'At 8:30 P.M. I had baby boy and he's 6 lb. Miss Edith Josie had baby boy and I give it to Mrs. Ellen Abel to have him for his little boy' (23). After a brief thanks to Miss Youngs at the nursing station, she reverts to reports of caribou sightings and, without missing a day, continues diligently to report other community events. The Edith Josie constructed here is less the heroine of her own drama (though her later visit to Whitehorse, because of its novelty, inspires more extended coverage) than the fellow participant in a network of communal relationships and activities whose depth is in the accumulation and layering of event rather than in introspective analysis.[3]

In Native American autobiography the self most typically is not constituted by the achievement of a distinctive, special voice that separates it from others, but, rather, by the achievement of a particular placement in relation to the many voices without which it could not exist. (Krupat, *Voice* 133)

Therefore, what 'we' get from literature is not an expanded 'we' but more of the same old 'us.' ... [Middle-class students] want to 'identify' with characters, and the only characters they can identify with are those with subjectivities (intro-spective, self-conscious, self-interested subjectivities) like their own. (Gagnier 136)

Is there a Beverly Hungry Wolf in this text?

'Nearly everyone who writes about American Indian autobiography mentions at some point that autobiography was not a genre indige-nous to Indian cultures,' notes H. David Brumble (131), though he and subsequently Hertha Wong do go on to document 'distinctly native traditions of self-narration' (Wong 4), including everything from picto-graphs (Wong's particular contribution) to coup tales, informal hunting tales, and vision tales. The question of whether *The Ways of My Grand-mothers* is autobiographical, at least by classic Western definitions such as Philippe Lejeune's – 'Retrospective prose narrative written by a real person concerning his [*sic*] own existence, where the focus is his individual life, in particular the story of his personality' [4]) – is somewhat beside the point. The question simply exposes the by-now-acknowledged narrowness of such definitions.

Even Gretchen Bataille and Kathleen Sands in *American Indian Women: Telling Their Lives*, while sensitive to differences between male and female Indian narratives and to the inappositeness of Western models, betray in their definition of the genre ethnocentric and individualist assumptions that would exclude Hungry Wolf. They describe autobi-ography as the 'rationalization of a life' that discovers the 'wholeness of the subject's identity' and proffers the life as 'a unique experience, not simply a typical representation of a tribal role.' Ethnographic autobiog-raphy they see as approaching 'genuine' autobiography only when 'the personality of the narrator breaks through' (13, 10–11). More interesting is the question of the nature of the subjectivity revealed in texts such as Hungry Wolf's.[4] What can I learn about ways of constructing identity that may vary from my own?

[A]n idea of one's ancestry and posterity is really an idea of the self. (Momaday 97)

One of the photographs in *The Ways of My Grandmothers* shows a Blackfoot woman from an earlier period turned away from the camera, her underexposed facial features barely discernible against the darkened sky (or backdrop). She displays a buckskin-covered cradleboard on her back, in which she is carrying a child. 'A Blackfoot mother and child in 1920,' the caption simply reads (176). Although no connection is drawn between the two photographs, the 1920 picture functions as a kind of prototype (or negative, with the tonal values of light and dark inverted) for the later picture of Hungry Wolf. Both photographs highlight what is characteristic rather than distinctive; the subjects' individual features yield to representative ways. The later woman stands in the place of the earlier. The similarity in pose, dress, accoutrements, and function serve as an intensification rather than a diminution or erasure of self.[5] Hungry Wolf is more herself, is more who and what she is, because she is so like this woman and others among her 'grandmothers.'

Hungry Wolf also looks forward self-reflexively to the future reproduction of shared (and changing?) cultural selves: 'I hope that some of the young women who read this book grow to become grandmothers, following ways that their grandchildren will one day consider valuable enough to record also' (10).[6] In not necessarily restricting her appeal to a Native readership, she extends the value of cultural dissemination beyond the transmitted specifics of her tradition to this broader ethos of filiative self-positioning. Although her formulation leaves her role only implicit, she takes her own generative place in this chain of successive generations,[7] modelling both traditional ways and the honouring of those ways through documentation. In my thesaurus, 'original' is linked simultaneously with both 'unprecedented, underived' and 'unimitated, unreproduced.' Hungry Wolf's meaning lies not in her being either novel or inimitable, not in an originality defined in contradistinction to others, before and after, but in her *un*singularity.[8]

On the psychological level, the text's dedication – 'FOR MY MOTHER / Whose apron strings / stretch clear across the / Rocky Mountains' (5) – conveys a similar value. In place of the differentiation from parents (especially mothers) and the establishment of clear ego boundaries that mark maturity and normative individuation in much of Western society, Hungry Wolf, with comic extravagance, appropriates the very symbol of maternal overprotectiveness to affirm her relational and familial interdependence.

Collective identities make me uneasy; I come from a family in which 'individuals' tend not to be, literally speaking, conceived individually. The oldest (but only by five minutes) of ten children (eleven, if one of the fourth set of twins, who died at birth, is counted), all born within seven years of each other, I favour strategies of self-differentiation. Apart from one sorry instance at the age of three or four (my first memory), when I buckled myself into the baby harness in front of our army-base bungalow in the hope of melding into the mass of younger siblings and having strangers mistake me for that apparently desirable thing, a baby, I have tended to pursue singularity. My family designated its members by groups – 'the big five,' 'the little three,' 'the smookers,' 'the pokers' – had its own school uniform when the school did not, and elicited the shouted refrain 'Here come the Hoys.' I resisted that common identity by mumbling my surname in new situations and am still inclined to set myself at odds with orthodoxies – setting out to be a single mother, for instance. And lest I seem to reduce a pervasive Western ideology to personal psychology or even neurosis, let me note that my own appetite for individual difference is more broadly determined by the competitive logic of late capitalism and other principles of contemporary Western culture, including individualist standards of artistic and scholarly originality. So I am startled and fascinated by a narrative self apparently untroubled by the compulsion to make its own mark, to distinguish itself by its divergence from the larger collectivity.

———•·•———

Although we cannot hope to stand free of what [Roland] Barthes termed the 'ideology of the person,' we can nevertheless seek to understand the nature of our necessary participation in it. (Eakin xiv–xv)

———•·•———

Much of *The Ways of My Grandmothers* consists of third-person passages of historical and domestic information, traditional stories, and the first-person narratives of others. I would argue that Hungry Wolf is none the less present even in resolutely impersonal passages and in these other women's stories – embedded in them, that is, not simply 'breaking through' occasionally within or between them. She is there, certainly, as one whose father's great-grandfather captured a Shoshone woman, whose great-grandfather's sister Makah is the woman pictured in the headdress of the Motokiks society,[9] whose great-grandmother's methods of setting up camp or butchering an animal inform those sections of the narrative, whose mother's mother has been a lifelong friend of Mrs Rosie Davis. She is there as the one to be initiated into the wearing of a sacred necklace by Mrs Rides-at-the-Door, the one lent a tipi liner by Paula Weasel Head.

There is more than just a genealogical and tribal positioning here, though, however self-defining this cumulative layering of relational mappings may be. Because the text documents the practices of *her* grandmothers, Hungry Wolf's selection and arrangement provide self-representation (though perhaps not in the highly individualized manner valued in Euro-American culture) in ways that a parallel document prepared by a visiting ethnologist (though highly revelatory of the compiler in its own fashion) would not. Aspects of a textual self are conveyed through Hungry Wolf's decisions (random examples, these) to include the story of a Kootenay woman (whose adoption of male gender roles parallels that of several Blood women), to detail children's games, to provide the German-derived recipe for head cheese, to discuss methods of contraception, to revert time and again to the subject of child brides, to incorporate photographs of a Beaver Bundle Dance or a Sun Dance initiation. More substantively, Hungry Wolf is implicated in the narrative as a whole because it lays out some of the materials from which her selves are cut.

———•—

selvage, -edge, n.: Edge of cloth so woven that it cannot unravel, border of different material or finish along edge of cloth intended to be torn off or hidden ... (15th c., f. SELF + EDGE, after MDu. *selfegge*). (*Concise Oxford Dictionary*)

This trade wool always had a white strip known as the selvage, where the cloth was clamped during the dying process. These white strips were always placed along the bottoms of dresses (as well as men's leggings and other apparel) as a form of decoration. (B. Hungry Wolf, *Ways* 230)

———•—

Selvages, self-edges. Vestiges of the manufacturing process, evidence of origins. Reminders of the bolt of raw fabric out of which finished garments are fashioned, of the shared discourses out of which selves are shaped. Not excised or concealed: in *The Ways of My Grandmothers*, these traces of the earlier, untailored, common stuff are made visible, even celebrated. Contours of the individual pattern conform to, or coexist with, or find heightened expression through, the strong, visible, ready-made margins of the larger fabric. Edges of selves need not be drawn at angles to, or over against, the original outline, the selvage, of the culture(s).

Without being the text's focus, then, Hungry Wolf pervades the narrative – or the narrative pervades her. Her position as auditor in the text is particularly revelatory of alternative discourses of the person. In reproducing stories that she neither originates nor necessarily augments, Hungry Wolf enacts and validates a self given little standing in the cultures most familiar to me – the self who listens rather than the self who speaks. Recent countercolonial, antiracist, and feminist work has urged the importance of voices and agency, the necessity for those marginalized by the 'over-culture' (Harjo, 'Q & A' 14) to speak and make room for their histories.[10] As narrator of *The Ways of My Grandmothers*, Hungry Wolf could doubtless be seen as joining that chorus of voices. Rhetorically, though, instead of positing a self through her own story, she locates herself primarily as the repository of what others have to tell, as one of the section headings, 'Learning from My Grandmothers,' suggests.

The Ways of My Grandmothers conveys a subjectivity constituted and sustained more by its receptivity than its productivity; more accurately, it is a subjectivity constituted and sustained by its productive receptivity. Hungry Wolf speaks of the only gradually released conviction held by her grandmothers, despite their strong faith in tradition, that no place in the world remained for descendants who might follow the old ways. 'I think it pleased them to know that they had something very special to offer us young people, even if it took a while for them to believe that times had changed enough to make us young people want to learn,' she says (109). Much of the text issues from the subject position she occupies here; she is one who gives renewed meaning and purpose to the accumulated knowledge of others rather than begetting meaning in her own voice. The self she constitutes in the text is one in whom a discourse lodges, through whom it finds expression.

––––––•–––––

My father told me ... that Hopi earth does contain my roots and I am, indeed, from that land ... But when I find them, he said, I must rebuild myself as a Hopi. I am not merely a conduit, but a participant. (Rose, 'Neon' 261)

––––––•–––––

In the caption beneath the photograph of 'Me and my son Okan in his cradleboard,' Beverly Hungry Wolf does go on from the description of historical uses of the cradleboard to speak of her own experiences. She notes that she finds cradleboards awkward in modern houses and towns but practical for walking or riding in a truck, and mentions an incident in which Okan's cradleboard tipped him onto his face in a restaurant. In a discussion on cradleboards from the section entitled 'Around the Household,' she is even more forthcoming. Here she comments on two incidents in which a child of hers in a cradleboard fell on his face. These were 'pretty hard on my mind until I was sure that no injury had happened' (248). Through such particulars, she inserts herself into the tradition as more than a static or faceless reproduction of an earlier model.

Struck as I am by the dispersed and transpersonal construction of self in *The Ways of My Grandmothers*, I may be underestimating the degree of self-portraiture and individuation in the text. Particularly in later sections on learning from the grandmothers, learning to camp tradition-ally, and managing the household, Hungry Wolf speaks in the first person, providing extended narratives on, for instance, her first attempt at preparing and using a tipi. She speaks of the tears she shed in adolescence over her brothers' strict supervision of her appearance and boyfriends, and of the pleasure she takes in watching babies stretch when she unlaces them from their moss bags. Personal emotion shines through her declaration, about the Sun Dance encampment: 'I love to wake up on an early summer morning to hear some old person singing in one of the lodges' (107). She sets herself against particular contemporary sentiments, defending the now-notorious boarding schools many Native children were forced to attend, on the basis that they provided good instruction in nutrition. She reworks traditional practices, adapting a Crow gut recipe to the modern taste for foods that are less plain, or sharing her appreciation of artificial sinew for moccasins and beadwork. She distances herself from some tastes, indicating that, despite the dish's nostalgic appeal for elders, she finds little merit in boiled hooves.

Hungry Wolf begins a section with the words 'One of my favorite childhood memories,' and, on first reading, I anticipated a specific personal anecdote (136). But the memory proves to be a generic one, central to tribal life. It is the memory of sitting by her grandmothers and listening to their ancestral stories. Even in (perhaps I should say 'especially in') passages of self-revelation, a ground-note of sameness, of shared experience, sounds. The early-morning Sun Dance prayer just mentioned, that Hungry Wolf finds exhilarating, is one that simultaneously 'brings cheerful tears into the eyes of all those in the camp who can hear' (111).

Within a context, then, where personal consciousness can coincide readily and propitiously with group consciousness, explicit self-representation takes a relatively unassuming form. Hungry Wolf situates herself through her particular selections among familiar options: she favours a two-piece pattern for everyday moccasins and prefers to work on a table in her tipi rather than on the ground as earlier generations had done. At times, a sense of collective responsibility inhibits the expression of a strong personal position, as when she acknowledges noncommittally that the absence of a central fireplace inside the tipi is both disorienting for elders and convenient for others. At times, personal forthrightness actually forecloses revelation, as when she indicates that she has never received the traditional treatment to terminate a pregnancy, and concludes, with uncharacteristic finality, 'So I won't be able to say any more about it' (203). And at times, she bypasses opportunities for self-disclosure, as when she ascribes to hearsay the conclusion that breast-feeding is an inadequate method of birth control. (*Shadows of the Buffalo*, a collaboration with her husband, Adolf, indicates that she has first-hand knowledge of this inadequacy [*Shadows* 267].) Still, a process of cumulative self-inscription occurs, through the accretion of numerous moments of self-positioning.

With self-development manifested through a deepening appreciation and mastery of tribal skills, through a practised understanding of which wood burns best or which skins make the sturdiest winter footwear, innovation is construed more in terms of functionality than of personal self-expression. Useful innovation is recognized by integration of the contribution into the community, not by the enhancement of personal stature. Or, rather, integration of such contributions into the community is the form personal credit takes here. Hungry Wolf does venture several reservations about traditional practices, hinting at alternatives. On the subject of cradleboards, she goes so far as to comment, 'I don't know why my grandmothers never made their cradleboards with a curved face protector like many other tribes used' (248). This, though, and a similar statement of incomprehension about the custom of restricting information on childbirth, is as far as such critiques go. She makes an opening within a discourse and lets the initiative rest, to await other responses within the discursive community. About her introduction of fruit and vegetables into the traditional diet, Hungry

Wolf expresses gratification that 'my grandmothers compliment my efforts, *even with* the new additions' (129; emphasis added) and then focuses on the continued merit of the simple diet of earlier days. A subject of the narrative does begin to emerge. It is the aggregate of various positions taken in the text, some more traditional than others. But the speaking 'I' seems to anchor certain alternatives and information more than accrue significance in its own right.

—————

This was the self of Victorian literature as it was studied in the academy. Subjects who did not assume creativity, autonomy, and freedom; who expressed no self-consciousness; who did not express themselves in individuated voices with subjective desires; who were regardless of family relations; and who narrated no development or progress or plot never appeared in literature courses. (Gagnier 28)

—————

As I was writing the first draft of this chapter, on sabbatical, I tromped up Palmerston Boulevard through the snow to fax off my teaching schedule for the following year. Toronto had had a twenty-centimetre overnight snowfall, and so at fifteen-metre intervals I was driven to reflect on the differences in sidewalk snow removal, from cattle trail through the drifts at one address to chiselled thoroughfare at another. Snow shovelling has occupied substantial portions of my time over the years; in particular, I can become relatively obsessive about it when I have an article to write. Clearly, there are differences in skill and approach involved, most perceptible to those dedicated to the art, as I had temporarily become. Some people settled for one or two shovel widths (perfunctory adolescents?), some shoved snowbanks past the curb altogether. Some ignored the snowplow's deposits at the driveway's end (hired workers?), some heaved shovelfuls far into the street, liberating curbside parking. One neighbour (who in summer sat on her flawless lawn in her black kerchief and dress, methodically plucking at weed sprouts) laboured with scraper and broom until the cement was bare and dry. For the enthusiast, there were opportunities to catch – the warm spell that permitted the cutting back of hardened banks; challenges to confront – the garbage truck that crushed the snowbank into the sidewalk; and decisions to shoulder – the snowcaps on the hedge that, for all their beauty, were destined to collapse onto the freshly cleared walk.

Snow shovelling defines some of us more emphatically than others.

Yet, if I were to write my autobiography, snow shovelling would not, I imagine, figure in it at all. It is repetitive, routine work, mere maintenance, not the stuff out of which a distinctive self emerges.

As previous references to the specifics of lodging, dress, food preparation, child care, and storytelling suggest, the pragmatics of the quotidian bulk large in *The Ways of My Grandmothers*. Narrators other than Hungry Wolf lace their life stories, too, with practical knowledge both uncommon and everyday: how to find stores of lily roots by tracing mouse trails, how to keep insects out of dried meat, how to care for a medicine-pipe bundle. The subjectivity displayed in the text is one, like my own consciousness over the course of a day, preoccupied in large measure with the necessary, the prosaic, the physical, and the repetitive, rather than with the highlights that retrospectively mark out a life story precisely because of their exceptional status.[11]

Literary conventions establishing what qualifies as real have altered substantially in recent years, thanks to the recognition of previously ignored or trivialized histories and stories. Still, the requirements of narrative continue to produce literary subjects defined through developmentally significant moments, at the expense of the iterative patterns and material responsibilities of daily experience. Structurally, *The Ways of My Grandmothers* represents reality as a repetitive process engaged with the workaday routines of maintenance, cultural transmission, and tribal interrelationships rather than as a drama of self-discovery or the trajectory of desire. Neither in the photographs nor in the narrative does Hungry Wolf attempt to develop what Sidonie Smith terms 'teleological itineraries' (18).

Information introduced in one narrative may be repeated in another, replicating the dispersal of cultural knowledge over multiple subjects and, in some instances, the process of cultural dissemination itself. So Hungry Wolf anticipates Mrs Rides-at-the-Door on methods of tanning, first paraphrases and later quotes her mother on the physical hazards of quillwork, includes both her mother's and Mrs Rides-at-the-Door's comments on the use of wild mint in rawhide parfleches, and retells Brown Woman's earlier story of sharing toys and scattering crumbs as a child bride. She also repeats herself in recounting elders' stories of spirits raiding babies' hammocks, for example, creating the effect not of a chronological or dramatic momentum but of an eddying, a return. The repetitions incidentally incorporate the reader into the circle of those already initiated into such knowledge.

Despite loose groupings of related material, the ordering of the sections communicates no sense of inevitability or progression. The final segment of the narrative – on traditional utensils – and the final sentence – on the strong flavour of deer-stomach canteens – through their anticlimactic homeliness speak to the arbitrariness of endings, repudiating structural notions of culmination. Like the self constituted within it, the text develops cumulatively, by accretion, gesturing towards a larger, ongoing story of which it is a part.

Notice, incidentally, the bizarre consequences of our tendency to seek an artist whose life can explain a text, in the case of a modern 'art' that is at least semicommunal: a series of movies written to star a particular actor, say, Clint Eastwood. (Revard 462)

The most obvious objection to all of this is that *The Ways of My Grandmothers* never proposes itself as personal narrative and that my conclusions follow from a perverse insistence on reading it as what it is not. Certainly one can argue that the subject produced here – collectively oriented, engrossed in the quotidian – is, even more directly than usual, a function of the genre, here the documentation of folkways. (Equally one could argue that the genre employed is congenial to, and so a ready medium for, a subjectivity unexercised by personal uniqueness.) For all my protestations, I may have been governed, in framing my approach to the text, by a preoccupation with the individual story (even when that takes the form of focusing on its absence). I may have implied an individual behind the text, differently constituted, perhaps, as communally based, but still fixed, coherent, and unitary. Speaking of *a* subjectivity, of *a* self, of 'Hungry Wolf' as a sensibility indirectly manifested, I may have obscured the degree to which Hungry Wolf, with an indifference to singularity, arises in the narrative variously, inconsistently, possibly not at all.

'The individual' will be understood here as simply the illusion of whole and coherent personal organization, or as the misleading description of the imaginary ground on which different subject-positions are colligated. (P. Smith xxxv)

One of the shifting positions Hungry Wolf occupies in *The Ways of My Grandmothers* is as auditor or audience, usually implicitly but on rare occasions explicitly: 'I am related to you, Beverly, because my mother and your grandmother Hilda were cousins' (52). She is present, at one point in her mother's account, as object of the narrative (as well as recorder of it): 'My daughter carries the name of her great-grandmother, SikskiAki, which means Black-Faced Woman. This is an honor that was bestowed on her by one of that great-grandmother's sons ...' (194). And, as we have seen, she speaks in her own voice.

As narrator, Hungry Wolf sometimes speaks to impart the cultural capital she has accumulated through trial and error (explaining how she uses stay stitches when sewing moccasins, to use a minor example), but rhetorically she often deflects attention from her own authority to constitute herself as initiate rather than instructor. The detailed personal saga of her efforts and misadventures in tipi making and tipi use situate her with the reader, as apprentice in the art. In the acknowledgments, she appears as two-time keeper of a medicine-pipe bundle; yet later, in Paula Weasel Head's narrative, she is given instruction in the most basic technique of employing a tripod to hang bundles.

Hungry Wolf shifts, too, between viewing change from the perspective of tradition and viewing tradition from the perspective of change. At some points, she stands with tradition, disparaging innovation, referring to the naïveté that young women display in adopting the male fashion of wrapping the ends of their braids with red cloth. More often, she assumes alteration over time, describing with equanimity women's adaptation of male fancy dancing, dance clothing, and even powwow drumming. For the most part situated within the culture, she does occasionally reveal the legacy of boarding-school colonization and speaks as epistemological outsider: 'Lacking the scientific knowledge of the modern world, my grandmothers *settled for* these legendary origins in any questioning' (137; emphasis added).[12] Disparately located, then, as 'I,' as 'you,' as 'she'; as novice and authority; as granddaughter, mother, distant cousin, and companion; as traditionalist and apologist for change; as cultural insider and outsider – 'Hungry Wolf' does not define a single, stable subject, nor does the diffuse narrative require one. The variety of her names (Beverly Hungry Wolf,[13] Beverly Little Bear, SikskiAki, Black-Faced Woman) underlines the disjunctures in her speaking positions. In teasing out her presence, I may be reconstituting the very notion of identity I am querying.

————◆————

One lesson of these narratives [testimonials] may be that our habit of identifying with a single subject of the narration (implicitly substituting her) simply repeats a Western logocentric limitation, a vicious circle in which only one center can exist. (Sommer 118)

My attempt to broaden notions of personal narrative, and of the personal itself, paradoxically risks reducing a richly communal text to the reflection primarily of a single author. Many narratives make up this text. Hungry Wolf's commitment to share grant money and royalties with her fellow narrators underscores its cooperative nature, as Barbara Godard has pointed out ('Listening' 149). And the older women's accounts contribute a somewhat different subjectivity, a sense of self more rooted in ceremonial responsibilities and status, than other portions of the narrative. 'I am an old woman,' says Paula Weasel Head, defending her outspokenness, 'and I have been initiated and given the rights to many, many things in life ... everyone knows that it is our tradition to back up what you say with your initiations' (80–1). Because the text is a collaborative one, the reader sometimes has trouble determining when an interpolated oral history has ended or who the speaker of a new segment might be (see, for example, 59, 190). And even when they are attributed to a particular person, many of the accounts of traditional practices speak the accumulated experience of generations.

Then there are the overtly collective narratives, the myths and legends, which I have not addressed. Apart from a vague suggestion that tales of women married to wild animals 'could have many more meanings for a life close to nature than we might understand in these modern times' (136), the narrative treats the myths as self-explanatory. (I am reminded of Angela Sidney [Tagish-Tlingit] in *Life Lived like a Story* who, when asked what children might learn from one of her traditional stories, replied cogently by repeating that story [Cruikshank 32].) Have I neglected these narratives – embodiments of a cosmology, crucial elements in the formation of a subject – because they are not cast in personal terms? In pulling on the Hungry Wolf thread, do I pucker the fabric of which she is a part? Do I conflate a genre capable of representing collective identity and of accommodating multiple narrative levels (cosmological, tribal, communal, and personal) with the narrower scope of the personal narrative?

[T]he present idealization of Native American women's lives by some white feminists is an extension of the primitivist tradition. (Carr 142)

Conversely, in making Hungry Wolf paradigmatic, do I succumb to nostalgia for an unalienated subjectivity? Do I subsume her narrative under a pan-Indian communal ethos, neglecting its tribal specificities, its gender implications, its particular historical juncture? Do I exempt it from political accountability, or, alternatively, do I blunt its political edge by treating it as the ahistoric manifestation of an ages-long tradition? To what extent does my account ignore the other contemporary discourses that help to shape *The Ways of My Grandmothers*, reading it instead as the unqualified expression of a collectivist ethic?

In particular, *The Ways of My Grandmothers* stands against the backdrop of a long-standing cultural project undertaken by Hungry Wolf's German-born husband, Adolf Gutöhrlein (now Hungry Wolf). Beginning with *Good Medicine: Life in Harmony with Nature*, published in 1970 by the couple's home-publishing company, Good Medicine Books, Adolf has been compiling books of traditional Native stories, teachings, and history as part of his personal quest to live the 'old ways.' (I have examined fifteen, but there are more, and the project continues.) In *Shadows of the Buffalo: A Family Odyssey among the Indians*, [14] Adolf betrays his romantic inspiration in a telling exchange with Blackfeet elder Jim White Calf, the irony of which seems to escape him: 'I asked if my race and modern upbringing would prevent me from learning his mysteries and powers. He said: "Anyone can live in harmony with Nature, if they try"' (*Shadows* 25).[15] At other points, Adolf ruefully acknowledges his persistent romanticism.

Since the early days of his project, Beverly has been involved in interpreting for Adolf and collecting material, as well as handling the business end of the enterprise. In *The Ways of My Grandmothers*, she draws on previously gathered stories, instructions, diagrams, and photographs from at least seven of the earlier books, some of them credited to the couple collaboratively.[16] Portions of *The Ways of My Grandmothers* then reappear in subsequent collaborative works both more and less personal (*Shadows of the Buffalo* and *Indian Tribes of the Northern Rockies*), placing no more premium on singularity of the text than on singularity of the person.[17] Beverly explains that, while Adolf felt this text should be her work, he helped 'by going through my many poorly typewritten pages and preparing them for publication' (*Ways* 10). Both agree that Adolf 'knew more about being a traditional Indian' than Beverly (*Ways* 16; see also *Shadows* 15, 28), setting aside in that formulation Beverly's Blackfoot language, family history, communal embeddedness, and discursive formation for a narrow focus on ceremonial practices.

The highlighting of a tribal narrative self in *The Ways of My Grand-*

mothers obscures the text's syncretic nature as a product of several cultures and discourses, including its complicated interconnection with Adolf's project. The book must also be read in the context of the social revolution and back-to-the-earth movements of the late 1960s and the 1970s, of works such as *The Whole Earth Catalog* and the Foxfire books, mentioned in Hungry Wolf publications (*Shadows* 15, *Indian Summer* 28, *Blackfoot Craftworker* 3). It enters into an uneasy relationship with ethnographic work such as Clark Wissler's *Blackfoot Source Book*, as its index and attentiveness to 'unusual' customs and to 'students' of Native culture might suggest (*Ways* 33, 243). Hungry Wolf includes Wissler and other early anthropologists of the Blackfoot in her acknowledgments and reproduces without credit – via *Blackfoot Craftworker Book*, where the drawings are given a blanket attribution – Wissler's sketch of quillwork stitching, for instance (*Ways* 241; *Blackfoot Craftworker* 2, 79; Wissler, Part 1, 56). The text's structure can be read as a reflection not only of a holistic philosophy, but also of the methodicalness with which a Wissler details the material culture, social life, societies and ceremonies, and myths and narratives of the Blackfoot.

At the same time, *The Ways of My Grandmothers* has its origins, Hungry Wolf says, in the often-repeated resolve of her mother, Ruth Little Bear, to write of the life of Blackfoot women (and in Little Bear's father's handwritten history of the people). The echoes within this text of a reiterative, participatory tradition of oral tribal narratives are critical, though less susceptible to bibliographic documentation than are its links with the work of Adolf or the anthropologists.[18] And Hungry Wolf's reference to the 'survival knowledge' inherent even in traditional techniques that are impractical in a busy modern household differentiates her undertaking in function if not in structure from the romance of salvage ethnography (205). Hungry Wolf's narrative is a heterogeneous one, simultaneously outcome of, and intervention in, multiple discourses, themselves not static but interpenetrating. Not archive, the text and its tribal tradition exist as historically engaged and evolving narratives.

How far am I, for that matter, from a collective subjectivity? To strangers and to my siblings' fellow-workers and friends, I appear indistinguishable from my sisters, in voice, appearance, mannerisms, and stories. 'Are you twins?' the store clerk asks, as my sister and I purchase identical, green, turtleneck pullovers. 'Well, ye . . es,' we reply. 'But not to each other.' As the obverse of this, what to my family appears anomalous, wilful, and perverse in me can, within another culture – that of feminist academia, say – merely mark the norm. There what differentiates me may be some quirk of family humour or my Canadian inclinations (if the setting is U.S.-American) or my post-Catholic moral anxiety or ... My Irish ancestors and kin have only recently laid claim to my imagination and hold little prospect of becoming my affiliative community. I have my clans, though, even if they reside outside the realm of consanguinity, clans defined by gender and political sympathy, by professional affinity, by sexual orientation, by nation – imagined communities with real toads in them (to conjoin Benedict Anderson and Marianne Moore). Much of my meaning lies in furthering those shared narratives. The ethnographic eye of the (true) outsider would, I suspect, perceive in my academic cohort, for example, common coloration and tribal uniformity. To that viewer, I imagine, the flashes of intellectual brilliance and administrative pugnacity that *we* remark would no more denote substantive individual distinctiveness than do the finer points of snow shovelling.

––––––•–•––––––

I wonder why it is that to be working class or a woman of color in America and to write a book about it is a radical action and one that must be published by the alternative presses. Why is it that telling our lives is a subversive thing to do? (Hogan 243–4)

Power is the ability to take one's place in whatever discourse is essential to action and the right to have one's part matter. (Heilbrun, *Writing* 18)

––––––•–•––––––

Gender, an organizing principle of Hungry Wolf's book, also complicates my analysis of *The Ways of My Grandmothers*. The collective identity I discern here coincides in troublesome ways with an apparent tendency in white female self-representation to downplay exceptionality and minimize authority (Heilbrun, 'Non-Autobiographies' 70; Spacks 177–81). Considerable potential for misconstruction occurs when Hungry Wolf's narrative finds itself within another literary tradition disposed to make self-dramatization the province more of one sex than the other, while simultaneously valorizing individual distinction. The subjectivity that Hungry Wolf enacts here risks being subsumed under the stereotype of female self-effacement.[19]

Simultaneously, the narrative can be viewed as a manifestation of one of the available discourses of the period: that of early North American second-wave feminism. Hungry Wolf tells us that many young women (a number of them non-Native, judging by the autobiographical details given in *Shadows of the Buffalo*) queried her about her grandmothers' natural methods of contraception, their interest presumably encouraged by the movement's focus on reproductive autonomy. *The Ways of My Grandmothers* draws on the language of oppression (Hungry Wolf characterizes the legendary Napi as the first to 'use and abuse' women [139]), of inequity (both Mary One Spot and Paula Weasel Head note the degree to which their fathers expected to be served, relic of an earlier division of labour), and of male norms (Ruth Little Bear ponders the marked nature of bestowed female names – Shot-Close *Woman* or Medicine-Capture *Woman* – and the unmarked nature of male ones). The text follows some of the early directions of white second-wave feminism both in revaluing the female sphere and in finding female instances of male accomplishment – here the warrior women of the past.

———•———

The literary, primitivist, and early feminist discourses that in one way or another frame this tale [*Papago Woman*] all claim to present Chona's subjectivity, yet they lead us to what they cannot encompass – the central oppressive power in Chona's life, which is that of the Euro-Americans, not of Papago men. (Carr 151)

———•———

Fundamentally, though, the polemical (and feminist) subtext in *The Ways of My Grandmothers* is a countercolonial one, directed against the dismissal or erasure of Blackfoot women's lives in the dominant culture and, by extension, within their own younger generations. Hungry Wolf speaks repeatedly to stereotypes of Indian women as drudges, to the neglect of their lives in histories, to her own youthful belief that earlier Indian women were sold and subjugated by their people. Her comments on women's superior tipi-raising skills, on evidence in tribal legends of the high social standing of women, and on the failure to collect Hate Woman's story of war exploits along with her husband's (perhaps even Paula Weasel Head's insistence on her own preparedness to lead ceremonies were the role not restricted to men) are aimed less at attitudes and practices within the tribe than at a colonizing epistemology and material practice that deny that 'Indian women have knowledge to contribute to world history' (17).

In fact, my examples may give a misleading prominence to the impact of feminist discourse. Hungry Wolf handles gender for the most part non-oppositionally. Instead, she rights the balance, she unobtrusively foregrounds the female dimensions of any aspect of tribal life, and she substitutes an alternative paradigm. Hers is an approach that might be called 'womanist' for its determination to counterpoise gender claims with other claims, such as those of race.[20]

The Ways of My Grandmothers unfolds always *against* the background of territorial and cultural imperialism – upon that background and in resistance to it. The political reality emerges matter-of-factly and incidentally in references encompassing a century of history – from an RCMP raid on a medicine lodge to the cutting of federal funding for Native education, from the enclosure of the land to the pollution of air and water, from forced labour in missionary schools to the demoralization of youth. In a colonial context, what is most orthodox and self-less and apolitical about Hungry Wolf's tribal subjectivity and narrative may prove, paradoxically, to be what is least orthodox and self-less and apolitical. Coming as it does at a period for the Blood of reduced resistance to Euro-American mores, her early advocacy of the 'ways of my grandmothers' represents an unconventional break with a tribal cultural trend. When she first applied to female elders for instruction, Hungry Wolf indicates, her interest was made light of and discouraged; even her own grandmother urged her to stop dressing like an old woman.[21] Her apparently ahistoric and unassuming transmission of tradition, then, can be construed as a moment of historic intervention, an assumption of agency, a gesture (ironically) of personal distinctiveness, a counterhegemonic political act.

One of the photographs in *The Ways of My Grandmothers* shows Beverly Hungry Wolf turned away from the camera, her over-exposed facial features barely discernible against the washed-out sky. She displays a carefully beaded cradleboard on her back, in which she is carrying a child. The photograph just catches the corner of a pair of eyeglasses glinting in the light.

How am I to read this figure? As an anonymous representative of a people and a culture? As the nostalgic reconstruction of an 'authentic' nineteenth-century Indian? As the link of transmission between Blackfoot mother(s) of the 1920s and Blackfoot mother(s) of the 2040s? As an enabling element in someone else's idealist dream of Indian mystery and power? As a product of the counter-culture of the 1960s and 1970s? As the embodiment of a resilient and adaptive Native tradition? As the self-reflexive object/subject of cultural study? As a token of resistance in a countercolonial struggle? As a stereotype of female nurturance and self-effacement? As an emissary for the claims of the practical and the quotidian? As one moment in an unstable succession of subject positions? As an integral component of a social unit, dependent for meaning upon that narrative of affiliation? As the self-construction of a craftsperson constituting a world with her needle and her pen?

How *can* I read this figure, when the narrative self is studiously absent, dispersed across multiple narrators and histories, refusing the self-aggrandizement of autobiography? How can I *not* read this figure, when the narrative self is defiantly present, writing herself back into history, refusing the voyeuristic distance and impersonality of ethnography with its curatorial dioramas? And why am I reading *this* photograph rather than one of the various pictures of Hungry Wolf within a group or, for that matter, a picture of other tribal members altogether?

6

'Because You Aren't Indian': Lee Maracle's *Ravensong*

In the Canadian context, I suggest that the term [First Nations] *is an ironic reinscription of the historical and cultural priority of the First Nations people and more than an innocent political gesture pointing to the role of nationalism in the oppression of indigenous peoples.*

(Srivastava, 'Re-imaging' 109)

The cult of origins is a hate reaction.

(Kristeva, *Nations* 2)

In *Nations without Nationalism*, Julia Kristeva describes 'the cult of origins,' the defensive human withdrawal into a 'sullen, warm private world, unnameable and biological, the impregnable "aloofness" of a weird primal paradise – family, ethnicity, nation, race' (2, 3).[1] '[T]he soil, the blood, and the genius of the language' that Kristeva considers the roots of a xenophobic national idea (40) are precisely the connections on which many First Nations peoples draw in resisting colonization. How does one reinvent oneself and one's connections in ways that avoid reductive and exclusionary allegiances? What does it mean to be a nation or, in less Eurocentric terms, to be a people? If the new nationalisms serve laudable, decolonizing ends, how does one avoid subordinating other claims, such those of gender, to the claims of solidarity? *Ravensong* (1993), by Salish-Métis writer and activist Lee Maracle,[2] provides an instructive opportunity to examine notions of nation, people, and tribe, and the subjectivities constructed by and within such imagined communities, because of the complexity of the multiple allegiances that the text negotiates.[3] The novel follows, among others, the stories of the Salish protagonist, Stacey, who moves increasingly into the world of white education, and the mythic Raven, who has designs on white and Native communities alike, to explore the challenge of transforming polarized worlds.

At a pot-luck gathering for Joy Harjo in Minneapolis just after the release of the movie *Dances with Wolves*, some of us (mostly Native), heads together, were exchanging low-voiced critiques of the movie. The slightly furtive nature of the huddle surprised me. Was it produced, I wondered, by the possible presence of some of the Lakotas involved in the project or by a concern, given the film's touted advancements in the representation of Native life, not to hurt the feelings of the non-Natives in the room.

'Are you Cree?' asked Houma film-maker Chris Spotted Eagle, misled perhaps by our group's sense of fellow feeling.

'No,' I said. 'I'm just Irish.'[4]

'Don't say that,' he corrected me. 'Irish is good.'

The 'just' had slipped out. Maria Campbell in *The Book of Jessica* had already begun to educate me on this subject. 'While you were being overwhelmed with my history and my oppression ...' she rebukes Scottish-Canadian collaborator Linda Griffiths, 'I couldn't understand why you didn't know your own history ... the history of your pain and all the things that happened to your people was exactly the same as our history ... It seemed that that would be a meeting place for us' (Campbell and Griffiths 35). Shortly after my conversation with Chris, I began reading up on the history of the Irish in Canada (and, inextricably, Irish history as well), on the Irish 'traveller' population, and on Irish mythology (from which Yeats's dramas had alienated me almost permanently).

I wouldn't say 'I'm just Irish' now. I don't think.

There is nothing as white as the white girl an Indian boy loves. (Alexie, 'Red Blues,' *Old* 86; 'Distances,' *Business* 18)

Am I Native American only when I am hated because of it? (Alexie, 'Because I Was in New York City Once and Have since Become an Expert,' *First* 81)

Lee Maracle's *Ravensong* seems to function antithetically, elaborating and in the process seeming to reinscribe the divide between Indians and 'white folk,' constructing identity through opposition, between 'us' and 'them people,' between 'the village' and 'the town,' between 'the people' and 'the others.' The text is set in the 1950s, in what Maracle has elsewhere called 'the stupidest of times' (*I Am* 90). It uses (my American-studies students argued) an era of white culture so self-evidently benighted and, to the contemporary eye, intolerable – I wish I were as optimistic as my students – as to throw into relief cultural tensions less nakedly at work today. Stacey, the nascent village thinker, compiles a 'grocery list of the differences' (115) between the two worlds. She begins with material differences – the amenities of the houses, landscaping of yards, size of community buildings, impact of the influenza epidemic, standards of female appearance – and modulates into broader cultural differences – connotations of the words for 'rain' or 'child,' strictures over sexuality, comfort levels with silence, sources of authority, community support systems, protocol (for socializing with unmarried females, giving thanks, voicing disagreement, responding to an offer of food), value of elders, gendered spheres of responsibility, nature of social sanctions, methods of teaching, handling of shame ...[5]

Eager not to disappoint, i try my best to offer my benefactors and benefactresses what they most anxiously yearn for: the possibility of a difference, yet a difference or an otherness that will not go so far as to question the foundation of their beings and makings. (Trinh, *Woman* 88)

The effect of Stacey's continuing anatomy of differences in *Ravensong* is not one of detached ethnographic documentation, as witness the piqued response of one reviewer, Marie Campbell:[6] ' "Is it prejudice or a gulf of difference too deep to cross?" Stacey asks in her relentless quest for "the why of this world." ... Although she dances around it with subtly-inflected and nicely visual language, however, Maracle's blunt approach never really takes us any closer to an answer – or even mutual respect' (46). 'Or even mutual respect.' Why this taking of offence? Affronts for the white reader, actually, are not hard to find in *Ravensong*.[7] It is not just that white people, individually and collectively, are held historically accountable ('while you're wishing, why don't you wish these people never came to mess up our lives' [105]); postcolonial revisionism is familiar enough. Beyond that, from the perspective of the Native culture, white assumptions – fundamental and still current assumptions – are rendered, literally, unthinkable. 'Unthinkable' is, in fact, the word used during Stacey's Momma's baffled incomprehension at the suicide of Stacey's white classmate Polly (150). The cultural vertigo first experienced by Stacey, as '[t]he Indian girl from across the river' at the white school in town (66), eventually becomes instead the portion of the white reader.

'Why compare *us* to them?' challenges Rena, one of Stacey's fellow villagers (115; emphasis added), and the novel works at reversing the direction of the comparison. Although from the context of the town ('I must be different when I'm out there' [134]), Stacey is tempted to adjudge her life as deficient, normativeness in the book is more often than not the prerogative of Native values. Maracle proliferates positions within *Ravensong* that decentre Euro-Canadian assumptions, while seeming to intensify a cultural/racial impasse. 'What is it with these people?' wonders Stacey, about the white readiness to demand commiseration for personal miseries after displaying massive indifference to the influenza epidemic's toll on the entire Native community (130). 'I would like to know something about these people before I die,' explains her brother Jim, requesting the occasional book as he announces his inability to continue with school, 'but I just can't stand them' (161).

Through Stacey's mother, in particular, Maracle author-izes a textual position from which the white world remains inaccessible and without meaning:

She tried to tell her mom how different white people were inside themselves. The littlest things were governed by the most complex rules and regulations ... She could tell that Momma didn't really believe her.
    'How can you live that way?' she scoffed. (151–2)

From Momma come the novel's most uncompromising refusals of cross-cultural negotiation. What could whites have to teach that would be worth learning, she asks at one point, worrying at other points that Stacey may in fact learn to be like them. Momma's dismissal of German Judy, Rena's partner – 'She's white and so she don't count' – reverberates through the novel (123, 127, 135, 194). And in her final implacability over the white town's callousness during the epidemic, Momma makes the most absolute and chilling repudiation of all: '"They aren't human," she had told Stacey a while back, categorically dismissing them all' (193). From this position, the dominant culture is more than simply dislodged from its hegemonic pre-eminence; its logic, its claim even to be a culture, is dismantled.

Ironically, too, parallel scenes between, first, Stacey and her white friend Carol and then Stacey and her mother only intensify the representation of the 'gulf of difference' between peoples. Taken aback by startling information about the use of native plants within the other community – that Native people eat weeds, that white people pull up and throw away native food and medicine – both Carol and Stacey's mother respond similarly. Both react first with shock, then with identically voiced verbal resistance ('you're kidding' [32, 76]), and then with hearty, relieved laughter, recuperating the anomalous back into familiar paradigms as a mere joke. Carol is never disabused of her mistake: 'It excited her [Stacey] to think that Carol knew absolutely nothing about her, while Stacey knew Carol so well' (32–3). The politics of privilege, *Ravensong* reminds us, permit whites an ignorance neither available to nor politic for marginalized others. Although provided with less overt correction – simply a look from her daughter compared to Stacey's unequivocal remonstration to Carol that she would never kid about such a subject – Stacey's mother quickly recovers herself, confirming that Stacey is serious. The information, though, proves unassimilable, simply confounding her. Carol remains oblivious to anything beyond her world to be comprehended. The more receptive of the two to new data about the other, Stacey's mother can only reiterate her bafflement and turn back to drying out the comfrey: 'I will never understand them people. Help me tie these up' (76).

In May of 1994, two of my sisters and I made our first trip to Ireland. The stock quality of this pilgrimage, the nostalgic return of the Irish-Canadian exile, we commemorated ironically in our scrapbook, with photographs, from the path alongside Torc Waterfall, of splayed, cross-hatched tree roots, polished with trampling. Irish roots. But when I stood on the groomed grounds of massive Adare Manor in County Limerick, I understood something that, for all the talk of the French Revolution, had been absent from my gawking at French chateaux in the Loire Valley. 'These people,' I thought, 'took this land away from my people.' I thought of my maternal grandfather generations later in Essex County, Ontario, who I discovered after his death had all his life rented the 'family farm' that he worked.[8] In recounting my reaction at Adare Manor to my therapist later, I was knocked sideways, not so much by the pain of past injustice but by the pain and power of that phrase 'my people,' by the anguish of that lost connection.

Of course, my sisters and I didn't fit in. 'No, you don't look like tourists; you're just colourful,' a tour guide at Trinity College lied charitably about our red and orange and yellow rain jackets. And for all our ease with Greek and Roman and Judaeo-Christian mythology, we could only respond with baffled laughter to the indecipherable sculpture, in Dublin's Merrion Square, of a bound, naked, male corpse attended by two standing women, one pierced by two swords, the other with a severed hand attached to her back and a large rock balanced against her neck (legend: 'As cranes / Chanting / Their dolorous / Notes traverse / The sky'). One complete and wonderful surprise of the trip, though, was to discover on every Irish street corner the faces of the women of my family. Not the dark-haired and ruddy-cheeked or red-headed classic Irish types of the picture books but familiar brown-haired women with features I knew, unknown aunts, lost cousins, possible sisters.[9]

The writing that emerges from this position [Eurocentric postmodernism], however critical it may be of colonial discourses, gloomily disempowers the 'nation' as an enabling idea and relocates the impulses for change as everywhere and nowhere. (Sangari 183)

It is this logic of opposition – this uncritical construction of an exclusive Self and an excluded Other – which links sexism, racism, and nationalism and brings nationalism as a postcolonial feminist strategy deeply into question. (Donaldson 10–11)

Reading *Ravensong* is, I have to confess, chastening for me as a white reader. I appreciate the decolonizing of history in the account of the Depression and the 1950s influenza epidemic, the challenging of a hegemonic perspective. I recognize the ironies of cross-cultural short-circuits, as in the account of the white itinerants during the 1930s who offend Native families with their open ogling of the young women and impertinent queries about the food. Sometimes I am 'simply' suffering from ignorance, unsure what exactly is denoted by the burning that follows Nora's burial and unfamiliar with the particular stories that I presume would explicate the terse allusions to Raven's foolish arrogance (16, 131). Sometimes I am brought up short by my own romantic (?) assumptions. The deprecation of Carol's simple grief at her grandmother's death, contrasted with the more profound horror and terror attendant on the loss of Stacey's Gramma, rudder of the Native community, disconcerts me. The scene confounds my initial expectation that Maracle would associate panic over death with white historical and spiritual deracination, and more philosophical approaches to death with Native values.

Even more tellingly, I misconstrue completely Stacey's family's shocked disbelief when Stacey explains Fascism, the absence of rights, to them. I naïvely explicate their reaction as incredulity at the existence of such an alien system. Their actual response, grounded in the utter commonplaceness, not the unwontedness, to them, of such practice – 'You mean our boys went to kill people they never met for that? Hell, we got that here. No one kills for that here!' (53) – catches me off guard: 'Gotcha.' The ironic twist, carefully crafted and darkly humorous, jolts me out of complacent solidarity, us democrats against the Fascists, into having to identify against myself, as some of us democrats turn out to be the Fascists. The text unsettles me.

It is over the representation of modern white mores, though, that I find myself more disturbingly defensive. I become a 'resisting reader' in the least attractive sense of that term, not an exegetical rebel but a recalcitrant foot-dragger, not a catechist of a text's unselfcritical ideological presuppositions but an outrider for my own. *We* always shared our car at funerals, I find myself arguing, resisting Maracle's – or more accurately Stacey's – contrast of white and Native funeral practices. Even with twelve passengers the everyday complement for our car (I savour the force of my evidence), we redistributed ourselves among vehicles, so that spinster aunts had rides and, more importantly, company, so that we all re-immersed ourselves, temporarily, in the bath of extended family. I bridle at the specific – three short sentences in the text on whites' half-empty cars – setting aside the novel's broader reflection on white familial disconnection, and its application to my story. Except for two short weeks in the summer, funerals were in fact the only time we enjoyed that extended family.

I resist, too, Stacey's critique of the artificial friendliness and false enthusiasm of Carol's mother, Mrs Snowden. At least she is making an effort, I rebut, positioning myself, according to a logic of opposition, with the whites, I who usually endorse the satirizing of bourgeois pretensions. With the representation of the influenza epidemic, I find myself looking past the textual foreground – the bigotry generated by school discussions of the epidemic, the white disregard for the deaths of elders, the coexistence of concerned rhetoric and actual inaction – to spy out exculpatory evidence, of a newspaper controversy over neglect of Indian patients or concern over the death of Native babies. And, although I am enlightened by the distinction drawn between shame assumed with dignity and shame partially deflected into a burden of guilt for others, I become an apologist for Stacey's white school friend Steve. However inadequate his response, at least he is being educated into shame over his physician father's abandonment of Native influenza victims, I protest. Taking offence on the basis of my racial affiliation, responding defensively on behalf of imagined members of that imagined community, as a reader I enact the politics of difference that the novel explores. I rehearse Stacey's father's dictum: 'Remember, if they ever have to choose between each other and you, they will always choose themselves' (89).

------·------

Full citizens lack culture, and those most culturally endowed lack full citizenship. (Rosaldo 198)

The risks of talking culture are immense ... While cultural considerations may be intended to promote sensitivity, dominant groups too readily adopt the cultural differences approach, relieved not to have to confront the realities of racism and sexism. (Razack 85)

------·------

'Culture talk,' as Razack suggests, is fraught: potentially conservative, ahistorical, and depoliticized. Does a focus on *Ravensong*'s anatomizing of racial/cultural difference shift the focus towards cultural awareness and away from political and social change? Is there a better way to read the novel? Certainly, Stacey's mother's final intransigence regarding the white world never presents itself as mere cultural chauvinism. What she repudiates is not simply a culture other than or even incommensurable with her own, but rather a particular, historically situated, and politically implicated culture capable of producing and sanctioning racist attitudes ('No small wonder they don't like us if they don't like their own' [153]) and genocidal practice ('One day they would all pay for watching a people die' [193]). In the background of the novel always is the haunting memory (literally haunting: it invades the mind and body of Stacey's younger sister, Celia) of the historic and destructive arrival of the first tall ship, with its physical and social contagion. In the foreground, functioning synecdochally, is the racially determined experience of the epidemic. The illness may hit white and Native communities alike, but power is shown to mediate the outcome: it is the village not the town that is stripped of its thinker, its keeper of medicine, its lineages, half its newborns. In the foreground are other reiterated reminders of the colonizing erosion of Native reality, such as the admonitions, from a subsequent, more knowing perspective,[10] that this generation and, specifically, Stacey's family will be the last to follow traditional practices. Read figuratively, Momma's lament, 'Our medicine don't work all that well on their illnesses,' gives an emphatically resistant cast to the novel's expressions of cultural dissonance (117).

'Is it because I am white?' he asked without bothering with the first part of the question.

'No,' she said softly. 'It's because you aren't Indian.' (Maracle, *Ravensong* 185)

I am no longer on the periphery of their world and cut off from mine; they are on the periphery of mine. (Maracle, *Sundogs* 139)

Maracle's focus on cultural difference takes a distinctly counter-hegemonic turn particularly through the situating of the narrative. Giving whites the accent, so to speak, the dialect, against the norm of Native speech, giving whites a non-transparent culture, is itself transformative, a political act. It repositions both white and Native reader, so that, within the discursive framework of *Ravensong* at least, the Native reader is the one with full citizenship, an epistemological shift with the potential to produce material sociopolitical change. Even Native exclusion from full entry into 'Canadian' society is inverted ironically into a strength and source of power, into an inevitable and delegitimizing refusal of assent to the self-evident foundations of the dominant culture: 'there were so many assumptions in the white world that had no meaning here,' the narrator notes (112).

This preliminary, levelling redistribution of cultural capital is modelled within the novel when Stacey and Rena's utter ignorance of the white world uncovers in German Judy a corresponding and disabling incapacity to fathom and so begin to address their incomprehension: 'All three women sat in a complete state of unknowing. In an odd sort of way they were all equal in their lack of knowledge' (113). Stacey's ignorance, we are told, has power in it. As Homi Bhabha says about the deployment of cultural difference as a disruptive strategy, the effect 'is not merely to change the "object" of analysis – to focus, for instance, on race rather than gender or native knowledges rather than metropolitan myths; nor to invert the axis of political discrimination by installing the excluded term at the centre ... It changes the position of enunciation and the relations of address within it; not only what is said but from where it is said; not simply the logic of articulation but the *topos* of enunciation' ('DissemiNation' 312). Making white culture marked and Native culture the standard foregrounds and calls into question the very naturalizing of normative cultures. It requires a new conversation and new power relations between the interlocutors.

———•———

Indians must see visions. White people can have the same visions
if they are in love with Indians. If a white person loves an Indian

then the white person is Indian by proximity. White people must carry
an Indian deep inside themselves. Those interior Indians are half-breed

and obviously from horse cultures.
    (Alexie, 'How to Write the Great American Indian Novel,' *Summer* 95)

———•———

In 1995, I was at an Anishinaabe White Earth land-recovery benefit, featuring Spokane–Coeur D'Alene poet and fiction writer Sherman Alexie. As I indicated earlier, my partner is Cherokee (-Greek), Canadian (-American), novelist (-academic) Thomas King, and we were there together. I have become fairly familiar with the uncomfortable position of outsider at gatherings where non-Native people are in a minority. Although the self-consciousness, vulnerable conspicuousness, and painful sense of representing the dominant race do not become less acute, I generally manage to experience this inversion of my usual position of race privilege as salutary. I compare it to the educative experience of men at early (second-wave) feminist meetings (though knowing what I felt towards those occasional men does nothing to make my position now more comfortable). I know, in my head, that the more discomfiting my decentring, the more effectual it is.

    From time to time, I find myself in smaller gatherings of three or four where the exhilaration and intimacy fashioned from a shared history, positioning, and politics are suddenly punctured by a necessary accommodation to the presence of a non-Native person in the company. A prominent Native artist, for example, recounting in exasperation the disproportionate effusiveness with which a white curator introduces her to white fellow board members, will recollect herself momentarily to say, 'Oh, Helen, I didn't mean ...' A Métis novelist, explaining how she and a typesetting friend sneaked into the press after hours to replace individual lines of text against the wishes of a white editor, will stop, apologetic about her use of 'white' as explanatory. And then I feel very white indeed.

At the reading, Sherman Alexie, wry and witty, read a song to brown-skinned women: 'because it's always easiest / ... / to watch an Indian woman / just this side / of beautiful / slow dance / to a sad song / and never have to worry / about making her any promises.' He read a poem about the white woman on Amtrak who thought two hundred years was an impressive stretch of history – 'while I ... / ... made plans / for what I would do and say the next time // somebody from the enemy thought I was one of their own' – and another about reading a love poem to a white woman, 'while you sat with another Indian woman, all three of you beautiful, listening' (*First* 108, 79, 110). He read poems about Spam and about powdered milk, poems that had those of us who have lived that story elbowing each other with pleasure.

The rueful poignancy of some of Alexie's poems was still with me when I turned to Tom before the lights came up. 'Is Sherman's wife Indian?' I asked Tom.

'I'm pretty sure ... yeah, she is.'

With me, too, was the image from one poem of brown hand comforting brown hand.

'I'm sorry I'm not Indian for you,' I said.

———•·•———

No nos podemos quedar paradas con los brazos cruzados en medio del puente (*we can't afford to stop in the middle of the bridge with arms crossed*). (Anzaldúa, Foreword [iv])

'I see you on the bridge almost every day staring at the water.'(Maracle, *Ravensong* 80)

———•·•———

Of course, Maracle doesn't stop with a depiction of two racial solitudes. One of the issues of the novel, from Raven's perspective at least, is that 'the people behaved as though they would have no part of the others' world' (44). Raven must find a way to bring the villagers 'across the bridge' to begin the transformation of white society (43). Stacey carries this narrative line, in her struggle over whether and how to enter the white world, her ambivalence about attending university.

The thesis Maracle advances is an audacious and provocative, even potentially inflammatory one (as much for Native readers and other anticolonialists as for apologists for empire). Summarized reductively, her teleological reading of historical pain seems to establish the European conquest and subsequent epidemics in Native country as necessary evils: 'Maybe we are being driven from our insulated little lives into the other world because they need something we have' (141–2). Even the contemporary demoralization of Native communities becomes part of this design: 'Until the villagers began to feel as ugly inside as the others, none could come forward to undo the sickness which rooted the others to their own ugliness' (191). Such a reading of history risks absolving Euro-Canadians of responsibility for colonization and racist oppression. It risks also seeming to facilitate Native assimilation or to undermine the radical sovereignty for the First Nations that Maracle herself advocates and that entails turning away from dominant political and social structures.[11]

At the same time, there is something grandly revisionist about such a history. Maracle inverts the significance of the entire European invasion, transforming it from a self-generated imperialist undertaking into Raven's salvific plan, a plan to staunch the far-away bleeding of the earth by transporting the ravagers to 'Raven's shore' and conferring Raven on all people (191). Maracle recontextualizes 'that "great narrative of entropy and loss" which is the Euramerican version of Native American history' (Owens, *Other* 22), restoring agency and salience to the First Nations. As a countercolonial great narrative, this account rivals the narratives of nation that Benedict Anderson describes, with their subjective antiquity (though actual modernity) and sense of destined inevitability (5, 11–12).

----·-·----

Lee Maracle speaks unflinchingly of the gulf between two cultures – a gulf that Raven knows must be bridged. (*Ravensong* cover blurb)

I've had enough
I'm sick of seeing and touching

Both sides of things
Sick of being the damn bridge for everybody

> (Rushin, 'The Bridge Poem,' *Black* 33)

Implacable in her representation of racial estrangement, Maracle counters with the figure of the bridge between village and town. Gulfs and bridges. The arc of the bridge, rising from opposing ramparts towards the sky and, in another context, defined as the strongest shape in nature, is shown both to obscure the view of the other side and to enable passage. Stacey returns to her own world across the bridge, neglects to stop on the bridge when she is shunning the complications of her relationship with the town boy Steve, and makes a symbolic passage across the bridge to town on foot with her mother before setting off by car for university. The bridge seems to correspond to various urgings within the novel for cross-cultural connection, whether old Dominic's call for a combined wisdom, a joining of all knowledge, or Gramma's conviction that sickness can only be deflected by learning to live with the others and seeing their ultimate nature altered.

Bridge Indians. Not village, not urban. (Maracle, *Sojourner's* 85)

Sick of mediating with your worst self
On behalf of your better selves

Sick
Of having
To remind you
To breathe
Before you
Suffocate
Your own
Fool self

Forget it
Stretch or drown
Evolve or die

> (Rushin 34)

A bridge is a span of connection between two banks, between two given, separate, solid, stable, and uniform entities. As a trope for cross-cultural relations, therefore, the figure of the bridge (and the river of difference beneath it) can capture one subjective reality – the peremptory experience of a natural communal membership produced by a shared subject position and of a fundamental rift with a contraposed collectivity, a rift requiring the construction of deliberate, intermittent avenues of exchange. But the bridge represents this reality only at the cost of fixing and flattening the contingent, enmeshed, discontinuous, and shifting nature of individual subjectivity and collective identity. On one level, Maracle constructs racial/cultural relations on a dualist model, reproducing Abdul JanMohamed's Manichean allegory of colonizer and colonized, but with the positive and negative valences reversed. In this model, a bridge operates as the alternative to a politics of separatism. (And even here, the mediation raises troubling questions about reciprocity of labour and power. Stacey's excursions across the bridge are more personally costly and collectively dangerous than Steve's. As Cherríe Moraga says about the antiracist interventions of women of colour: *'How can we – this time – not use our bodies to be thrown over a river of tormented history to bridge the gap?'* [Moraga xv]). But Maracle's text, presided over by the figure of Raven, is trickier and more multifarious than the trope of the bridge might suggest.

I have seen a refusal to submit to white feminist essentialism turn to an identity essentialism in a strange twist of theory and politics. (Bannerji, *Returning* xxiii)

Intervening in an interconnected world, one is always, to varying degrees, 'inauthentic': caught between cultures, implicated in others ... Identity is conjunctural, not essential. (Clifford 11)

Simultaneously with its affirmation of racial/cultural absolutes, *Ravensong* works to subvert the simple binarisms of this model. The setting of the novel bears some resemblance to what Mary Louise Pratt defines as a 'contact zone' of colonial encounter.[12] So the novel invites reading from a 'contact perspective,' treating the relations among colonizers and colonized 'not in terms of separateness or apartheid, but in terms of copresence, interaction, interlocking understandings and practices, often within radically asymmetrical relations of power' (M.L. Pratt 7).

Binarisms break down, as the white world is repeatedly found to be internal rather than external, on this rather than that side of the river. Both Stacey and the Native man known as 'the snake' are perceived to have brought the town into the village. Stacey's subjectivity is multiply constituted, of 'white' as well as 'Native' perspectives among others, as she finds herself judging her mother's sexuality (through white eyes) in terms of public perception, for instance.

More than this, though, the constructs of white and Native themselves are shown to be mutually dependent, problematic, and unstable. One of the moments that crystallizes racial identity for Stacey – 'She had never felt this Indian in all her life' (89) – constitutes the category 'Indian' entirely in structural rather than substantive terms, over against the Other. What produces Stacey's feeling of Indianness is Carol's apparent gesture of race loyalty in betraying Stacey's confidences, to another white friend, Steve. Whiteness produces Indianness. And, only pages later, this categorical sense of racial difference not only begins to falter but threatens to invert itself. Stacey is led to wonder whether Carol's indiscretion doesn't align Carol instead with Stacey's brother, her uncle, and Ella in their scheming over Momma's love life.

One of the features of *Ravensong* that one of my senior classes in Canadian Native literature commented on most was its contradictoriness. Some of this is explicit in the text, in Stacey's recognition that whites draw and repel her, or her resentment simultaneously of her mother's collecting of 'weeds' and whites' discarding of them, or her critique and defence of Carol's rudeness in refusing tea. Students pointed out other unnoted instances also, though, such as the inconsistency between the emotional reserve and the ease with intimacy that Stacey alternately attributes to whites or between the absence of sexual prohibitions and the courtship protocol that she ascribes to her people. Features of white culture that Stacey deplores, such as the inability of wives to leave their husbands, coexist – unremarked at the time – in the village, in the snake's household, as well. Madeline's appreciation for the letters of the alphabet that jump out of character, that cannot be counted on always to sound the same, could be read as a metatextual endorsement of this principle of inconstancy. The space of contradiction that Stacey inhabits was, one student felt, the space that as reader she too was invited to occupy.[13]

Telling Tom that I was sorry I wasn't Indian for him was a lapse in resilience on my part, a singular and momentary lapse. I recognized it as maudlin – the tears in my eyes, after all, were more for me than for him – and retracted it almost at once. The timing was ironic because my therapist had that morning given me the assignment to practise being what I was (Popeye style: 'I yam what I yam'). To live through the contradictions of my position. Even though my partner is male, I was to eliminate the defensive qualifiers, the tentative deferring to someone else's homogenizing categories, to stop saying, even or especially to myself, 'I am a *non-practising* lesbian' or 'I am a *self-defined* lesbian' or 'I *consider* myself a lesbian.' I was simply to say, 'I am a lesbian.' 'I am a lesbian who lives with a man.' Simple enough.

'I am what I am.' ... 'I'm sorry I'm not Indian for you.'

Tom and I talked about my comment later, and I apologized for it again.

'You did hurt my feelings,' he said. 'You made me feel different. What I spent most of my childhood trying to get away from. You wouldn't expect me to apologize for not being white.'

I acknowledged the truth of that.

'My difference from you,' Tom said, 'became greater than your difference from me.'

People resist all forms of extinction, including homogenization. (Jahner 184)

The brilliant suggestion of Uma Narayan, that we grant epistemic privilege to the oppressed, falls apart when the subject positions are so confused. Unless we want to fall into the trap of demanding that the oppressed speak in a unified voice before we will believe them, we are still left with the difficult task of negotiating our way through our various ways of knowing and towards political action. (Razack 49–50)

The opening images of *Ravensong* are of Raven's song spiralling outward from the deep, through layers of water stacked in sheets of varying greens. And of the river, shoreline, and houses of the present giving way, before Stacey's sister Celia, to the landscape and bighouses of another era. The images of superimposition, like the superimposition of at least three time periods within the text, point to a strategy of narrative density, devised to convey the plurality of affiliations, histories, and desires comprising each subjectivity and community. From the multiple, unsynchronized bathroom stops required for a carload of individuals who have eaten and drunk at the same time, to the greater sensitivity to sun of mixed-blood women, *Ravensong* provides ample evidence, physical and figurative, of the heterogeneity within Stacey's community. The language of chasms and bridges extends into descriptions of *village* relations, complicating earlier dualities. Stacey has to use the arc of family history to connect with her own cousin Stella, who is distanced by residential school, motherhood, and a 'womanly' rather than intellectual realm.

'Context' is the word Maracle repeatedly evokes for the shared subject position essential to connection. Talking to Ella is insufficient, Stacey warns Steve; he would have to have suffered through what an epidemic means to the village.[14] And, while Stacey knows that Steve does not have sufficient context even to assess her attractiveness, her mother similarly suspects that Stacey lacks context to appreciate her mother's sexual needs. From the Christian villagers whom Stacey doesn't comprehend to the lesbians shunned by some others, Maracle multiplies the disjunctive, even conflicting claims of subjectivities constituted within the tribe. The figure of Nora, who justifies her 'illegal' fishing not with her Aboriginal rights but with her obligations as a mother and who is passed over for Speaker because she is a woman (and whose outspoken voice from beyond the grave is often at odds with the more thoughtful advice of tribal members), is only one of a number of female characters contributing to a feminist analysis that refuses to subsume 'woman' under 'Native' in the constituting of identity.

Within that dualism of white and Native, too, Maracle introduces tribal difference in the person of Madeline, of the Manitoba Saulteaux, who has married into the village.[15] With her distinctive physical type, her different accent, her communicative directness, her indifference to gender roles, her physical expressiveness, and her emotional abandon, she disrupts by her mere presence the cultural transparency (Rosaldo's term, 466) of the village, in the way that *Ravensong* disrupts white cultural normativeness: 'It was annoying to have your whole self challenged so innocently' (173). Intriguingly, Maracle singles out Madeline for the textually marked speech – 'dey jiss do' (175) – used in other literary contexts to distinguish Native characters generally. From within a Native perspective, she also ironically has Stacey remark upon the 'exotic' otherness of Madeline's classically 'Indian' features, her chiselled nose and prominent cheekbones (166). In psychodynamic terms, Madeline even represents for Stacey the repressed libidinous self – 'wildness,' 'desire,' 'freedom' (173–4) – so often figured in white literature through the presence of the Native character(s). Maracle is ironically deploying a lexicon of othering from *within* the very category that it has been used to construct. Her strategy explodes the category 'Indian,' with 'Indian' becoming a signifier of racial difference rather than of a given racial group. And it signals the presence of systems of racial inclusion and exclusion even within that carefully circumscribed category of identity, the village.

———·•·———

'We all go through the same things – it's all just a different kind of the same thing! If it weren't why do you and I know – what we know this minute?' (Glaspell 220)

Everyone had the feeling that there was more to be considered than who shot whom. While the woman was not one of them, the children were. (Maracle, *Ravensong* 159)

———·•·———

Intertextual reverberations emphasize Maracle's attention to the complexity of social collectivities. The scene in *Ravensong* in which Madeline shoots her abusive husband, 'the old snake,' echoes similar narratives by early-twentieth-century U.S.-American writer Susan Glaspell in 'A Jury of Her Peers' (1917) [16] and, following her, contemporary Canadian writer W.P. Kinsella. Kinsella's story 'Yellow Scarf' (1981) explicitly adapts Glaspell's plot to a Native context. His position in intervening between Glaspell and Maracle is particularly ironic because his stories of the Hobbema reserve have been at the forefront of the Canadian controversy over the appropriation of Native voice by white writers. Kinsella has exacerbated the tensions by inflammatory comments, such as his claim that minority writers 'don't have the skill or experience to tell their stories well' (McGoogan C1).

In all three stories, an isolated and mistreated wife turns on her husband – in Glaspell's and Kinsella's versions fatally. In all three, the case is investigated informally by the woman's 'peers,' other women in Glaspell's account, other Indians in Kinsella's and Maracle's. The evidence – or, in Maracle's case, the fact – of the attack is kept from the authorities. Glaspell's story is the revelation of a devalued female culture that enables the neighbour women to detect the untold story from the 'trifles' of domestic life and to join in solidarity to suppress the evidence of a motive, the strangled bird found in Minnie Foster's sewing basket. In 'Yellow Scarf' the collusion is transposed to Indian characters, dismissed by a white coroner contemptuous of their perceptions and of the 'junk' of the Crier household (including the latent evidence of the squashed kitten). Maracle's version continues the motif of the search for explanation in the detritus of everyday, 'as though the history of the moment were mysteriously locked into the piles of things tucked into the bags in disarray' (160). In a twist on the original, though, the physical discovery is not of a presence – the dead bird or kitten – but of an absence: '"It's in what she doesn't have," Stacey whispered plaintively to Kate' (160).

The greater elusiveness of the evidence signals the comparatively more nuanced analysis Maracle develops of the experience of affiliation. Whereas Glaspell's and Kinsella's stories end with renewed solidarity in the face of gender or racial othering, Maracle's version (the authorities relegated to the periphery) moves on to the subsequent ramifications of the crisis. Community, *Ravensong* suggests, cannot be affirmed simply by a banding together against outsiders but entails the harder *internal* work of balancing the different needs and obligations of the various participants in the tragedy and of the group. Kinsella's story complicates issues of affiliation (but does not address possible split allegiances) in that, like the colluding witnesses, both the protected assailant and her victim are Native. By contrast, assailant and witnesses in 'A Jury of Her Peers' close ranks along gender lines against both male victim and authorities. 'Yellow Scarf' does not, however, address the matter of the male victim's claim to community. By having the husband survive the attack, Maracle in *Ravensong* makes even more central the problematic of divided allegiances. Madeline's second attempted assault, which threatens Momma's life, also moves the witnesses beyond their role as mere bystanders in the aftermath of the crisis (as in the earlier versions), graphically enacting the community's implication in and vulnerability to the divisiveness of the conflict.

Even before the old snake's greater offence of incestuous abuse is discovered, detection in the episode reaches beyond the motive for Madeline's attack to another question of equal import for the community: 'What could possibly drive the old snake to this level of neglect?' (161). In contrast with the other stories, the wife's assault on the husband is never in doubt, so that the quandary is less whether she acted (or why), and more how to intervene constructively, to resolve the conflicting claims of wife, husband, children, and village. For affiliations here are not clear-cut. Madeline is an abused woman (and the framework of analysis is feminist), but she is an outsider in a matrilocal society. The snake is an offender, but he is one of the tribe. The snake is a member of the tribe, but he is also a bearer of white patriarchal values. The final decision, to banish the snake, is an unprecedented one, entailing the loss of a group member in the interests of other members (the children) and of the whole. Gender, tribal, and racial solidarities are all real here, but they are neither entirely compatible nor definitive.

As Maracle's rewriting of Glaspell suggests, affiliative networks do not always cohere with social/political structures. The village is greater than the tribe (it includes Madeline); the tribe is greater than the village (it includes individuals such as Shelly, who married out, married a white man, and is lost to the village). Gender in particular produces allegiances pulling against the racial/cultural centres of gravity established in the novel. Until Stacey learns of the vulnerability of white women within their family structures, she 'had bagged white men and women in the same sack. White women started to look different' (81). Thereafter gender connections, such as vague links between Polly, Carol, Shelly, and Gertie, two young women from town, two from the village, all somehow caught in the wreckage of sexual politics, trouble Stacey's sense of cultural/racial allegiance.[17]

What the various narratives of *Ravensong* produce is a three-dimensional Venn diagram of overlapping and layered circles of affiliation, except that the colours keep running and bleeding into one another. The interpenetration of various communities is most emphatically established by Raven. Raven, that tutelary figure specifically of Northwest Coast Native culture, the novel tells us in a far-reaching claim, can 'never again be understood outside the context of the others,' of non-Native cultures (191). And, extending the interconnections beyond the human, Raven warns Cedar, 'These people are heading for the kind of catastrophe *we* may not survive' (44; emphasis added). (The existence earlier in the novel of a version of this declaration reading 'they may not survive' [14] heightens the impact of 'we' here.) The nearly imperceptible textual slippage from one subject to another in the later sentence – 'these people' becoming 'we' – replicates syntactically both the ease and the inextricability of the implication of one world with another. Far from glib declarations of global oneness, these interconnections point to the painfulness of being unable to maintain separate destinies, while still not sharing the lived context necessary for coexistence.

The presence in *Ravensong* of what Maria Lugones calls 'thick' group members (as opposed to transparent ones), individuals whose ways, needs, and interests fail to cohere exactly with those of the group, requires a logic other than the logic of purity (however politically mobilizing that logic may be and helpful to strategies of separation). Maracle's representation of powerful cultural/racial identities and simultaneously of plural subjects who exceed those constructions may configure the strategy of curdle-separation that Lugones advocates (her trope is of the inevitably incomplete separation of the oil-in-water emulsion of mayonnaise) in place of the impossible purity of split-separation ('Purity' 474, 459). Solidarities of tribe, race, gender, and nation remain but engage plural rather than fragmented subjectivities.

[B]eing Indian at this time is political. (Coke 89)

Through its insistent dichotomizing of white and Native, I have argued, the text of *Ravensong* constructs me emphatically as white, and it constructs white ultimately as deficient. The otherness, the alienness of white culture, which helps reconsolidate the villagers as a people in a new, more self-conscious fashion (and in response to the very threat it poses to that community), shuts me out. 'As a white reader ...' Anne Campbell, one of my students in a joint graduate–undergraduate Canadian Native literatures class, writes in her reading journal, 'you can't help but be able to understand (sometimes – sometimes definitely NOT) what the whites are thinking or going through at a particular instance.' Being *unable* not to understand what the whites are thinking creates a split positioning. It separates me from the protagonist and other Native characters, who at times emphatically do not understand what the whites are thinking, at the same time as narrative perspective positions me with the protagonist and her culture. But just as the village, constructed in opposition to the town, to whiteness, itself contains a white person, so *Ravensong* offers several possible interpellations (none entirely comfortable) of the white reader into the text, through white characters who cross the bridge into the village.[18]

There is Carol, who visits the village only once and then in a moment of personal need, observing the differences with silent curiosity before returning to her own world. There is Steve, who, as the best kind of white liberal, visits persistently, accommodates himself to the role of listener and learner, makes himself useful to Ella, and discovers that, from his side of the river, he will be unable ever to experience Native life adequately. But it is German Judy, Rena's partner, in but not of the village, ignored for the most part, entering into aspects of village life, shut out from private moments, who most fully enacts the potential positioning of the serious outsider reader within the text, in terms both of possibilities and constraints. Judy, from her shared context with Carol, is unable to continue enjoying Stacey and Rena's laughter over Carol's culturally inappropriate and inflexible expectation of a telephone in the village. Judy's response and Stacey's dismissal (echoing her mother's) – 'She's white so she don't count' (135) – implicate white readers as well. So, too, however, does Nora's subsequent reappraisal: 'Of course they count, but not right now' (194). Repudiation is real but not absolute. 'Not right now' – for the space of the novel, at least – can be a substantial period, though, for readers accustomed always to counting.

———•———

[W]e (people of colour) are always being asked to tell our stories for *your* (white people's) edification, which you cannot *hear* because of the benefit you derive from hearing them. (Razack 48)

———•———

Here I catch myself, yet again, in an irony. My extended attention to the experience and interpellation of the white reader in the text is in direct contradiction to the conclusions such analysis produces. It ignores the agenda of *Ravensong* to foreground Native perceptions and issues. It is at odds, too, with the model provided by German Judy, largely unobtrusive, who tactfully absents herself from scenes such as Stacey's departure where she knows she does not belong. The space of the novel that I've just mentioned, the space where white experience – even the experience of white reading – is beside the point, can more helpfully be seen as a substantial period for Native readers (and, in some fashion, other readers of colour) instead. It provides a site, disproportionately rare in North American literature, where the terms of reference are set by and within a non-Anglo culture, giving precedence to that beleaguered perspective. In so doing, for many readers it replicates (or, where that has been absent, gestures towards) the lived experience of the normativeness of non-Anglo positioning. It places the burden of explanation or self-justification on white culture (and readers): 'Ahead

lay a land of strangeness – a crew of sharp-voiced people almost unintelligible to the people behind them.' More importantly, it lifts that
burden of relentless (self-)scrutiny and difference from the insider reader:
'Behind the women stood the homes of people so familiar to them that
no questions about their lives were ever exchanged' (196). As in Maracle's
Sundogs, when white reality loses its centrality and recedes to the
periphery, so for *Ravensong*'s primary readers, the world, no longer
upside down, 'has righted itself' (*Sundogs* 139).

At the same time, insider experience and readership are emphatically
not construed as monolithic. After my conference presentation of a
version of this chapter, an Anishinaabe graduate student recounted to
me her resistance to *Ravensong*, specifically to scenes of Stacey's challenges to the school principal. Such confrontations with figures of authority she found discordant with her own traditions of respect. Other
readers of colour, too, invited to enjoy a textual interlude where hegemonic assumptions are displaced, may none the less find that the
specifics of Salish culture locate them in some ways outside the narrative.[19] The text, itself a critique of a white culture that 'lack[s] the will to
labour to see from more than one angle,' that has 'no other story but its
own' (65, 187), accommodates such readers, I would argue. Madeline,
tribal outsider integrated into the village, models such a positioning.
So, too, though, does Nora, a tribal member, but one whose two-
spiritedness has lost its place in the village's story. An explicitly liminal
figure, Nora cannot be contained by either of two apparently comprehensive alternatives: in the course of game warden raids, '[n]o one
knew what Nora did during those moments when she was suspended
between being caught and remaining undiscovered' (22). Psychologically and socially indeterminate (like the legendary warrior woman,
'[n]ameless ... for want of definition' [97]), Nora is marginalized further
by death before the book's opening. Yet the text, the community, and
Stacey's psyche continue to resonate with her intractable presence. As
Ravensong insists on making room for Nora (even when her difference
precludes full acceptance by her community), so it embraces the variety
of readers for whom whiteness does not speak. Whether like Jim, who
experiences in the village a perfect consonance between personal and
cultural expectations, or like Stacey, whose questioning nature produces a less comfortable fit, such readers are offered in the text respite
from a dual consciousness that must accord pre-eminence to the logic
of white culture.

Many of us don't consider ourselves Canadian citizens. I'm one of them.
(Maracle, 'Native')

[T]he modern nation, either as a state or as a body of people aspiring to form
such a state, differs in size, scale and nature from the actual communities with
which human beings have identified over most of history ... the question still
remains why, having lost real communities, people should wish to imagine this
particular type of replacement. (Hobsbawm 46)

Just when the city of St Paul added boxboard to its list of recycled
materials, and Northwest Airlines began non-stop flights from Minneapolis to Montreal and Vancouver and four other Canadian cities, and
the missing groundhog returned to her burrow in our St Paul backyard,
I gave up a satisfying position at the University of Minnesota because I
wanted to be home, in Canada, to re-place myself within the Canadian
cultural matrix. From the beginning of my five-year tenure in the United
States, it was clear to me that I was not in Canada, from the tellers
casually doing their nails in the august institution of the Bank, to the
campus proselytizer ('hellfire' on one side of his sandwich board, 'dam-
nation' on the other) declaiming, 'Do not be deceived. Liberalism is a
plague.' From the beginning I constructed my position there as 'critic
(of the U.S.) in exile.'[20]
   My own Canadian nationalism is in many ways simple anti-Ameri-
canism, including necessarily a distaste for nationalism as exemplified
so dangerously for the rest of the world by the United States. In Minneapolis, a Hungarian student and I were shaking our heads together
over the number and size of flags in the United States. I told her that all
the Canadian flags I own were given to me by U.S.-Americans. That
wasn't quite accurate. I do have a teasing, going-away gift from a
Canadian friend: salt and pepper shakers of a U.S. and a Canadian flag
in the form of a single heart, interlocking along a jagged break through
the centre.
   So I returned to Canada. Or I would have if there were an airport at
'Canada.' More accurately, I moved to Guelph, Ontario. Guelph was, in
my case, the concrete manifestation of the abstraction 'Canada.' My
anxious concern was whether the particularities of life in Guelph could
carry the burden of gratification generated by my desire for Canada. I
worried, too, about whether I was giving up a productive (if/because

uneasy) site of contestation in pursuit of an unproblematized sense of belonging.

I know that 'Canada' is an invention, that, to adapt Tim Rowse adapting Raymond Williams, there 'are in fact no [Canadians]. There are only ways of seeing people as [Canadians]' (Rowse 257). I know that 'Canada' is constructed these days in large part against the United States (Q: 'What is the difference between a Canadian and an American?' A: 'The Canadian knows the difference'). I know, increasingly, as I teach literature by Native writers and other writers of colour, that the Canada I connect with (Q: 'How many Canadians does it take to screw in a light bulb?' A: 'Oh, that's okay, really; I can see just fine') has almost nothing in common with the Canada many people of colour experience. I know that my attack on U.S.-American cultural, economic, diplomatic, and military imperialism (like Canadian superiority to U.S. racism) makes it all too easy to overlook the colonizing and racism perpetrated abroad and domestically in the name of Canada.

Still, I was coming home.

————·•·————

Academic theories
are but the leaky summations
of human stories   (Maracle, '*Ka-Nata*,' *Bent* 107)

————·•·————

With each of Maracle's novels, *Sundogs* and *Ravensong*, I was nonplussed to find myself unsure, days after reading the book, of whether or not I had finished it. The epilogue to *Ravensong*, set twenty-five years later, seems to derail the narrative. It announces abruptly and then leaves unexamined the thwarting of Stacey's dream to teach the village children and is silent on the status of Raven's scheme to enlist Native people in the transformation of the non-Native world. (My students also found the ending of *Ravensong* curtailed and incomplete. In particular, they had anticipated seeing Celia's role as keeper of the people's earlier history developed more fully.) In part, though, that inconclusive quality results from a genre error in my reading. I was familiar with but mainly puzzled by Maracle's goal, spelled out in the preface to *Sojourner's Truth*, to combine Native oratory with European story. In her monograph *Oratory*, she clarifies what she means by oratory, not so much the general art of rhetorically elevated address, as I tend to think of it, but 'theory presented through story' (Maracle, *Oratory* 14).[21] It was when I was rereading *Ravensong* for theory, in light of the questions about collective identity that I raise here, that I began to appreciate the textual integrity and fullness of the work (I now hesitate to use the misleading word 'novel') – and to get a sense for what Maracle means by oratory. Reading *Ravensong* as story in the service of theory removes certain narrative burdens from characters and plot, enlisting them in a more reflective enterprise. Radical inconclusiveness, a narrative about-face, even, that seems to nullify what has gone before, fits Maracle's description: 'Most of our stories don't have orthodox "conclusions"; that is left to the listeners, who we trust will draw useful lessons from the story – not necessarily the lessons we wish them to draw, but all conclusions are considered valid ... Our stories merely pose the dilemma' (Maracle, *Sojourner's* 11–12). In the final line of *Ravensong*, Stacey's son, Jacob, is reassured about his failure to understand an explanation of his mother's (in a line that echoes earlier passages in the book [16, 49] and other writing by Maracle): 'You'll know the answer when you need to' (199). At the end of *Ravensong*, I don't know the answers about communal connections, othering and belonging, unstable categories, and multiple allegiances. But that is, in part, because theory through story does convey, with a complexity that theoretical cerebration cannot, the layered experience simultaneously of absolute membership in an imagined community and of other affiliations transecting that identity.

7

'How Should I Eat These?'
Eden Robinson's *Traplines*

I didn't want to start with native stories. Once you've been put in the box of being a native writer then it's hard to get out.

(Eden Robinson, quoted in Penner 8)

I am a full-blood contemporary artist, of the sub-group (or clan) called sculptors ... I am not a Native 'American,' nor do I feel that 'America' has any right to either name me or un-name me. I have previously stated that I should be considered a mixed-blood: that is I claim to be a male but in fact only one of my parents was male.

(Jimmy Durham, quoted in Churchill 107)[1]

Traplines, a collection of three short stories and a novella by British Columbia Haisla-Heiltsuk writer Eden Robinson, appeared in 1996 with some fanfare, including advertisements touting her as the 'J.D. Salinger for the millennium' and a *New York Times* review dubbing her a 'Generation X laureate' (Marcus 21). [2] In contrast with virtually all the fiction published by Native writers in Canada, most of *Traplines* does not overtly feature Native characters or focus on Native communities. A Native context can (but need not) be inferred for the first, title story, with its contrast between the world of the protagonist, Will, and his friends from the village on the one hand and that of the 'townies' on the other hand, and with Will's family's marten trapping and gillnetting. The final story, 'Queen of the North,' a belated contribution to the published collection, is the most conventionally 'Native' in its account of a young Haisla woman and her response to sexual abuse. (The story that it replaced, 'Terminal Avenue,' a futuristic narrative after the Uprisings when Native reserves have been Adjusted and Peace Officers prey on Indians, also deals explicitly, albeit in a temporally displaced fashion, with Native material.)[3] But 'Contact Sports,' for example, the novella that comprises over half of *Traplines* and that depicts protagonist Tom's entanglement with his increasingly sadistic older cousin, Jeremy, contains no obvious markers of Indianness.[4] By default, within the current reading culture that produces white as the unmarked location, the characters may well be read as white.[5]

Moreover, Robinson resists the label of 'Native writer' for herself and of 'Native stories' for her fiction (Penner 8). (In addition, her fiction moves away from immediate personal sources by focusing more often than not on young male rather than female protagonists and on the primarily male worlds of those characters.) What characterizes the stories of *Traplines* more than any Native subject matter is their focus on the anxieties and adjustments of adolescence (hence the Salinger analogy), and their chilling and matter-of-fact explorations of violence. When I commented to Robinson that some reviewers of her stories assumed that her characters were Native and other reviewers that they were non-Native, she replied, 'I just assumed they were really young and really poor' (conversation, 10 September 2000).

In reading *Traplines*, I find myself wanting to read the text through the lens of Robinson's background, to ask how the author's racial/ cultural biography engages intertextually with the stories. How does the Indianness of *Traplines* signify? Or does it signify? (This is not the same as asking that gatekeeping question of whether the text qualifies as a Native text. Written by a person who identifies, has reason to identify, and receives community recognition as Native, it functions automatically as a Native text, I would argue, even if it were to function thus primarily by contesting the constricted territory assigned to Native texts.) But, particularly given the history of what has manifested itself as Native fiction in Canada to date, the conjunction of Robinson's Native background and her text's apparently non-Native emphasis provokes reflection.

'Oh, it's simple. All I want you to do is be good.'

Tom stared at him suspiciously. 'When you say "good," what do you mean?'

'... You listen to me when I tell you what to do.' (E. Robinson, *Traplines* 98)

A little freedom lost. A little financial security gained ... How bad could it be? (E. Robinson, *Traplines* 98–9)

Certainly, the violence and desperation of Robinson's characters and stories echo the history of First Nations–European contact in Canada. 'Contact Sports' (with the potential word play of its title), in particular, lends itself to a figurative reading: the protagonist's family agrees to receive cousin Jeremy into its home and then is subjected to Jeremy's increasingly dangerous violence, so that the protagonist, Tom, finds himself resorting to desperate strategies. The narrative systematically replicates facets of early and continuing settler–Native interaction.[6] In terms of specifically Haisla experience, Gordon Robinson, Eden Robinson's uncle, in his *Tales of Kitimaat*, dates the missionary influence in Kitimaat at 1876, noting that the shamans and secret society members accurately identified – and resisted – the new way of life as 'a threat to the social order' (41). Eden Robinson has indicated that the residential-school experience is still manifesting its devastation through family dysfunction within her village. In such a context, historically freighted phrases in 'Contact Sports' – 'you got no right to tell me what to do' (95), 'I can take care of myself' (95), '"I'm trying to help." "We don't need your help"' (95) – acquire ironic, allegorical force.

Reviewers always comment on the 'anger' in my work, for example (anger having been categorised as a particularly 'Black' emotion), and on its portrayal of 'the Black experience.' White work, on the other hand, is never questioned for its portrayal of 'the white experience.' (Brand, *Bread* 159)

I am aware that my indigenousness never leaves the minds of white folks. I am a Native writer, never just a writer ... (Maracle, *Sojourner's* 60)

Colonial paradigms, it could be argued, structure the narrative in 'Contact Sports.' Tom's mother, Christa, welcomes Jeremy – whose murky past includes dishonourable, apparently murderous activity, in a military context – as a guest and relation into her home.[7] Tom, though reluctant, is initially willing to receive his cousin on an equal footing, sharing a bedroom that, especially in the context of Jeremy's prosperity, feels none too large. Jeremy, like the European newcomers, brings with him the novelty of world travel (as an army brat), unfamiliar foods (sushi), and refinements in transportation (his Jaguar XJS convertible), as well as material benefactions (the gift of an entertainment centre that is rejected when his unsavoury behaviour is revealed, but whose reappearance marks the power of its influence). Although Tom is at first uncertain how to read Jeremy's display of affluence (for whom is the fridgeful of food intended?), and their communication about it is marked by awkwardness and discomfiture, he reaches the conclusion that 'Jeremy had been trying to be nice' (88). Almost from the moment of Jeremy's arrival, though, his presence, as with the Europeans, disrupts the existing patterns of interaction and affiliation: 'Things had already shifted so that it was Jeremy and his mom on one side and him on the other' (81). Significantly, the realignment manifests itself over Tom's attempt to signal his economic independence when Jeremy offers to treat them to dinner.

The parallels play themselves out in the historically weighted areas of education, economics, mobility, and norms of appearance. Jeremy assumes supervision of Tom's education: ' "It's late," Jeremy said. He was standing in front of the door with his arms crossed. "And it's a school night"' (95). He then proceeds to interfere with Tom's studies (literally pulling the chair out from under Tom while he is reading and interrupting or prescribing homework at Jeremy's pleasure), as though Tom hasn't been demonstrating notable maturity and responsibility for his own learning already.

Jeremy offers Tom a way out of his newly straitened circumstances, although, in a departure from the model of European incursion, Tom's loss of his previous means of support merely coincides with, rather than resulting from, Jeremy's arrival.[8] Caught between desire (for a school trip) and self-respect, alerted by Jeremy's incipient superciliousness over the likelihood of being paid back, Tom seeks a reciprocal arrangement, proposing to wash Jeremy's car in exchange for his cousin's financial contribution. During the car washing, however, Jeremy proceeds to vitiate the mutuality of that agreement, through high-handedness, bullying, and threats. Later, significantly, he defaults on his part of the agreement. As in many narratives of colonization, though, that delinquency occurs parenthetically and at a point where the aggrieved party is in a position barely even to take note of it, other forms of control having superseded the initial inducement.

Violating Tom's privacy, identifying his area of vulnerability (his overdue bills), and taking a proprietary interest in his personal affairs, Jeremy subsequently proposes a 'deal,' one that Tom envisions as temporary. Although Jeremy's use of the phrase is itself parodic, his 'let's make a deal' allows Robinson to conflate the sleaze and shamelessness of game shows (another 'sport') with other forms of economic manipulation and treaty making (98). In exchange for material assistance (discharge of debts, contributions towards food and rent), Jeremy asks for 'one itty bitty little thing,' that Tom be 'good.' Tom must seek permission for his comings and goings and overnight absences (as with nineteenth-century travel-permit regulations on western-Canadian reserves),[9] cede control of his life, and submit to Jeremy's authority: 'You listen to me when I tell you what to do' (98). (Less obtrusive or humiliating means of compensating for temporary exigency, from within Tom's own circle, predate Jeremy's advent, incidentally – in Tom's friend Mike's tactful provision of surplus lunch supplies – just as the communal responsibility of Native life predated European interventions.) In a historical context, the irony of Tom's musings about the deal with Jeremy – 'How bad could it be?' – is palpable (99).

The subsequent cutting of Tom's long hair to meet Jeremy's specifications (achieved through the circumspect application of force) is, for me at least, the single most obvious signal, in 'Contact Sports,' of a correspondence with the historical record, with the culturally calculated cutting of Native children's hair. From their positions of power and expertise, respectively, Jeremy and the hairdresser are able to decide, to Tom's consternation, how he should look. As with the introduction of European goods and culture, the accompanying radical transformation of Tom's dress to conform to Jeremy's standards is initiated with a gift – though a gift on the giver's terms ('Rules of the game. One. You pick a jacket. Two. I approve of the jacket. Three ...' [105]). The civilizing mission quickly proceeds, however, to more coercive measures. Jeremy confiscates Tom's clothing, returning some later at his discretion (actions reminiscent of the censorious – but profitable – seizure of Native ceremonial dress and artifacts, and the arbitrariness and inconsistency of modern demands – simultaneously – for Native assimilation *and* authenticity).[10] Jeremy's declaration that Tom can earn back his clothes and Tom's response – '"Earn them?" He stood up. "Those are my clothes! I bought them!"' (126) – echo and challenge government approaches to self-determination or sovereignty not as inherent but as a favour to be conferred, and conferred according to someone else's conditions.

As with Native cultures, Tom must pay both financially and socially for changes that he has actively resisted; his insistence that he cannot afford the purchases has metaphoric, but also allegorical, force. His outward transformation produces division and animosity, and new alignments, within the social group – peers gape or snicker, Mike accuses him of having sold out, Paulina Mazenkowski smiles apprecia-

tively. The change entails self-alienation as well. With Jeremy's introduction of new forms of intoxication – cocaine standing in for the
recreational alcohol promoted by European traders – Robinson traces a
depleted capacity for self-fashioning and resistance to interference.
Tom realizes retrospectively on one occasion, as he experiences the
social consequences, that he has allowed Jeremy to dress him. Stoned
and hungover, he has neither noticed nor cared how he has been
decked out.

Jeremy's gratuitous requirement of meaningless speech or ritualized
observances, specifically his requirement that Tom repeat accurately the nonsense word 'supercalifragilisticexpialidocious' at Jeremy's
whim, replicates familiar forms of colonial control and colonized self-
alienation around issues of language or even religious practice. Even in
the absence of overtly derisive comments, Jeremy's more subtle undermining of Tom's self-esteem, his muffled laughter when eliciting confidences, his implicit and assumed superiority, the paternalism that makes
Tom feel six years old, all figure forth the dismissal of minoritized
culture and history that accompanies more dramatic acts of domination
and cruelty.

As potential allegory, 'Contact Sports' does not limit its implication,
though, to some safely distant historical period. Particularly in Jeremy's
conciliatory overtures to Tom, the story embodies the self-deceptive
disingenuousness of contemporary white expedients for liberal guilt.
Early in the story, when Tom proves obdurate after the extorted car
washing, Jeremy appears to embark upon an apology: 'does Tommy
forgive Jeremy for everything? Hmmm?' (101).[11] Dismissively conde-
scending and simultaneously coercive, the 'request' for forgiveness
takes place in the context of physical duress. And, in its supple shift to
accusation and aggrieved demands for apology over Tom's resistance –
'Tommy's not going to sulk anymore, is he?' and 'If you are really,
sincerely sorry for being a pain in the butt, I think you'll want to prove
it, won't you, Tommy?' (101, 102) – by an insidious sleight of hand, it
inverts transgressor and complainant. (Compare the resentful charge:
'Your anger about racism makes me feel guilty.') The passage presages
a later, more substantive and telling attempt at apology. Again under
circumstances of physical intimidation, a stoned, maudlin Jeremy demands forgiveness for having caused Tom's epilepsy by dropping him
on his head as a baby. Curiously beside the point – Tom counters that
his epilepsy predates Jeremy's baby sitting, but in any case that historical moment is past – Jeremy's apology manages ironically to ignore the

chronic coercion and violence in Tom's present that Jeremy has no intention of ending. As with token white compunction for the theft of Native land, Jeremy, in a moment he need not take seriously later, apologizes for a long-ago wrong (and one for which he may not be directly responsible) while continuing to inflict harm in the present.

The denouement of 'Contact Sports' provides a haunted conclusion to the narrative of colonization, past and present, as the sport of contact grows more violent. Various stances of the colonized – attempted reciprocity, temporary endurance, repudiations of consent, coerced cooperation – having proved unavailing, Tom's resistance becomes more vigorous. An appeal to the social contract, to external arbiters – revealing the suitcase of cocaine to Tom's mother (like Native recourse to the courts in cases of blatant illegality) – achieves only temporary results. The interloper is dislodged (the keys to the apartment retrieved), and, when that proves insufficient, physically barred, but the injunction and the barricade (or in this case, deadbolt) are circumvented. Jeremy appeals to a higher level and brings his mother, Tom's aunt, into the negotiations. Tom is impelled to replace futile, impulsive acts of defiance (a rock thrown at Jeremy's windshield, which only results in Jeremy's use of the car itself against Tom) with more calculated and risky depredation (the arranged theft of Jeremy's prized Jaguar).

Resistance, the narrative suggests bleakly, seems only to entail an escalation and entrenchment of the violence. Jeremy moves from random, equivocal, and primarily psychological cruelties to forcible confinement and overt sadism, taking Tom prisoner (with the complicity of one of his own group, Paulina), holding him in bondage, and torturing him with cigarette burns to the point of unconsciousness. (Jeremy's ultimate identity as sadist – hitherto ambiguous – is affirmed, in the end, too, by his viciousness towards Paulina.) As an anatomy of the politics and psychology of colonization, the text portrays both colonizer and colonized in downward spirals of abuse and impotence. Any acceptable resolution seems to lie in the realm of fantasy: 'He wanted to have never met Jeremy' (179). (This echoes, at the figurative level, Ella's challenge to wishful thinking in Lee Maracle's *Ravensong*: 'while you're wishing, why don't you wish these people never came to mess up our lives?' [105].) Precluded from an individual solution, from flight, because his vulnerability and responsibility extend beyond himself – '"You can leave," Jeremy said. "But your mom's not going anywhere"' (182) – Tom finds himself condemned to a home that has been permanently invaded by his (now proven) enemy. The despair in the story's poignantly ironic penultimate line, 'They were going home' (182),[12] evokes Chinese-Canadian May Yee's reflection, 'I feel this country is nobody's real home, except the First Nations people, who have had so much taken from them I wonder that they must not also feel profoundly homesick' (21).

Read as a pun, the novella's title, 'Contact Sports,' refigures the European–Native encounter, casting it as simultaneously capricious frolic and sanctioned violence, entertaining diversion and physical collision, mere amusement and contest of win and lose. (Frolic, diversion, amusement, that is, from the perspective of the colonizer: it is Jeremy in the story who initiates the power games, sets the terms of play, and organizes matches to his own advantage.) 'Sports' in the title tends to emphasize a sardonic sense of colonization's gratuitous side, with 'contact' weighting the metaphor more heavily towards the brutal, although each of the words paradoxically carries both benign and ominous implications. 'Contact' is associated with both communication and contagion, for example, 'sports' with both the ludic and the combative.

Even simply as a category of athletics, without reference to colonial history, the term 'contact sports' contains curious ironies and ambivalences that Robinson's use here exploits. 'Contact,' often designating minimal forms of touching or meeting, shifts ironically, in conjunction with 'sports,' to designate the most intense and punishing forms of physical interaction.[13] Concurrently, 'sports,' in this combination, shifts to denote precisely those games marked least by either 'sporting' or playful behaviour. Brought into conjunction with each other, two innocuous words, with primarily neutral or positive connotations, produce a potent charge, reorienting each towards the most extreme and violent of its meanings.

The marked transformation that the ostensibly bland word 'contact' effects upon the noun phrase of the title represents in small the concussive impact that an ostensibly neutral 'contact' between nations has produced historically in North America. 'Contact' is revealed to be the euphemism it is, in relation both to athletics and to the European invasion of the Americas. After 'contact sports,' 'contact history' as a designation takes on a new and grimmer resonance: what less restrictive rules, more vigorous activities – for participants or historians – are mandated within this category?

In the context of the European invasion and its five-hundred-year aftermath, 'sports' obviously carries most of the title's ironic power because of the metaphor's mordant inappropriateness. Even before one begins to explore the specific applicability of notions of fun, of play (and fair play), of rules, of contained and equable competition, the term stands out as belonging to the wrong register – or at least an unlikely register – for rendering historical events of this gravity and complexity. In addition, the word introduces other quite various denotations – from dandy to genetic mutant ('sport of nature'); from good loser ('what a sport!') to misfit ('what a sport!'); from gambler to plaything ('sport of the gods'). These denotations – which shift substantially from deliberate self-fashioner to haphazard product, in the first instance; from exemplar to outcast, in the second; and from agent of chance to object of chance, in the third – proliferate possibilities for the title. Entailing this range of significations, the story title 'Contact Sports' can be applied to persons rather than to activities, to the players in the drama rather than to the drama itself, to the 'Sports of Contact.' Configured thus, the title produces a detached and irreverent or derisive reading of North American colonization as more freakish than inevitable, its products more ludic/rous than ominous or tragic.

Despite all the story's satiric potential when read allegorically, the title 'Contact Sports' signals a range of possible meanings and connotations, reflecting all the ambiguities of the narrative itself. For one of the most unnerving and original features of Tom's contact with Jeremy (and one of the greatest strengths of the story) is the equivocal nature, until late in the narrative, of the relationship. This, along with its humour and freshness of contemporary detail, is what takes the novella, read figuratively, beyond a predictable excoriation of the inexorable depredations of colonization, although it certainly exposes those power politics. During much of the narrative, I found myself, as a reader, like Tom, unsure how to gauge Jeremy's behaviour, wary of overreaction, disconcerted and forced into reassessment by moments of reprieve and camaraderie, caught out in anticipating worse from Jeremy than his next actions always warranted. Jeremy's flip, parodic manner, his glib, endless quoting – '*Heal* this bliiind soul, that he may finally seeee the light' (116) – make intensity and confrontation seem naïve, uptight, even paranoid. With his infantilizing baby talk, his supercilious raillery, his ironic pseudo-seriousness – 'Does Tommy want to go for a ride?' 'Hah! It speaks again!' '"No hump," he said, looking at Tom's back. "Decent teeth"'; '"Thought we needed to talk." "About what?" ... "Oh, I don't know. The plight of the Amazon rain forest ... Maybe some golf tips"'

(101, 100, 84, 149) – Jeremy makes sport both of his cousin and of attempted resistance.

Until the final scenes, I was hesitant to make – indeed precluded, by the ambiguities of the behaviour, from making – a final judgment about Jeremy. Explicating the realist level of the narrative, my students found themselves having recourse to notions of fraternal or homoerotic or homosocial underpinnings to account for the complexity of Jeremy's involvement. Eden Robinson, in an interview with CBC's Shelagh Rogers, speaks of the story finally taking shape when she perceived Jeremy as a person rather than a caricature, when she saw him, on the brink of truly evil deeds (and Robinson does use the term 'evil'), fighting against something, without his even being conscious of the struggle. At the same time, Robinson has indicated that what fascinates her about violence and abuse is the point of view not of the abuser but of those nearby, not the Unibomber but the Unibomber's brother. What fascinates her are the dynamics of coming to realize, slowly or quickly, through nuances or abrupt revelation, that one's brother is a fearsome being (Rogers interview). Part of what makes Jeremy so disquieting is his convincing performance of cool, intelligent attractiveness, his disconcerting capacity to meld the brutal with the unexceptionable, the ordinary, and the witty. This is a character who uses the '*meep, meep*' of coyote-roadrunner cartoons to police Tom or complains of a 'nic-fit' while holding Tom captive (103, 180). 'Between you and me, I think that girl has a few problems. You might want to ask someone else to the prom,' he advises Tom, with incongruous avuncular concern, after having kicked Paulina in the head and encouraged her in criminal, possibly lethal, sadism (181). Tom's response, plausibly enough, is often confused and inconsistent, including appreciation for Jeremy's snoring companionship and a pained apprehension that 'The only person who really gives a shit if I live or die is a whacked-out drug addict who likes playing God' (144). Robinson's success is to create, in Jeremy, a monster who is, for most of the story, not a monster and, so, much harder to decipher or circumvent.

Nor does Robinson idealize the 'pre-contact' period. The story opens with Tom already fantasizing about an alternative home, Mike's, as preferable to his own. We learn parenthetically that he has, in the past, been removed from his mother and placed in foster care. He must exercise vigilance to protect her from disappointments provoking sudden drunken absences. His mother hearkens back to an earlier period of harmony in her family of origin (the childhood of the Nation, perhaps, allegorically speaking), coded with signifiers of 'natural' Indian existence – 'She was describing horses she had ridden, berries she had picked' (113).[14] Her memories, however, are explicitly framed as self-delusions, complete with revelatory, romantic capitalization. As the story unfolds, 'Uncle' Richard, Tom's mother's current lover, proves just as capable of physical viciousness as Jeremy. No simple contrast of Edenic and post-Edenic periods is possible. Reading 'Contact Sports' allegorically, then, foregrounds not simply the damaging coercion but, more disturbingly, the confounding ambiguities and profound ambivalences of colonial interactions in process.

Aunt Genna told me other things. She told me there were monsters and bogeymen in the world, but all you had to do was be a good girl and they wouldn't get you. I always believed Aunt Genna until Mama killed her. (E. Robinson, *Traplines* 44)

Although the most sustained in its historical parallels, 'Contact Sports' is not the only story in *Traplines* lending itself to an allegorical reading. 'Dogs in Winter,' the story of adolescent narrator Lisa Rutford, whose mother has killed at least eight people including Lisa's father and later the aunt who cares for Lisa during her mother's first imprisonment, also carries postcolonial weight. Lisa is haunted, intermittently suicidal, and the story documents the permanent, damaging impact of her mother's destructiveness even in Mama's absence. Directly and indirectly, Lisa witnesses her mother's violence – the knifing of a dog, the ritual sacrifice of a moose, the stench of the defrosting freezer full of body parts, the splatters of Aunt Genna's blood on her mother's shoes. So she must confront the irruption, in even more extreme form than must Tom, of apparently gratuitous or irrational violence into everyday life. The intimacy of the family connection, closer yet than in 'Contact Sports,' similarly evokes the impossibly embrangled and confounding conditions of Fourth World existence, where the menace resides within one's own home. The intimacy reflects ironically, too, on the trope of the 'great white mother,' the colonizer figured in maternal terms.[15] In Robinson's hands, the family romance, whether at a literal level or as a figure for the postcolonial nation, becomes a blood-splattered narrative.

Certainly, 'Dogs in Winter' cannot be read for the systematic allegorical correspondences of 'Contact Sports.' But the profound and chronic insecurity of Lisa's existence, her debilitating sense of impending peril (made explicit in Robinson's working title 'Seven and Counting' and substantiated by Mama's continued, ominous interest in Lisa) together with manifestations of past trauma, replicates the colonial condition. The story's final reference to Mama, heading out after her initial killing spree, 'smiling and happy and lethal,' provides a powerfully sardonic and original image of the insouciant deadliness of the colonizer (70). In the black humour of Lisa's bleak conclusion – 'Everything would be perfect, I thought, if only Canada had the death penalty,'[16] – 'Dogs in Winter' captures the intensity of the problem, the paradoxical contra/dictions of its imagined eradication (57). Read as a postcolonial text, the story – bloody acts and homicidal mother as background to a 'normal life' of camping trips, lab projects, and McDonald Happy Meals – proffers an almost surreal or expressionistic take on Native history.

[I]f the motivating force for history here is ... the unitary 'experience' of national oppression (if one is merely the *object* of history, the Hegelian slave) then what else *can* one narrate but that national oppression? Politically, we are Calibans, all. (Ahmad 9)

[The literary-critical industry] at the moment seems to find these two central terms – 'post-colonial' and 'resistance' – positively shimmering as objects of desire and self-privilege ... (Slemon 31)

Ah, here's the rub, the difficulty with my entire preceding analysis of Robinson's fiction. Aijaz Ahmad has challenged Fredric Jameson's definition of the 'Third World' exclusively in terms of its experience of colonialism and imperialism, and Jameson's reading of Third World texts as necessarily national allegories. '[O]ne may indeed connect one's personal experience to a "collectivity,"' suggests Ahmad, ' – in terms of class, gender, caste, religious community, trade union, political party, village, prison – combining the private and the public, and in some sense "allegorizing" the individual experience, without involving the category of "the nation" or necessarily referring back to the "experience of colonialism and imperialism"' (15). Must all Native writing be reduced to a singular narrative of colonization and resistance? While postcolonial analysts have long rejected essentialist notions of Native authenticity, we have hovered avidly around textual manifestations of postcolonial resistance. Or we have conjured up those manifestations.

Does my allegorical reading do violence to Robinson's texts, constraining them within a biographical/cultural matrix from which they might seem to have removed themselves? Why focus on the Native implications of *Traplines*? I could equally well, for instance, read 'Contact Sports' as a socialist allegory rather than a postcolonial one. Jeremy's progressive capacity to appropriate Tom's labour, control his time, and constrain his options models the relations of capital and labour, as does his use of (unearned) capital to corrupt the relationships he touches. His simultaneous arguments for Tom's opportunity to improve and Tom's personal responsibility for failure echo capitalist ideology. The struggle between the cousins invites class analysis. When Tom considers in the mirror the new image that Jeremy has imposed upon him, 'The person who looked back at him belonged to a debating club, got his assignments done on time, and never, ever worried about money' (109). Like the capitalist enterprise, Jeremy is offering not unencumbered affluence, but its illusion, the consumerist treadmill; Tom can pay him back, a little at a time, for goods he had no initial interest in acquiring. Tom's flailings against subjection – 'Jeremy could take his money and shove it' (99) – and the illegal but unchecked violence punishing his own wildcat action (assailing Jeremy's property) culminate in a final state of proletariat abjection, with Tom economically and psychically in thrall to his prosperous cousin. The reality out of which Robinson writes, in other words, is not simply – nor, by some lights, primarily – a Native one.

My students were quick, too, to produce gendered readings of 'Contact Sports.'[17] In particular, they pointed out the parallels between Jeremy's control of Tom and domestic abuse in patriarchal culture. As the product of a woman writer, 'Contact Sports,' they suggested, offered a displaced rendering of a familiar abusive scenario, from Jeremy's coercive grip above the elbow to his surveillance, his isolating, and his interference with Tom's contacts.[18] Specifically, they called attention to the markedly patriarchal overtones of Jeremy's contract with Tom: 'I'll help with rent and food, and all you have to do is one itty bitty little thing ... No staying overnight anywhere without phoning ... You ask me if you can go to parties. You listen to me when I tell you what to do' (98). After coerced hours of scrubbing not only Jeremy's car but also the apartment floors, Tom angrily defines himself as 'Jeremy's fucking maid' (99). So the narrative allows for a displaced exploration of the psychology of conjugal subjection and violence, through Tom's emotional ambivalence, economic dependence, fond memories, uncertainty about the borderline between playfulness and meanness, fear of attracting attention, and inability to speak out even when endangered. Reframed outside their usual context, the unsettling effects of domestic abuse can be investigated, uncoupled from rote responses.

And apart from various emblematic readings, *Traplines* is clearly an account of a contemporary youth culture of anger, vulnerability, and disconnection, family insufficiency and volatile peer relations, North American consumerism and grunge sensibilities. Through characters such as Adelaine in 'Queen of the North,' who engages in vicious brawls with other girls while confronting her own childhood sexual abuse, Robinson unflinchingly explores the disconcerting complexities of this world – a world whose Native context is only one of its features.

All of the Indians must have tragic features: tragic noses, eyes, and arms. Their hands and fingers must be tragic when they reach for tragic food. (Alexie, 'How to Write the Great American Indian Novel,' *Summer* 94)

There are times when I feel that if I don't have a circle or the number four or legend in my poetry, I am lost, just a fading urban Indian caught in all the trappings of Doc Martens, cappuccinos and foreign films but there it is again orbiting, lunar, hoops encompassing your thoughts and canonizing mine, there it is again, circle the wagons ... (Dumont, 'Circle the Wagons,' *Really* 57)

Earlier I wrote that, as with token white compunction for the theft of Native land, Jeremy in 'Contact Sports' apologizes for a long-ago wrong while continuing to inflict harm in the present. I have to ask now whether this chapter engages in the same process. While deploring the historical colonialism I read figuratively into Robinson's stories, does my allegorical reading, by deploying fixed and static signs of Indianness, participate in present-day neocolonial 'strategies of containment' (Bhabha, *Location* 31)? Do I reinscribe the 'invented Indian,' the 'dead voices,' the 'terminal creeds,' the 'tribal simulations' that Gerald Vizenor inveighs against in what he calls the surveillance and simulations of dominance (*Manifest* 5, *passim*; *Dead* 7; *Bearheart* 195, 197)? Vizenor, postmodern herald of cross-blood tricksters and 'postindian warriors,' and one of the foremost Native critics of essentialist Native identities, proposes 'postindian simulations of tribal survivance' and 'shadow stories' in place of the representational straitjackets he deplores (*Manifest* 4, 66, 178). He seems to be seeking less predictable imaginings, alternatives to both the old negative stereotypes and the well-meaning replacements.

Accompanying this ethnographic present tense is a generalizing of individual utterances so that they illustrate an argument, or fulfill a pattern, rather than function in the context of any dialogue. (D. Murray 141)

I am not trying to 'show cultural differences' in my writing; I am not even trying to portray a 'racial group.' What you read into the text so far as that is concerned depends on your stance, your location ... The white reader may perceive cultural difference, but I am merely writing myself. (Brand, 'Interview' 276)

Some years ago, my friend Carol, a Cherokee scholar in American studies, and I were discussing the raising of our daughters, then about six and five years old. In particular, we were focusing on what mattered to us, which behaviours were getting more of our attention at the moment.

'One thing I do make sure she knows,' said Carol, 'is that she needs to watch what comes out of her mouth. She just can't go around saying things, using any words at all, hurting people without thinking what she's saying; she has to pay attention to how her words are going to affect people. I don't let her get away with much on that score.'

'That's interesting,' I said. 'That seems like a particularly Native concern, your emphasis on the careful use of language.'

Well, okay, I didn't sound quite that stuffy, but that was the gist of what I said. And Carol's words did echo much of what I'd been reading, by Douglas Cardinal, by N. Scott Momaday, by Basil Johnston, by Jeannette Armstrong.

I could have invoked other identities, and ones that we shared, as explanatory. I could have invoked gender – and for all my theoretical compunction about reductive universalizing, I do in everyday conversation make suspect generalizations about 'women's' sociality and attentiveness to interpersonal nuance. Most obviously, I could have concluded that a passion about language's power, its potential for good and ill, arises predictably enough for literary scholars, knee-deep as we are in words. Or I could simply have attended more specifically to what Carol was telling me about herself and Halley and child rearing.

'That seems like a particularly Native concern,' I said.

'Mmmm,' said Carol.

A polite, noncommittal response, a strategic blankness. A rare moment of withdrawal in what is a fairly rambunctious, teasing, and sturdy friendship.

[B]oth American Indian and Native Americanist discourses continue to be preoccupied with parochial questions of identity and authenticity. Essentialist categories still reign insofar as more of the focus of scholarship has been to reduce, constrain, and contain American Indian literature and thought and to establish why something or someone is 'Indian' than engage the myriad critical issues crucial to an Indian future. (Warrior xix)

[T]he task ... is not to reduce difference to sameness nor to exoticize or fetishize it. Rather, the task is to become aware of our tendencies to do any of these things. (Sarris 92)

When I taught *Traplines* for the first time recently, I wanted to consider reading the violence of Robinson's stories as a possible allegory of the violence of Native history and experience, a history and experience that are, at most, implicit in the stories. *And* I wanted to problematize that approach. Among topics assigned before class discussion, I asked students in my second-year English course to reflect on Robinson's apparent decision as a Haisla woman to focus a considerable portion of *Traplines* on white male protagonists. I proposed that they reflect, too, on whether the collection was about 'First Nations women in literature' (the course was a 'Women in Literature' course, my selection of the text deliberately provocative, counterintuitive) and whether this was a useful question. Students didn't need much prompting to consider a Native context. Before our class discussion of 'Contact Sports' (or any of the other stories), one student asked, 'Are we supposed to read the title as a metaphor for first contact?' Several others, following the discussion, persisted in calling the story 'First Contact,' the title of its initial section. Another student, whose seminar presentation interpreted the stories cumulatively as revealing 'layers and histories of victimization and colonization' in the context of 505 years of oppression, noted that she had read the book first, early in the semester, with the dust jacket off and seen it quite differently, without Native significance. (She also identified and decried the disturbing power of stereotype in her assumption, rereading later *with* the biographical information, that Will's family in 'Traplines' must be Native because his parents are alcoholic.)[19]

The second half of my undertaking – problematizing this approach to Robinson, without simply eliding the issue of race – proved more difficult. Students who had not found an allegorical reading persuasive welcomed the opportunity to return to the literal aspects of the narrative, drawing on Robinson's wariness of being categorized as a Native writer. Many of the white students, however, took a liberal-humanist approach to the question of Robinson's subject matter – with the risk, I would argue, of what Ruth Frankenberg defines as race- and power-evasion (142–3, 156–7). They spoke the discourse of equal opportunity –'Robinson is free to write about whatever she wants'; of aestheticism – 'she's just writing for creativity's sake'; and of humanist universalism –'she's showing that everyone can be [or even 'everyone *is*'] abused, not just women, not just Native people.' One of two Black students in the class, by contrast, was the most passionate in arguing for 'thinking through race,' to use Frankenberg's term (142). She defended anticolonial figurative readings, demanding to know 'why do you want to wipe out Robinson's Native origins?' and insisting that where the voice was coming from was key to the book. And sometimes other student arguments against allegorical readings were, in fact, also 'race cognizant' (Frankenberg 157), interpreting Robinson's selection of subject matter as strategic and transformative, as a resistance to ghettoization.

Exploring possible implications of Robinson's text was complicated by the junior level of the course (for a number of the students this was their first English course), by my desire not to intervene prematurely in the largely student-directed discussion, and by the preliminary status of my own grapplings with these issues. What I think I was trying to move us towards was something like Homi Bhabha's distinction between 'diversity' (as totalizing) and 'difference' (as dynamic). 'Cultural diversity,' Bhabha argues, 'is an epistemological *object* – culture as an object of empirical knowledge – whereas cultural difference is the *process* of the enunciation of culture as "knowledgeable," authoritative, adequate to the construction of systems of cultural identification' (*Location* 34; emphasis added). Difference in this formulation could be minted anew among author, text, and reader, could be something *Traplines* performs, rather than an ethnographic given that is brought ready-made to the text by either author or reader. What we seemed to get caught up in, during class discussion, instead of Bhabha's distinction of 'diversity' and 'difference,' was the false either–or dichotomy of 'diversity' or 'sameness.' Either we appealed to the 'cultural diversity' of *Traplines*, drawing on the 'recognition of pre-given cultural contents and customs' (Bhabha, *Location* 34), or, in the interests of not categorizing, we fell back on universalism. Suspicious of the recuperative effects of reading 'Native' within the narrow discursive repertoire available, I was still taken aback by the extent to which dismissal of the text's (and author's) social location presented itself in the class as the primary, plausible alternative.

Was there – and is there – a way, without being formulaic and reductive, of none the less remaining race cognizant in reading *Traplines*? Is taking the dust jacket off Robinson's book, figuratively speaking, an adequate response to the inadequacies of preconceived racialized readings? As long as race remains anything but neutral and as long as the 'neutral' reception of racially unmarked texts can casually subsume diverse narratives and characters under a white or Western rubric, both naming and not naming the racial context of *Traplines* contain pitfalls.

———————

One of the finest things about being an Indian is that people are always interested in you and your 'plight.' ... Our foremost plight is our transparency. People can tell just by looking at us what we want, what should be done to help us, how we feel, and what a 'real' Indian is really like. Indian life, as it relates to the real world, is a continuous attempt not to disappoint people who know us. (V. Deloria 1)

The publishing world only knows how to deal with categories. If they didn't have categories, they would have to read the books. (Owens, 'American')

———————

In 1997 I attended the St Malo Book Fair in France, where the 'Festival Etonnants Voyageurs' highlighted western American writers and, in particular, Native writers. The fascination of the French there with things Indian, uncomplicated by North American white guilt and resentment or, for the most part, by a sense of implication in the history of North American colonization, was intriguing. At the book-signing tent, Native novelists were approached by a French woman wearing a four-strand bone choker and elaborately beaded, fringed buckskin; by a man with a pile of anthropological books looking for more material on Indian pictographs; and by two very young women determined to 'work for the Indians,' who had already unsuccessfully written to Ron Irwin, minister of Indian Affairs, and some of the reserves to which he had referred them. At the panel on 'Etre indien à la fin du XXe siècle,' a woman wept continuously in the back of the audience. (At a subsequent panel on American Indian literature, another woman who began with tears in her eyes soon left the room, as the Native novelists, repudiating solemnity, engaged in teasing and banter with each other.) Later, as the drumbeats began, people sprinted madly down the hall for an unexpected chance to catch the drumming and dancing of the Ute Red Spirit Singers.

And the Indians they were running to see were the Indians of legend. 'You have the eyes of a wolf. You are like an animal. Really. I cannot look you in the face,' a French female journalist told Cherokee-Choctaw novelist Louis Owens. 'Is there such a thing as *social* drinking, anything between abstinence and alcoholism?' asked a young German emigrant to France, who had visited Lakota reservations in the Dakotas, Blackfoot reserves in Alberta. ('Yes,' was the reply, 'we'll be doing some of that right after this session.') 'There are no real Indians today,' declared another member of the audience with finality at the end of the 'Being Indian' panel, after two-and-a-half hours of discussion by eight Native panelists: activists, traditionalists, singers, and novelists. (The panel host hastened to correct her English; in French what she had said, he insisted, was that the panel had not accurately represented the reality of Indian existence, the poverty, the injustice, the suffering. Her translation, though, 'There are no real Indians today,' had its own plausibility.) 'Is there anything you can do,' asked another listener, 'ever to overcome your pain?'

———•———

While contemporary Native American writers do create devastating critiques of European American society, they express wider and deeper concerns than those of social criticism. (Ruppert 7)

Shadows tease and loosen the bonds of representation in stories ... The shadows are the silence in heard stories, the silence that bears a referent of tribal memories and experience. (Vizenor, *Manifest* 72)

———•———

Of course, other mappings of the violence in Robinson's fiction exist, apart from what Marcia Crosby (Haida-Tsimshian) calls 'the ultimate colonization of "the Indian" into the spaces of the West's postmodern centre/margin cartography' (86). If a story lies behind the recurrent patterns of Robinson's imaginings, why need it be the one central to a Western imagination? In the early history of Kitimaat village, and indeed in the Haisla imagination today, the Haida loom as a powerful, aggressive (even arrogant), and warring people, whose enmity with the Haisla was officially ended little more than a hundred years ago (G. Robinson 30). Stories about the naming of Kitimaat ('people of snow') still circulate among the Haisla, stories intended to sustain Haisla pride while taking the mickey out of the Haida. The stories begin with a Haida raiding party coming upon the Haisla obscured behind shoulder-high snowbanks and, in some cases, end with the Haida fleeing and an English pun 'hide-us, hide-us.' (One of the ironies of Robinson's 1996 book promotion was the number of times journalists and others mistook Haisla for Haida.)

A variety of monsters also inhabit Haisla stories, the most prominent being the one protecting Kitimaat Arm. This monster with a huge opening and closing mouth, which had to be braved for the founding of Kitimaat village, proved to be millions of gulls rising and settling, feeding on herring roe or small fish (G. Robinson 22). In some of the Haisla dances that I attended at Kitimaat village in May of 1996, a threatening, monstrous figure advanced upon other dancers.[20] (The presiding elder admittedly identified one of these monsters, in passing, as the Indian agent – a symbolism more in keeping with my allegorical reading above.) The story of the founding of Kitimaat begins, too, with acts of violence, Waa-mis's accidental killing of his wife with a stone tossed at her head and his flight with his relatives from the people of her village, bent on putting them all to death (G. Robinson 21). Given my own minimal exposure to Haisla culture, I don't so much want to elaborate such alternative subtexts as to propose their possibility. Clearly, the psychology of struggles over power, of painful clashes, of confrontations with the fearsome and unknown and monstrous, is not restricted to the narrative of European colonization.

If this limited criticism [of Native texts] has a sociological orientation, it asks questions concerned with the way Native American society has decayed or how the work criticizes American society and its values ... Or [Western criticism] may adopt what is believed to be a Native perspective as it searches for

the key referent in traditional culture such as a specific ritual or oral narrative, which the critic sees as representing the complexity of the text. (Ruppert
16–17)

Pomo people – indeed all Indian people ... are victims of a battle that continues
to destroy what is left of them and what they might tell others, not only of their
culture but simultaneously of the others' culture. (Sarris 57)

Are there yet other ways to read Native stories of racially unspecified
characters and communities, ways that refuse to lay a scrim of Native
history onto quite different material, while at the same time recognizing that a Native author's depiction of abuse, abandonment, isolation,
and violence may have a special provenance? If Native subjectivity has
developed in circumstances of violation both external and internal to
the community, then an author such as Robinson can be read as bringing distinctive resources to explorations of mainstream power relations
and a contemporary culture of violence. Like the Unibomber's brother,
like Patricia Hill Collins's 'outsider-within' (*Black* 11), a Native writer
may have a distinctive angle of vision on dominant culture. One could
read Robinson's inclusion of stories of violation within both Native and
white communities in *Traplines* as a signal of this continuum.[21] By this I
don't mean to suggest the liberal sense of a universal human condition
or the romance of an inherent wisdom or spiritual profundity that
Native culture can offer a morally depleted Western world, but rather a
historically and materially situated sense of social and cultural co-
implication. Robinson's two 'white' (or racially indeterminate) stories,
'Dogs in Winter' and 'Contact Sports,' are buttressed by more 'Native'
stories, 'Traplines' and 'Queen of the North.' The lurid sadism and
sociopathic mayhem of the central stories are held in place by the
chronic and endemic familial dysfunction of the opening and closing
ones. One can read the structure as encoding Robinson's relationship to
her 'white' material. Perhaps, the structure may imply, the logic of the
patterns of psychic and social damage within Native communities
offers a new angle of vision, new contexts in which to understand more
apparently gratuitous outbreaks of violence elsewhere.[22]

Perhaps the question that feminist critics should ask themselves is not 'Is there
a woman in this text?' but rather: '*Is there a text in this woman?*' (Jacobus 109)

In May of 1996 the Haisla sports day opened, to the siren of a fire engine, with a bicycle parade and contest. Small children in costume, their bicycles and wagons festooned with streamers and crêpe-paper flowers, advanced on the sports field, led by the drumming of a half-dozen elders in traditional regalia. One little boy in the traditional vest and red-and-black colours of the tribe sported the sign, 'Haisla Nation.' The women of Kitimaat Village had set up tables around the perimeter of the field, with crabs and hot dogs, seaweed and herring roe, soft drinks and shish kebabs for sale. Three judges conferred and announced the winners of the contest. Third prize, shin and elbow pads, went to 'The Spirit of Kitslope' (Kitslope being a river and region in the area); second prize, a bicycle helmet, to 'The Lion King'; pride of place and a new bicycle to ... 'Pocahontas' in full Disney regalia. Multiple texts of Indianness were operating here during sports day.

'Once you've been put in the box of being a native writer then it's hard to get out,' says Robinson (Penner 8). To some extent, though, she is being marketed precisely as a Native writer, daughter of a Haisla father and a Heiltsuk (Bella Bella) mother. The publicity packet for *Traplines* prepared by her agent included a map of the Haisla territories and nineteen Haisla reserves, decorated with ovoid West Coast Native designs (hummingbird, killer whale) and drawn by her cousin Lyle Wilson. (Robinson proudly displays the original on her apartment wall.) The same designs appeared on the cover of the packet and the title page of excerpts of the novel-in-progress *Monkey Beach*. The photograph in the packet was of Robinson, back to the camera, displaying the elaborately adorned Native button blanket sewn to celebrate her Master's degree. (The success of this marketing is reflected in the six-figure, two-book package deals negotiated with publishing companies in Canada, the United States, Britain, and Germany.) On the back flap of the *Traplines* dust jacket, too, Robinson is identified as 'born in 1968 on the Haisla Nation Kitamaat reserve in British Columbia.' Not surprisingly, most reviews and promotional copy identify Robinson as Native or Haisla.[23] But what does that identity mean, and to whom?

———•—•———

As so often happens with Aboriginal works, there is an easy conflation of the text and the author. (Warley, 'National')

Nevertheless, these aspects of an individual which we designate as making him [*sic*] an author are only a projection, in more or less psychologizing terms, of the operations that we force texts to undergo, the connections that we make, the traits that we establish as pertinent, the continuities that we recognize, or the exclusions that we practice. (Foucault, 'What' 150)

Traplines complicates simplistic assumptions about authorial identity and self-expression. Already the unexpected disjunction between author and text has become a staple of interviews and profiles of Robinson, not in the terms I raise here – of race and gender – but in terms of temperament and tone. The stark, shadowed photograph of the author on the jacket of *Traplines* is the work, as Robinson enjoys repeating, of a photographer determined to produce a picture not like Robinson but like her stories (implicitly insisting upon the incongruity of the two).[24] (The haunted jacket photograph contrasts strongly with the campy photo on her agent's promotional brochure, a photo – snapped by her sister – of Robinson with head thrown back flamboyantly in teasing movie-star fashion.) Interviewers are taken aback by the cheerful disposition of the author of these sometimes macabre stories. CBC's Shelagh Rogers, for example, notes the irony of discovering a woman who laughs more than Rogers herself, while producing fiction that Rogers describes as 'sombre, dark, excruciatingly painful to read.' Robinson appears intent on sabotaging direct connections between her own experience and her fiction. Asked about the personal origins of her material, she speaks with apparent seriousness but ultimately parodic effect of having been slapped by her mother for setting a couch on fire between the ages of four and six, and of getting into some fights ('rolling around on the ground') in grade one with a boy who called her 'monkey face' (Rogers). From the author of characters she herself describes as 'flamboyant psychopaths' (Marchand, 'World' C6), the reply manages to convey not only its own utter inadequacy as explanation but also the folly of such originary quests more generally.

Rather, Robinson suggests, the bizarre and gruesome catch her imagination from bits of stories, from newspapers: 'If I read something or hear something and go home and can't get it out of my head, then that's what I'll write about' (Penner 8). (In conversation, as a recent example of what captivates her, she offers the newspaper account of a man arrested naked while stealing shrubs from a nursery – naked, he explained, so as to escape detection.) While notions of imaginative and discursive autonomy untrammelled by personal and social history are naïve, Robinson's autobiographical 'explanations,' like her stories, may mark a self-conscious refusal of reductive etiologies. She and her stories are not so easily corralled.

'They gave me other presents, too.'
  'Cause you're such a good storyteller,' said Harlen.
  'I don't know,' said Lionel. 'Maybe cause I'm Indian. You know, I didn't see any white storytellers over there.' (King, *Medicine* 174)

At the Canadian Embassy in Paris, a week after the St Malo Book Fair, Thomas King read chapter twelve from his novel *Medicine River*, being launched in its French translation. The chapter introduces a Blood elder and storyteller who is thinking about getting a credit card. Lionel James concludes that the world is crazy because people in the countries he visits, Germany, France, Japan, want him to talk about what it's like to be an Indian, and only want to hear stories about old-time Indians. Lionel, for his part, hankers to tell also the story of Billy Frank and the Dead River Pig: '"It's a crazy world," Lionel said, as he walked me to my truck, "them people living in the past like that"' (King, *Medicine* 174).

At the end of the reading and the translation, Tom fielded questions. The first question came from a senior official at the embassy. 'Can you tell us,' he asked, referring to a peripheral detail in the story, 'what is a medicine bundle?'

When I included these observations about France in my paper on Eden Robinson at the Learned Societies meetings in Newfoundland in 1997, Renate Eigenbrod of Lakehead University told me her own story, of teaching a non-credit course on Native literature in northern Germany. Aware in advance of possible preconceptions or exoticizing assumptions held by her students, she deliberately began the course with two poems that self-consciously address notions of Indianness, (Mi'kmaq) Rita Joe's 'I Lost My Talk' – 'You snatched it away / I speak like you / I think like you' (32) – and Jeannette Armstrong's 'Indian Woman' – 'I am a squaw / a heathen / a savage' (*Breath* 106). At the end of the hour, she asked the group whether this was what they had anticipated for the first class of the course. Many shook their heads. 'No,' said one student. 'Where is the culture?'

Difference is all in the framing.

'You know the difference between you and me?' my partner said to me, out of the blue, the other day. 'I like to be in the company of women.'

He paused for a minute, and reformulated his thought: 'And so do you.'

Other writers have a collective identity *and* are respected outside their identity. The papers I see written on Indian writers always find our influence in other Indian writers. (Bell, 'American')

Here the strategy and the end result are the same ... nail down the Indian in order to nail down the text. (Sarris 128)

Greg Sarris has warned of the dangers of attempting to identify, or extrapolate from, an 'Indian' presence or 'Indian' themes in a text, without inquiring how one discovers or creates what is defined as Indian (123). Even reading Robinson as exploring issues of violence in mainstream culture from her Native perspective may participate in this dynamic. While the extremity of the violence and abuse in Robinson's fiction would seem to demand explanation, similar tendencies in fiction by white writers, say, rarely inspire recourse to larger racial and historical connections. Any attempt to recognize the salience of Robinson's Native background seems to reproduce the self–Other dualities of colonialism and to enact the liberal strategies of containment directed at heightening the 'visibility' of visible minorities and the unmarked status of the dominant culture. (Ruth Frankenberg has noted how 'the category of "American" represents simultaneously the normative and the residual, the dominant culture and a nonculture' [198]; Trinh Minh-ha how bounded cultures are relegated to the periphery [*Woman* 80–90].) Despite Toni Morrison's invitation in *Playing in the Dark*, where are the equivalent, automatic investigations of the salience of race and culture – the tropes of colonizing power, for instance – in the gritty contemporary urban fiction of white authors?

---

growing up in rural Alberta
in a town with fewer Indians
than ideas about Indians   (Dumont, 'Helen Betty Osborne,' *Really* 20)

You scour the reservation landfill
through the debris of so many lives:
old guitar, basketball on fire, pair of shoes.
All you bring me is an empty bottle.
                    (Alexie, 'Introduction to Native American Literature,' *Old* 3)

I find myself resisting the term 'serial killer,' used by Robinson's agent, her publisher, interviewers, and reviewers for the narrator's mother in 'Dogs in Winter.' Despite its functional economy in describing the perpetrator of at least eight murders, most of them involving strangers killed without explanation and apparently for the pleasure of killing, the term seems to substitute the reductive reassurance of a familiar designation for what in the story remains a series of barely glimpsed and possibly inexplicable acts. Mama is a haunting figure in the story precisely because she eludes understanding. Terms such as 'Native writer' and 'non-Native subject matter' contain the same danger, functioning as empty signifiers purporting to convey or specify meaning when that meaning is, in fact, what is under negotiation.

'Where is the culture?'

Where are the medicine bundles?

The experiences with school obligations or epilepsy or weekend breakfast rituals or teenage irritability or blueberry Kool-Aid hair that Robinson details in *Traplines* are just as constitutive of Native life as of non-Native life. And they are just as constitutive of Native life as are abuse and violence, for all the historical resonance and contemporary prominence (material and discursive) of the latter. I thought of using adolescent sexual interplay, so important in the collection, as an example here but realized that, in reference to Native peoples, sexuality is so racialized that such instances won't serve my purpose. (Using Edward Said's terminology, Terry Goldie identifies sexuality as one of the 'standard commodities' in the '"economy" created by the semiotic field of the indigene' in literature [*Fear* 15]). Similarly, the family intimacy – of Lisa and Aunt Genna in 'Dogs in Winter,' for example – which I was going to conjure up as a counter to the constrictive narrative of oppression and survival fails to serve my purpose. Though with a positive valence, the notion of relational affiliation can be a racialized one as well, a 'tribal' attribute, drawn from a predictable romanticizing archive and earning the designation of stereotype precisely for its totalizing quality. Stereotypic responses aside, though, every facet of the stories –

and not just those comprising a familiar narrow repertoire – is susceptible of being read as a component of Native culture.[25]

Greg Sarris argues that critic David Brumble, III, 'identifies anything nonrecognizable or unfamiliar in a narrated American Indian
autobiography, such as the presentation of seemingly disconnected
deeds or actions, as authentic, as Indian as opposed to Euro-American' (89). What's different, according to a particular outsider interpretive community, becomes the defining characteristics of a group. The
process proves to be primarily an exercise in self-revelation. What
Robinson's stories share with my own I am less likely to define as
'Native.' So colonized status or Haisla stories become my key to the
'Nativeness' of the collection, while other narrative details drop out of
sight: *Cheers* reruns, explorers of Africa, personal estrangement, Ror-
schach tests, Janis Joplin, headaches, Baby Duck, abortion, *America's
Funniest Home Videos*, astronomy, fireweed ... Fireweed? Hmm. What
about blueberry picking? Marten trapping? Cleaning halibut? What
about powwows? Where do I mark the border of the reserve and how
narrowly do I configure it? – fry bread on one side of the line, Rice
Krispies on the other, northern Native broadcasting on one side, *Sesame
Street* on the other – when Robinson cannot and does not separate
them? And where does karaoke fit in? What about Haisla characters
with their hair in pink and purple Mohawks? Attempts at definition
raise the political question of whose interests are being served? Which
cultures shrink, which expand during the exercise?

———•———

'Are you Indian then?'
   A hundred stupid answers came to my head but like I said, bullshit is work.
'Haisla. And you?' (E. Robinson, *Traplines* 207)

———•———

In identifying the bannock and the biker parties of *Traplines* as equally
part of Native experience, I'm not simply raising the much-ballyhooed
matters of cultural mutability and cultural syncretism, although these
are certainly relevant here. Beyond these is the point that any non-
museum culture is necessarily comprehensive, articulated through and
by all hours of the day, not readily hived off into a few, select, historically persistent manifestations. What nexus of contemporary 'Native'
signifiers could one possibly evoke that would not either instantly
disenfranchise nine-tenths of Native people and activities or alterna-

tively provoke instant challenges over the validity of such inclusive touchstones? By what criteria did I initially determine that 'Contact Sports' 'contains no obvious markers of Indianness'? By what further presumptuousness could I suggest to students (even hypothetically and under the influence of Robinson's rejection of the 'Native stories' label) that what did not meet my criteria of 'Nativeness' by default registers therefore as 'white,' so confirming white as the residual category?

In 'Queen of the North,' Robinson herself punctures the othering of Native people, the bracketing of their practices as somehow inherently 'different.' In the introduction here, I have already noted Adelaine's silent rebuff, while selling fry bread at a fundraiser, of a sexually and racially titillated powwow spectator, on the prowl for cultural novelty:

'How should I eat these?' he interrupted me.
  With your mouth, asshole. (E. Robinson, *Traplines* 208)

Ironically, Philip Marchand interprets the customer's overtures – which are accompanied by the flashing of twenty-dollar bills and which I read as cultural and sexual predation – more sympathetically, as a 'quiet, fumbling but oddly heartfelt attempt to make contact.' They are evidence, in his view, of the positive narrative presence of white people that, in two Robinson stories, offers temporary respite from the anguish of the Indian reserve ('Steely' G20). [26] This strikes me as an exculpatory move by the reviewer, exonerating in advance the outsider reader/ reviewer who may share the customer's propensity to produce and consume alterity. 'With your mouth, asshole' exceeds Marchand's efforts at containing the scene. Adelaine's gibe works, I would argue, as a curt metafictional injunction to readers bent on fetishizing the Native writer and characters. Earlier, Adelaine, subjecting her inquisitor in turn to a query about *his* racial or tribal identity, has insisted on reciprocity. Similarly here, sweaty in her cutoffs and baseball cap, pale and bleeding from a recent abortion, she refuses, through her silent rebuke, to permit the romancing of culture at the expense of – and as somehow separate from – the everyday routines and challenges of her life.

––––––––––

Indeed, the inability of most contemporary criticism to speak with any clarity to the science fiction of Russell Bates (Kiowa), the mystery writing of Martin Cruz Smith (Senecu del Sur/Yaqui), the political humor of Will Rogers (Cherokee), and the host of other Indian writers whose work does not fit into standard definitions of Indian writing seems more than enough justification for some fundamental reworking of scholarly understandings of American Indian literature, culture, and experience. (Warrior xx)

However impeccably the content of an 'other' culture may be known, however anti-ethnocentrically it is represented, it is its location as the closure of grand theories, the demand that, in analytic terms, it be always the good object of knowledge, the docile body of difference, that reproduces the relation of domination and is the most serious indictment of the institutional powers of critical theory. (Bhabha, *Location* 31)

———•———

Rather than redeploying given notions of Native history and culture in my analysis, I might more profitably read *Traplines* as a site of contestation of such notions, as enacting (in dynamic ways) and not merely (re)articulating Nativeness. Through the eclecticism or unpredictability of her text, Robinson can be seen to perform her culture, to inhabit Homi Bhabha's 'Third Space' of enunciation and cultural translation, evading the stubborn binarisms of tradition and modernity, of Indian and non-Indian.[27] (And it is her own particular version of her culture that she performs here; even if she writes about her Haisla community, as some community members have urged and as she goes on to do in *Monkey Beach*, she is still, she points out, telling her story, not theirs.) Just as soccer games have replaced canoe races at Haisla sports days, so in Robinson's text the translating or re-presentation of 'white' narratives by a Haisla author becomes a version of Nativeness – except that the categories 'white' and 'Haisla' are (misleadingly) mine and not those of *Traplines*. By its existence, the text effects the traversal of one term by the other, emptying out the criteria that constitute the distinction between them. (Robinson, incidentally, is also doing gender creatively here; with her male protagonists and especially the casual representation of extremes of violence, her hard-nosed, minimalist fiction breaches gender protocol.)

To rework Mary Jacobus's comment about women writers (Jacobus 109), Robinson redirects us from the question 'Is there an Indian in this text?' to an alternative formulation, 'Is there a text in this Indian?' Through their *absence* she evokes and queries some of the fictions used to constitute her difference and, in her own hand, rewrites the texts that formulate her. When a Native writer takes as her purview the pop culture of the young and the restless, the hype of the tabloids, the tragedies of contemporary urban males, she seriously damages the capacity of white culture to allocate to itself all that remains after the racial/cultural reserves have been allotted. In so doing she makes 'Native writer' a less constricting designation and helps move us towards a point where the asymmetrical deployment of such categories becomes less pervasive and problematic.

So, while some of us continue to ask, 'What is the use of reclaiming difference when it is already given to us?' some others among us refuse to concede theory and history to the Master all over again, and work carefully at expanding the term from within as we continue to displace it. A new hearing may then be produced on our own terms that makes difference not an inherited attribute but a politics of articulation (or disarticulation). (Trinh, 'Undone' 11)

The postindian warriors hover at last over the ruins of tribal representations and surmount the scriptures of manifest manners with new stories; these warriors counter the surveillance and literature of dominance with their own simulations of survivance. (Vizenor, *Manifest* 5)

Eden Robinson tells the story of asking her grandmother, when Robinson was ten, to sing her a Haisla song. Her grandmother agreed and began to sing:

Wha-wha-whiskey and wild, wild women,
They drive you crazy, they drive you insane.
Once I was married and had a good wife[28]
....

'That's not a Haisla song,' Robinson objected.
'Yes, it is.'

The stories in *Traplines* aren't Haisla stories. Yes, they are.

In/conclusion

But as there is no such thing as an innocent reading, we must say what reading we are guilty of.

(Althusser 15)

That's how the tales started, all the gossip, the wondering, all the things people said without knowing and then believed, since they heard it with their own ears, from their own lips, each word.

(Erdrich 9)

At a literary reading in St Paul, Minnesota, in the early 1990s, Leslie Silko (Laguna Pueblo) described a plant growing in the desert that feeds on radioactivity and converts it into harmless matter. She celebrated the plant as a corrective to the human arrogance that would insist upon our capacity for planetary destruction, ignoring the regenerative power of the natural world. I am reminded of her argument when I think over my anxieties around potential cultural violation of the Native texts that I am studying in *How Should I Read These?* The texts are more resilient than I imagine, proliferating possibilities in interaction with other readers, hardly reducible to a singular, interested reading. This is not to downplay the issues of power and access (and Silko is far from dismissing or underestimating the global dangers posed by the contemporary military-industrial complex, as anyone can testify who has read her *Almanac of the Dead*). Like the Chippewa characters in Louise Erdrich's *Tracks*, I am certainly capable of producing, from what I read, a tale of my own devising. And along with readers of similar background, I can believe my version of the text the more readily because it conforms so well to my culture-specific understandings, because I have indeed heard it from my own lips, each word. But Erdrich's own ironic formulation gestures towards a wry, compensatory awareness of the presence and sources of such gratifying inventions. Like the First Nations themselves, devastated, yes, in many ways by centuries of colonization but flourishing, too, despite all the proclamations of their imminent demise, these texts can withstand meddling.

———·•·———

S: Frankly, I'm very *tired* of having other women interpret for us, other women empathize for us, other women sympathize with us. I'm interested in articulating our own directions, our own aspirations, our own past, *in our own words.* (Osennontion and Skonaganleh:rá 7)

We need to move away from a picture of cultural contexts as sealed rooms, with a homogenous space 'inside' them, inhabited by 'authentic insiders.' Western feminist reflections on their own experiences should teach them that there are many ways to critically and creatively inhabit a culture. (Narayan, 'Contesting' 412)

———·•·———

At the Haisla sports day in 1996 in Kitimaat Village, British Columbia, where we were being hosted by one of the leading families in the village, my seven-year-old daughter teamed up with a seven-year-old Haisla girl. With coaching from her brother ('walk, don't run, so you avoid falling down'), Elizabeth was delighted to win one of the three-legged races, to place well in another, and to have found a ready companion for the rest of the day. My ten-year-old son, Benjamin, though a good runner, was more chagrined to discover that the age categories ('hundred-yard dash, boys twelve and under') grouped him with much larger boys, making competition disheartening, for all my encouragement about doing his personal best. When the hundred-yard dash for women thirty-five and older was announced, I headed for the starting line with alacrity. I run almost daily and enjoy pushing myself in the occasional race. But no one else appeared. 'Come on, ladies,' encouraged the announcer and our host, 'hundred-yard dash, thirty-five and older. Where are the competitors to take on the Ontario Nation?' Eventually, one of the women seated on the sidelines rose and joined me on the field.

'If you came in together, you could each win a toonie,' joked the organizer at the starting line, referring to the three-dollar and one-dollar prizes. I knew what he was saying. I know that joking is an important technique for couching advice. I knew that Donna, the announcer's daughter, was in the race solely as a courtesy to their visitor. I didn't need to win. We started off together. But I couldn't do it. Not because my pride was on the line. Not because winning took precedence over fellowship. I couldn't run alongside Donna and cross the finish line together, because doing so felt wrong, felt insulting to Donna. With our natural paces so much more divergent than I'd anticipated, I felt increasingly that I was patronizing her with my laboriously slowed gait, showing her up by attempting not to. I had to pull away, pick up my pace. 'And the Ontario Nation wins,' the announcer teased, tongue-in-cheek. 'Donna has let down the Haisla Nation.' (Later, appropriately enough, in the four-hundred-yard race for women eighteen and over, three young women blazed past me, me an afterthought huffing along half a course behind them, as they battled for first place.)

———•—•———

Moreover, we tend to privilege experience itself, as if black life is lived experience outside of representation ... Instead, it is only through the way in which we represent and imagine ourselves that we come to know how we are constituted and who we are. (Hall 30)

The fact that women will not be determined in advance should not make women any less determined to ask what they may turn out to have been. (Elam 32)

———•—•———

The structure of *How Should I Read These?*, linking texts on the basis of shared identity categories, as Native (and to a lesser extent as female), implicitly and explicitly organizes understandings of the writing in terms of these categories. So, what's so Native about ...? Or, as I have been asking throughout, how does the Native provenance of these texts affect my reading and teaching of them? And yet, as we have seen, particularly in the previous chapter, quite other questions could have been asked about these books. Armstrong's *Slash*, Slipperjack's *Honour the Sun*, Maracle's *Ravensong*, and Robinson's *Traplines* could be used to explore the literature of trauma or the narrative functions of violence. Along with Culleton's *In Search of April Raintree* and Hungry Wolf's *The Ways of My Grandmothers*, they could illustrate, expand, and challenge the category of the *Bildungsroman*, the narrative of maturation. Several work as instances of popular culture (Culleton, Hungry Wolf), or formal experimentation (Hungry Wolf, Campbell and Griffiths), or pedagogical writing (Armstrong, Hungry Wolf). Zeroing in on their Nativeness – as if that is a known quantity – can restrict or skew their significance, homogenize, even quarantine them.

Within a mainstream culture that produces certain kinds of difference and ignores other kinds, the Nativeness of these writers will none the less be a prominent feature of their reception. Several of the books – *Slash, In Search of April Raintree, The Ways of My Grandmothers* – moreover, were written expressly to remedy gaps in the literature, silences around recent First Nations history and activism, Métis experience, or Native women's stories. All the authors (Robinson more partially, notably in 'Queen of the North') write self-consciously out of the cultural specificities of their peoples and, more generally, the colonial history of First Nations in Canada. Campbell and Maracle frame and explicate their dramas directly through this history (Campbell with metaphors of homesteading and treaty making, Maracle with flashbacks to the tall ships and smallpox epidemics), a history that they show re-enacted in the present. Armstrong structures Tommy Kelasket's search around actual (sometimes unnamed) events in the political struggle of the Indian movement of the 1960s and 1970s, contextualized as these events open backwards onto earlier stages of conquest and resistance. By contrast, Slipperjack (like Robinson in 'Traplines,' if that story's protagonists are read as Native) lets the history speak only by implication, through the indirect evidence of its often insidious, continuing impact on Owl's (or Will's) isolated community.

How the authors communicate tribal or Native realities differs also. At one extreme, Beverly Hungry Wolf's ostensibly ethnographic voice, reporting on the dances, medicine bundles, household customs, and traditional values of the Blood people, risks reducing culture to a preset content fixed in the past, an 'object of empirical knowledge,' a constraining lot of 'terminal creeds' (Bhabha, *Location* 34; Vizenor, *Bearheart* 197). Hungry Wolf does, however, wrest ethnography from the outsider-anthropologist in favour of ongoing self-definition, sets insider voices in conversation with one another, foregrounds cultural change, and slides from one subject position to another, challenging efforts to pin her and her culture(s) down for dissection. Similarly Armstrong, Campbell, and Maracle specify distinctive tribal or Native ways – of learning without repetition (Armstrong), of giving freely

(Campbell), of waiting comfortably through silence (Maracle), and so on – in part to represent or revalue what has hitherto been ignored or misprized. All three reflect in part Pra-cwa's sentiment in *Slash* that 'We live different than them and they live different than us' (18).

That difference or cultural identity, though, is immediately opened to scrutiny, made the substance of the narrative's investigation, and revealed to be fractured internally or even within the individual. Maracle's *Ravensong* builds narrative and theory upon the disparate, sometimes incompatible allegiances that persist between but also within communities. For all her articulation of how village ways differ from town ways, for example, Stacey proves unable to share the context or perspective even of her own mother or to recognize that she shares a context with her clanswoman Nora. Values prove to be distributed across cultures, as in Campbell's discovery within herself of the Catholic repression that she deplores in Griffiths. Despite a clear sense of a recognizable Okanagan tradition in *Slash*, the novel's dilemma involves how that tradition is to be successfully articulated with current youth disaffection, and the book stages even-handed debates, between First Nations characters, about how best to pursue Native self-determination. Specific cultural norms coexist with an active, open-ended process of self- and community definition and discovery.

By contrast, although *Honour the Sun* conveys a strong sense of a distinctive ethos, Slipperjack enacts rather than verbalizing it, implicit communication being central to that ethos. Even the rare injunctions from Delia – to listen to the silence or honour the sun – or the Medicine Man's reassurances in the epilogue do not directly formulate generalizations about Owl's Ojibway culture. Rather, they place readers in the culturally apt position of having, like tribal members, to determine the lessons' meanings by and for themselves. Overall, the narrative's obliqueness, its descriptive richness paired with interpretive restraint, and its cumulative rather than dramatic structure induct readers into the ways of knowing modelled by the characters (Ojibway readers having a cultural advantage here). So the text communicates, exemplifies, and promotes a particular culture without overtly talking about it.

At a further extreme lie Culleton's and Robinson's texts. Although Culleton reviews Métis history in *In Search of April Raintree*, except for a brief reference to early Métis as 'an independent breed, freedom lovers' (171), her characters ascribe no specific cultural characteristics to that people. 'Métis,' the identity around which the plot revolves, stands as an undefined category whose meaning remains to be determined beyond the novel's end. Discrediting earlier damaging representations, Culleton leaves 'Métis' not as a cultural given but as an open site for affiliation and political mobilization.[1]

Robinson goes even farther in rejecting preformulated identities. The characters in her stories, with their contemporary urban cool, challenge preconceptions. References to amplifiers, chug buddies, roller rinks, nachos, biker chicks, scorpion tattoos, jacuzzis, body piercing, granola bars, shaved heads, and VCRs, to Disneyland, Ritalin, Armani, Jehovah's Witnesses, *Kiss of the Spider Woman*, and Oodles of Noodles abound.[2] The prominence in Robinson's work of the material and symbolic features of North American mass-media, consumer, and youth cultures confounds any attempt to confine understandings of Native reality to a nineteenth-century cultural preserve. The racial indeterminacy, too, of some characters and stories in *Traplines* works to redefine and expand the sometimes dismissive designation of 'Native author.' From Hungry Wolf to Robinson, textual strategies for representing and imagining Native experience can encompass, at one pole, a reclaiming of early traditions and, at the other, a revisionist disregard for the boundaries of 'us' and 'them.'

The centrality of the larger tribal, racial, and historical context (however represented) to many of the individual stories here is unsurprising, given the racialization of individual identity for Native people in North America and threats to the survival and self-determination of their Nations. Unsurprisingly, community, a sense of responsibility or connection to 'all my relations,' figures prominently in these texts. This connection may be only belatedly achieved, as in the ending of Culleton's novel (in April Raintree's invocation of 'MY PEOPLE, OUR PEOPLE' [228]). In the case of *Traplines*, the obvious exception to this generalization, the connection may be invoked by default; in Robinson's collection, grievous *failures* of family and community are what propel each story. But, one way or another, these texts suggest the importance of membership in a larger collectivity. Armstrong, Slipperjack, Culleton, Maracle, and, in part, Robinson, while recognizing colonial determinants, probe difficulties or breakdown within the group (alienation, violence, substance abuse, despair) – central concerns, given the crucial function of community.

Intriguingly, too, while the focus is on the tribal or racial community, accountability and membership often extend farther.[3] Armstrong's Tommy Kelasket looks towards a continued struggle, 'until Indian people did what they had to, not only for their survival but for the survival of what is human in an inhuman world' (*Slash* 251). *Ravensong*, similarly, is built around the necessity to deliver Raven's vision to the entire earth. At the end of *Honour the Sun*, Owl defines the community to which she belongs as comprising the elements of the natural world around her. Urging the necessity for healers and teachers and connections in a time of ecological devastation, Maria Campbell speaks to Linda Griffiths of the stolen sacred things 'that belong to all of our old people, all over the earth' (102). Clearly growing out of a tribal ethos in some cases, such concerns draw on broadened notions of community, in imagining how the Native person is constituted.

What this responsibility or connection to community entails, of course, is far from self-evident. In fact it is the crux of several of the books, including Armstrong's, Culleton's, and Maracle's. How does one 'find a way back' as an Okanagan youth or best pursue a Native future (Armstrong, *Slash* 87)? What does it mean to be Métis? How does one manage simultaneous membership in more than one group, with incongruent group interests? What happens when attempts to give something back to a community risk offending some members? How does change over time fit with long-standing tribal values? Can one leave a place and still remain a part of it? What sustains or destroys a nation? How and with what difficulties do members of First Nations take responsibility for a global community? Acknowledging a location, a community, in these books opens up rather than foreclosing the question of what that positioning or that membership might mean. Being human, being Native, being Ojibway or Métis or Blood, while all demanding accountability, pose exacting questions rather than providing ready answers.

Although less a focus within *How Should I Read These?*, questions about gender also arise from the grouping of these particular authors. The framing texts, Jeannette Armstrong's at the beginning and Eden Robinson's at the end, through their male protagonists, enact alternative performances of female authorship, simultaneously traditional (invoking women's 'soft power' as educators of men) and revisionary (claiming authority beyond constrictive gender boundaries). Beverly Hungry Wolf is most overtly feminist in her structuring of *The Ways of My Grandmothers* around gender difference, singling out the lives and stories of women of her tribe, to redress an imbalance. But the narratives of Owl's developing subjectivity in Slipperjack's novel and the Raintree sisters' in Culleton's are also very much gendered narratives, in their scrutiny of what the development of Native *girls* entails (the physical and emotional harassment that Owl and her mother face, the 'Native Girls' Syndrome' in Culleton). ('Women' is even a category Cheryl Raintree wields to escape her marginalization as Native.) Lee Maracle uses connections among women to complicate the racial binaries that initially seem all encompassing in her novel. And Maria Campbell and Linda Griffiths grapple with how their shared status as female – through tropes of matriarch, goddess, bad girl, sister, dark mother, old whore, sibyl, Virgin Mary, White Buffalo Calf Woman, or Lady of Shalott – inflects the attractions, projections, and tensions between them. Revealingly, sexual (sometimes incestuous) assault against women is a common element, and pivotal, to five of the seven books: against Maria Campbell and her stage persona, Jessica, against Owl's mother, against April Raintree, against Madeline's daughters in *Ravensong*, and against Adelaine in Robinson's 'Queen of the North.'

The texts identify and critique the larger patterns, the social structures within which individual gender relations operate, as in *Ravensong*'s dramatization of Mrs Snowden's symptomatic exclusion from political discussion in favour of her young son. Maracle's narrative goes on to analyse the place of women's divorce, suicide, sexuality – straight and lesbian – domestic abuse, childbearing and child rearing, and independence within the norms and power relations of their societies. Using the greater gender equity of Salish culture as a measure, her judgments are most unsparing regarding the vulnerability of white women, unprotected by ownership of their own homes and bodies. But she does also scrutinize the incapacity of the Salish village to accommodate the sexual and gender nonconformity of a character such as old Nora or to draw on Nora's potential.

Reassessing the contract disputes over *Jessica*, Maria Campbell identifies a recurring scenario in which men produce a problem and evade its consequences, profiting from the resulting conflict between women. More broadly she discusses her recovery of the abandoned figure of the mother, celebrates the circle of the grandmothers, and ponders with Griffiths the causes and costs of the historic loss of matriarchal power to male conquerors.[4] Much of the import of Campbell and Griffiths's struggle with each other, though, lies in their understanding that their shared female and even feminist identities are saturated separately, differently, with racial and ethnic histories and operate within systems of power reproducing colonial relations between them.

The Ways of My Grandmothers works to dispel misapprehensions regarding earlier Blood practices, such as the marriage of girls in childhood, the 'selling' of daughters, or the heavy labour of women. A major thrust of the text is to provide, as do the oral narratives that Hungry Wolf records, 'evidence of the high social standing achieved by the women in my grandmothers' times' and to counter a bias dismissing Native women's contribution to world knowledge (136–7). At the same time, as part of her project to reinstate the value of women's ways, Hungry Wolf does not shy away from noting instances of tribal gender inequality. Paula Weasel Head criticizes her father's spoiled expectation of domestic service, for example, a possible holdover from an earlier, more equitable, gendered division of labour.

Beatrice Culleton, tracing the debilitating anguish and the indignities of the judicial process in the aftermath of April Raintree's rape, explicitly invokes a social ignorance around sexual violence that her narrative sets out to remedy. Although Slipperjack's critique remains more implicit, *Honour the Sun* traces, in hyperreal detail, the progressive enculturation of a young girl in a colonized, economically straitened environment conducive to female beleaguerment amid the erosion of family and communal responsibilities. Owl is shown increasingly to take for granted an atmosphere marked by male intimidation and a sexual vulnerability that finds skewed expression in her mother's indignation over Owl's first period. The sexual assaults in five of the narratives occur not as individual aberrations but within broader contexts – of community breakdown, racist misogyny, infiltration of white values, and the legacy of residential school abuse.

Much of this analysis, particularly that of Campbell, Hungry Wolf, and Maracle, is self-consciously feminist or womanist, expressly including gender within an anti-oppression framework. Strategies for addressing gender, though, prove to be quite various. Besides exposing and denaturalizing patriarchal practices, authors here explore more transgressive female scripts, most obviously with the girl brawls of Robinson's 'Queen of the North' and the happy-go-lucky killer mother of 'Dogs in Winter.' Through her male-focused stories, Robinson may also be discovering less predictable, more figurative ways to tell female stories of domestic abuse. She may, equally, be challenging such confining definitions of femaleness, staking a claim to broader territory, enlarging her sphere of authority as woman writer. Jeannette Armstrong, most clearly of all, resists the notion that feminist literary work consists in telling women's stories. Instead, by undertaking the educative narrative of a young man reconnecting with his nation, she models a female cultural responsibility for guiding and reshaping an entire people.

Warning about the constrictive potential even of liberatory labels, Judith Butler has concluded, 'This is not to say that I will not appear at political occasions under the sign of lesbian, but that I would like to have it permanently unclear what precisely that sign signifies' ('Imitation' 14). Similarly, the texts here raise and reward questions that broaden rather than confirm assumptions about the meaning of signifiers such as 'Native' or 'woman.' The texts refuse to be confined by these terms; they refuse to abandon them either. Instead they demonstrate the many ways, both critical and creative, of inhabiting female and Native cultures, of asking what women and Native people may turn out to have been.

———•———

To be a creative listener first requires that you be uncreative. (Corbett)

To put our beliefs on hold is to cease to exist as ourselves for a moment – and that is not easy. It is painful as well, because it means turning yourself inside out, giving up your own sense of who you are, and being willing to see yourself in the unflattering light of another's angry gaze. (Delpit 46–7)

———•———

I was abashed to discover, at the Haisla Sports Day, that knowing the culturally appropriate response wasn't enough. What confounded me were the simultaneous demands of apparently incompatible norms, my deep conviction that to do what was right was to do what was wrong. Either way. I experienced the moment as an invitation to evacuate my role as my own ethical arbiter, to show respect in a form that to me felt disrespectful. (By failing/refusing to do so, I failed another ethical imperative, to honour different cultural values – in the process proving that imperative less central to my constitution of my ethical self.) Was there a means of reconciling two different notions of respectful behaviour – or should I have simply set aside as inapposite my fear of condescension, knowing that, however negatively I judged my slow pace, a social context that understood it otherwise took precedence over my private reading?

Camaraderie, good humour, and community building clearly were the order of the day in Kitimaat Village that Saturday. At the boisterous, men-versus-boys soccer game in the afternoon, raillery ruled, especially among the adults, with the men entering into mock disputes with the referees over egregious fouls, carrying the soccer ball under their

shirts, shouting playful encouragement in Haisla, and carting off opposing players, ball and all. Earlier, the older, stocky, Tsimshian mayor
of nearby Hartley Bay and other adult contestants were subjected to a
novelty race that involved being swaddled in oversized diapers and
sucking on infant soothers.

Looking back on the women's hundred-yard dash, with more than a
split second for consideration, I can see that being able to run slowly
and comfortably alongside my race partner required finding a more
effective way to reconfigure the event, for myself, as the social rather
than sporting occasion that it was. I needed to enter into engaged
enough conversation (we had chatted briefly during the first moments
of the race) that we would clearly be companions rather than runners,
rendering our pace and hence my perceived capacity to patronize irrelevant. (Viewing the event as social rather than sporting figures me
rather than Donna as the person in danger of being 'shown up.' I
wonder whether she felt that her own graciousness in humouring my
need to race was, like my slowed pace, blatant and, so, potentially
shaming.) At the time, I regretted, as I do now, my failure in courtesy.
Given a chance to replay the incident, I would hope to use conversation
more successfully to resolve the dilemma. Yet I am still seeking to enter
into the spirit of the day 'comfortably,' without having to come into
conflict with my own values. What remains disconcerting is the evidence of how intractable I can find a difference between another (admi-
rable) ethic and my own.

———•———

[C]ontemporary [Native] texts contain the critical contexts needed for their
own interpretation and, because of the intertextuality of Native American
literature, the critical commentary and contexts necessary for the interpretation
of works by other Native writers. (Blaeser 59–60)

If they had asked and listened, they would have heard the answer ... (Armstrong,
Slash 249)

———•———

'How should I eat these?' Chapter one on Jeannette Armstrong begins
with the pursuit of an 'intrinsic approach,' a way of reading from the
inside out, drawing on a text's own cultural and aesthetic assumptions.
Chapter seven on Eden Robinson ends with cautions about the risks of
using a text's Native origins as a source of explication and about nar-

row, imaginatively fettered notions of Native culture. All my chapters address difficulties arising from the possible inappropriateness of the cultural and aesthetic understandings that I bring to my readings. At the same time, the texts studied here address multiple audiences and provide guidance in their own reading. 'More and more we will be required to read across lines of cultural identity around us and within us,' advises Louis Owens (*Mixedblood* 11). Recognizing, as does Owens, that readers may themselves be ambiguously located, and the texts as well, one needs to be wary of monolithic cultural explanations. These are transcultural texts, not reducible to alternatives of 'authentic' self-representation or 'contaminated' assimilation. Still, without reifying Native culture(s), there is profit in considering how the 'critical voice that comes from within that tribal story itself' (Blaeser 61) assists in the reading not only of its own narrative but also of those by other Native (and non-Native) writers. Stressing knowledge of specific tribal contexts, Craig Womack has argued for a radical 'Red Stick' literary criticism by Native critics, 'the assumption that Indian viewpoints cohere, that Indian resistance can be successful, that Native critical centers are possible, that working from within the nation, rather than looking toward the outside, is a legitimate way of examining literature ...' (12).

Jeannette Armstrong's *Slash*, through narrative emphasis on the substance of community debates and rhetorical attention to the characters' process of hearing and grappling with ideas, implicitly proposes a way of reading that listens for 'the deep thinking that's hard to convey in words' (Armstrong, 'Rights' 37). The novel's repeated triad of asking, listening, and hearing requires of the reader the same kind of thoughtful attentiveness and respect for difficult views modelled by the novel's characters. Slash's comment about a later encounter with his cousin Chuck – 'this time I didn't argue with him. I tried to hear what he said and make some sense out of it' (238) – comes to function as metafictional instruction for readers of this and other texts.

In a related fashion, Ruby Slipperjack establishes silence, whether textual subject or textual strategy, not simply as withholding or resistance, or even as an alternative form of communication or 'silent words,' but also potentially as meditative receptivity. 'The stillness itself lasts forever but the noise can be silenced,' suggests the Medicine Man (*Honour* 211). Like the persistent sun unconcerned by the passing clouds, to which he also refers, the stillness points to internal depths and consolations that outlast distractions and annoyances, depths and consolations to be discerned in the undifferentiated details of everyday. As we have seen, *Honour the Sun*, paradoxically using words to communicate wordlessness, trains the reader in the process of attending to underlying (and sustaining) significances beyond the surface, beyond words.[5]

This analysis, though, is taking on an unwonted solemnity. As counterpoint, let me revert to the passage from Eden Robinson's 'Queen of the North' with which my introduction begins. Read as metacritical illumination, advice to the reader, the passage – '"How should I eat these?" ... With your mouth, asshole' (*Traplines* 208) – reaffirms the importance of gustatory and aesthetic pleasure. Stop worrying the issue of cultural difference, you asshole, Adelaine's rejoinder declares, and enjoy. Take delight in what you are offered. Taste what you are eating; don't just classify and anatomize it. (It's worth noting also that much of what Slipperjack's characters discover beyond words is the comic, with silent, restorative laughter a frequent shared pleasure.) *In Search of April Raintree* too, with its pursuit of emotional intensity, particularly through the tragic arc of Cheryl's promise and then destruction, reflects an aesthetic of feeling. Beatrice Culleton promotes the worth of responsiveness in a reader's engagement with texts, reclaiming the sometimes disparaged value of sentiment.[6]

Maria Campbell's contributions to *The Book of Jessica* emphasize reciprocity, responsibility to community, openhandedness, and healing as requirements of art. True art, she tells Linda Griffiths in a self-reflexive moment, gives back by empowering, creating beauty, bringing joy, and raising questions. Campbell invites the reader into a communal teaching and healing cycle that is mutually restorative: 'Every single little time that somebody reads a word in here that makes them feel good, it means we made them a little bit stronger ... and we make ourselves a little bit stronger'(103; ellipsis in the original). (Lest this sound utopian, Campbell also notes the precipitousness of the project's desire to heal a personal/sociopolitical wound that may not mend for another hundred years.) The responsibilities that Campbell details for the artist are responsibilities for which the reader/critic becomes answerable as well: '"Whether you're a storyteller, a painter ... whatever you are, you're a healer first. Whatever you do with that, it will come back one day. And if it's good energy, and it's healing, it will heal you too." ... Just know the responsibility' (90; initial ellipsis in the original). Pleasure, feeling, healing: the texts here identify responses of engagement that they seek from readers.

In chapter six on Lee Maracle's *Ravensong*, I drew on the Native concept of oratory as defined by Maracle – 'theory through story' – in analysing Maracle's book (*Oratory* 14). In fact oratory can serve more broadly as a guide to reading a number of the texts discussed here. Maracle argues that the aim of oratory is to pose rather than resolve dilemmas and, since ideas must be applied and must be manifested socially, to use narrative to convey thoughts and values: 'When our orators get up to tell a story, there is no explanation, no set-up to guide the listener – just the poetic terseness of the dilemma is presented' (*Sojourner's* 12). Confounded by unexplained adult behaviour in *Ravensong*, Stacey decides 'to let it sit there until life imaged up some sort of answer,' demonstrating the patience and receptiveness that Maracle expects from readers, who will similarly 'get the answer when it was time' (16, 49).

Armstrong's *Slash*, in particular, makes sense as a form of oratory, bodying forth crucial dilemmas around personal location and tribal self-determination.[7] Like the historical symposium near the end of the novel, the book, while giving special weight to the elders' perspectives, provides 'a representative voice from as many points of view on the question as possible, from the most assimilationist to the most radical' (245). Although the symposium misses some of its intended audience, the narrative, as oratory, offers parallel opportunities to readers: 'The listeners are drawn into the dilemma and are expected at some point in their lives to actively work themselves out of it' (Maracle, *Sojourner's* 12). Armstrong herself describes the book as raising 'questions which make things clearer,' and discusses story or art in a Native tradition as working by implication, as 'a way sign *toward* something which the reader/viewer constructs' ('What' 16; Isernhagen 164).

The oral tradition's capacity to convey values without elaboration is clearly relevant to *Honour the Sun*, as amplified above, but may equally apply to *In Search of April Raintree*, a text more readily associated with popular or sentimental fiction. Through an emotionally charged story, Culleton embodies complex theoretical issues around institutional and discursive power, racialized identities, and the production of meaning. And critical and readerly baulking at the novel's apparent resolution suggests that the dilemmas it raises do remain in effect unsettled, to reside thenceforth within readers.

Dee Horne has proposed that Robinson's *Traplines*, too, be read in light of Maracle's description of oratory, noting that 'In the vein of oral traditions, these stories do not tell us what to think. Instead, they are open-ended and leave readers to ponder the dilemmas and issues that they raise' (Rev. 162). Even more than some of the examples just mentioned, Robinson's stories stop short with the fleshing out of serious, unresolved social problems – of poverty, social segregation, parental abandonment, adolescent bullying, consumerist superficiality, emotional and sexual abuse, frenetic self-stimulation, and arbitrary (or all-too-explicable) violence. They leave us more with the intensity of characters' distress, the relentlessness of their entrapment, than with directions for change.[8] While the graphic details and startling extremes of the narratives may seem to signal sensational fiction rather than a fiction of ideas, Robinson is theorizing (and inviting the reader to theorize) through story.[9] Tracing the subtleties of power, social pressure, and deprivation, the twists of self-preservation, she gestures towards values through the anguish of their absence or distortion. And in documenting the losses of her characters, she provokes speculation about origins and alternatives. The distance between Armstrong's methodical reasoning and Robinson's sometimes grisly dramas may seem great, but the various authors here are working in different ways from within common traditions of orature that require readers to determine themselves the analysis contained within the stories.

Readers, for instance, cannot be separate from the history of their reading, of all that makes for their encounter with and response to that which they read. Mabel once said, 'Don't ask me what it means, the story. Life will teach you about it, the way it teaches you about life.' (Sarris 5)

Texts can be remarkably resilient, offering their narratives anew to fresh readers for fresh readings, whatever the interests of past interpretations. For both good and ill, readers can be similarly resilient – resistant or simply impervious to particular textual directions. My daughter, Elizabeth, aged ten, was recently reading aloud from *Little House in Brookfield*, a prequel to the Laura Ingalls Wilder 'Little House' series in which an indomitable pioneer family overcomes the physical and psychological rigours of homesteading in the nineteenth-century U.S. Midwest.[10] The series, attentive to the vulnerabilities of the newcomers, is unforthcoming on the historical context that produces the tensions in the texts between encroaching whites and Native peoples of the region. Indeed, like much history, the 'Little House' books tend to invert the relationship of the two groups, figuring the Native character rather than the white as invader and threat. When two unknown Indians arrive without warning at the door of the orphaned and widowed Quiner family (bringing assistance in the family's straitened circumstances, as it turns out), the *Brookfield* narrative is initially rich with signifiers of racial menace. At the sight of an Indian, Mother pales and steps backwards; Caroline's breath catches in her throat. The intruder bears a jagged scar from eye to chin across his red-brown face, speaks in a strange, rapid, deep, and incomprehensible voice, and gesticulates excitedly, his long black hair flying. That the Indians here prove to be benefactors, and thus hypothetically either friends or foes, does nothing to redress the historical and structural distortion that positions the pioneers and their incursion as resolutely benign. And the familiar initial positing of the Native figure as freakish, so necessary to the narrative of ultimate kinship, vitiates that eventual liberal gesture, even while enabling it.

As reader, my daughter remained wonderfully un(in)formed by the fearsome implications of this scene and by the history of representation of Native people that undergirded it,[11] drawing instead on her own reassuring repertoire of signification. 'So,' she asked obliviously, 'is he their father?'

Like me studying the texts discussed above, but in a different direction, Elizabeth was embarked upon a 'cross-reading,' the term Louis Owens uses to describe 'the way in which all of us engage texts across some kind of cultural boundary or conceptual horizon' (*Mixedblood* 5). Just as I must confront my assumptions as they encounter genres, aesthetic standards, or cultural principles that they do not fit or a politics that calls me to account, so the commonplaces of a white text here are exposed and transfigured by a reader unsusceptible to its world-view. A novel that would deem herself and the people she knows as unnerving Others is too strange itself to fathom, and so my daughter must reconstruct it more plausibly. With Elizabeth as reader, little houses on the prairies, in the big woods, on rocky ridges – or in the towns and cities of contemporary North America – along with their imagined inhabitants, Native and non-Native alike, take on intriguing possibilities.

'So, is he their father?' Emma LaRocque, Jeannette Armstrong, Lenore Keeshig-Tobias, Lee Maracle, Connie Fife (Cree), Marie Annharte Baker (Anishinaabe), Janice Acoose, Kateri Damm (Ojibway-Pottawotami), Suzanne Methôt (Cree), Jo-Ann Thom (Métis), Cheryl Suzack (Ojibway), Gloria Alvernaz Mulcahy (Cherokee), Patricia Monture-Angus, and

Marilyn Dumont are just some of the Native women in Canada, often also creative writers themselves, who are reviewing and critiquing, reconfiguring with fresh conclusions and questions, the literature of both Native and non-Native writers. The increasing presence and authority of Native women *readers* are the necessary correlatives to the growing number and authority of Native women *writers*. Native texts need Native readers; non-Native texts need Native readers. Native texts profit from explication by readers educated in relevant cultural references and implications, generic conventions, oral antecedents, tribal language, and social dynamics, broadly informed by a tribal ethos, attuned to the power relations of a racist society, or simply positioned, like my daughter, Elizabeth, alongside the Native characters.[12] Non-Native texts are illuminated by sometimes resisting readers who can render the texts' assumptions visible, even strange, and ask unanticipated questions of them. These Native readers and readings, though, must have critical and institutional authority within the broader culture and literary and academic worlds, the authority that has allowed me, even as a cultural outsider, to write this book.

———·———

I sit by talking grasses now
with nothing more
to make a good world of
than thought paint
and dance talk in lines,
but song colours
pour over my world
and my good time
still goes on.   (Armstrong, 'World Renewal Song' *Breath* 110)

———·———

New representations have power to reproduce themselves, to enter into the lexicon, in quite unexpected and enduring ways. When I commented sardonically on the celebratory picture of Columbus's ships that my son, Benjamin, then aged seven, had been asked to colour at his Minnesota school ('Imagine that you are an explorer!' the assignment read), he pointed out some red spots on the sails that I had overlooked. 'I put blood on it,' he explained, adding, somewhat pedantically, 'to express my anger.' Evidently he had remembered Tom's and my appreciation of the incident the previous June, during the 1992 Columbus quincentennial, in which American Indian Movement co-founder Vernon Bellecourt (Anishinaabe) had thrown his own blood on the replica of Columbus's *Santa Maria* displayed at the St Paul Science Museum. (In a typical display of 'Minnesota nice,' the curator had inquired whether Bellecourt wished to be arrested, an opportunity that Bellecourt with corresponding civility declined.) Although it was apparently sponged away at the next site on the replica's tour, the blood, with all its historic and contemporary import, remained on view throughout the St Paul exhibit. Bellecourt's intervention not only disrupted an all-too-persistent Western narrative of cultural triumphalism but, just as importantly, opened positive new sites of self-location for others importuned by the same disabling narrative.

'I am your worst nightmare: I am an Indian with a pen.' (Bell, *Faces* 192)

New readings. New writings. Taking for granted perspectives and perceptions underrepresented in North American culture, Native women, both as readers and as writers, are engaged in what Emma LaRocque calls 'reframing cultural information' ('When' 122). Widening the discursive repertoire, struggling over representations, imagining themselves, their communities, and the world creatively, as readers and as writers they are inevitably altering as well the political, social, ecological, economic, and legal realities that are so enmeshed with representations. In his discussion of the pragmatic function of ceremonial chant, the perception that language can produce change in the physical world, Craig Womack points to a similar element in contemporary Native writing, the use of 'language as invocation [rather than evocation] that will upset the balance of power' (17). '[T]he song for rain and green / and good,' Jeannette Armstrong suggests in 'World Renewal Song,' can revive a world of dying grasses (*Breath* 110). The responsibility and the potentiality are not Native women's alone, of course. For all readers and writers of the texts of Native life – both the literary and the sociopolitical texts – the challenge is to move, as Sherene Razack argues, beyond a politics of inclusion (which may leave structures of domination intact) to a politics of accountability: 'Accountability begins with tracing relations of privilege and penalty. It cannot proceed unless we examine our complicity. Only then can we ask questions about how we are understanding differences and for what purpose' (170).

'How should I eat these?' The tourist at the bannock booth in Eden Robinson's 'Queen of the North,' titillated by novelty, eager to commodify and consume, offers a cautionary model of one type of reading practice. By contrast, the reader of Native women writers in Canada has an opportunity to reframe and renew understandings, within unequal structures of power, in a spirit of pleasure, engagement, and accountability, in the interests of change.

————•·•————

There is an element of hope in the forwardness and the huge desire that Native women have to rectify, not just life for ourselves, but the colonized land and the impoverished people capitalism naturally creates. (Maracle, 'Infinite' 167–8)

> In the end, it will pick you up from the pavement
> & take you to the tribal cafe for breakfast.
>
> It will read you the menu.
> It will not pay your half of the bill.
>   (Alexie, 'Introduction to Native American Literature' *Old* 5)

Notes

Introduction

1 Philip Deloria (Lakota), in his historical analysis of the white U.S.-American fascination with 'playing Indian,' points out how knowing or reading about Indians replaces more engaged social and political interaction: 'As a result, the ways in which white Americans have used Indianness in creative self-shaping have continued to be pried apart from questions about inequality, the uneven workings of power, and the social settings in which Indians and non-Indians might actually meet' (189–90).

2 The interaction in this scene is more complicated than I may have suggested. Arnold is the only person in the story to inquire about Adelaine's pallor, result of her recent and traumatic abortion. His final request, to which Adelaine accedes, to see her hair loose, is made blushingly, with disquieted awareness (finally) that his need oversteps what he is entitled to ask. Adelaine's use of a phony name and her dismissal of Arnold, as he continues to talk – '"Goodbye, Arnold," I said, picking up the money and starting toward the cashiers' (E. Robinson, *Traplines* 209) – with its implicit restoration of their exchange to a financial transaction, however, confirm the impertinence of his overtures.

3 For a parody of white Othering, see Beverly Slapin's *The Basic Skills Caucasian Americans Workbook*, dedicated to 'all boys and girls who love white people and animals.' Its 'Note from the Publisher' mordantly illustrates the power of indirection and denial to construct a people and culture as past, singular (both odd and monolithic), and inconsequential: 'Our purpose for publishing *The Basic Skills Caucasian Americans Workbook* is to provide young readers with accurate accounts of the lives of the Caucasian American people, who, long ago, roamed our land. Caucasians are as much a

part of American life as they were one hundred years ago. Even in times past, Caucasians were not all the same. Not all of them lived in condos or drove Volvos. They were not all Yuppies. Some were hostile, but many were friendly' (np).

4 Mollie Travis discusses this problem in relation to Black writers: 'When readers fault African American writers for attempting to transcend race ... we display what Nadine Gordimer calls "the essential gesture" of criticism, which mandates that a writer living in a politically conflicted country write about the conflict, that a female writer represent the female experience, and that the culturally marginalized author write about the experience of marginality. In the essentialist mandate, white male writers from politically stable Western countries – thought of as being unmarked by gender or race – are the only ones free to construct ahistorical, apolitical, and unrepresentational narratives. This essential gesture ... reveals the white critic as a manufacturer of otherness, a curator of difference to valorize and preserve her/his own autonomous essence – a sign of the institutional necessity of race in reading and a sign that we need to read more closely this criticism which passes for cultural work' (195).

5 During his 1997 reading tour in France, Cherokee-Greek author Thomas King, in the face of persistent Othering, took to turning the tables on his interlocutors, asking them to explain the French practice of supplying *pink* toilet paper in public facilities. Foregrounding French people's own enculturated existence, the question also presumably pokes fun at reductive approaches to culture as a superficial curiosity rather than, in Chandra Mohanty's words, a 'terrain of struggle' (196). 'How should I eat these?' 'Why is your toilet paper pink?'

6 See also the discussion in *Signs* 22.2 (Winter 1997) among Susan Hekman, Nancy Hartsock, Patricia Hill Collins, Sandra Harding, and Dorothy Smith on the knowledge claims of feminist standpoint epistemology.

7 See also Terry Goldie's term 'indigenization' to describe the 'impossible necessity,' for white settlers, of becoming indigenous, sought through literary representations of Native peoples (*Fear* 13).

8 Philomena Essed rightly observes that 'the idea of tolerance is inherently problematic when applied to hierarchical group relations' and demonstrates, in her study of everyday racism experienced by Black women in California and Surinamese women in the Netherlands, '[t]he compatibility of cultural assimilationist practices and cultural pluralistic discourse' (viii, 17).

9 Dionne Brand has spoken of how, when North American media represent Blacks at all, the reassuring image chosen is often that of the gospel choir ('Jazz').

10 This demarcation of Maracle's audience is somewhat qualified by her addition, 'and those who are not offended by our private truth' (*I Am* 11).

11 Smaller Native presses such as Moonprint (Winnipeg) and Rez (Kwantlen First Nation, Langley, British Columbia), Native-focused presses such as Fifth House (Saskatoon), and presses run by women of colour, such as Williams-Wallace (Stratford, ON) and Sister Vision (Toronto), have also contributed to this change.

12 The Weesageechak Begins to Dance Festival, providing workshops for new Native playwrights and choreographers, is a separate undertaking of Native Earth.

13 The Saskatchewan Indian Federated College (University of Saskatchewan) might be another example, along with the First Nations House of Learning (University of British Columbia), First Nations House (University of Toronto), and so on, but their location within dominant-culture institutions makes their contribution somewhat different.

14 Rather than as a genteel conversation, I could have imagined Canada as a clamour of stipulations, protests, voices in the wilderness, decrees, whispers, contracts, backroom chats, chants, judicial reports, gossip, private phone lines, party lines (in both senses), shrieks, red tape, royal commissions, songs, and multilateral agreements. Intrinsic to that formulation, though, would have to be an understanding both of the quite disparate authority of the various discourses and of the systemic interrelations – economic, legal, and so on – of the forums in which they had weight. In any case, either formulation gives undue precedence to discourses over economic, political, and social organization.

15 Willie Ermine (Cree) explores features of an 'Aboriginal Epistemology,' including a holistic sense of immanence connecting all of existence, to be known by inwardness and developed through community: 'Ancestral explorers of the inner space encoded their findings in community praxis as a way of synthesizing knowledge derived from introspection' (104).

16 I am unclear about the political valence of Spears's poem, in terms of the issue of appropriation. Certainly it mocks the righteousness of its presumably white protagonist: 'she is tender to the slightest slight / in conference papers people raced to finish.' At the same time there is poignancy and rich suggestiveness, along with mockery, in the ambiguity of the final enjambment: 'She does not want to hurt any more, not to hurt / any more.' There, the object of hurt seems doubled, with the protagonist's capacity to cause hurt represented simultaneously as the cause of her own hurt. As an exposé of her excesses and personal investments and neo-exoticizing in the name of cultural sensitivity – 'She stands at the contaminated boundary /

she has raised' – does the poem ultimately extend or discredit challenges around cultural appropriation (89–90)?

17 In this regard, it is important for majority critics like myself to develop other areas of intellectual focus, so as not to become invested in the field and unprepared to 'move over' for those Native scholars who choose this as their specialty.

18 See, for example, the familiar joke in *The Crown of Columbus*, by Michael Dorris (Modoc) and Louise Erdrich (Chippewa), expressing gratitude that Columbus was looking for India and not Turkey, when he named the Indians (23). Or the lines by Chrystos (Menominee) in 'I Am Not Your Indian Princess': 'This is Indian food / only if you know that Indian is a government word / which has nothing to do with our names for our-selves' (*Not* 66). Jeannette Armstrong, on the other hand, defends the term 'Indian' as reflecting Columbus's perception of Native people as being '*in deo*, meaning in with God' ('What' [116]). (See also Russell Means, quoted in Vizenor, *Manifest* 11–12.) And Drew Hayden Taylor (Ojibway) jokes that, upon arrival in an unfamiliar town, he doesn't find himself asking the first Native person he meets for directions to the nearest 'First Nations Bar'(53).

19 Armstrong also discusses the 'commonalities' of colonization shared by the First Nations, both internally in the effects on Native traditions and exter-nally in terms of distorted assumptions or stereotypes (Isernhagen 136).

20 'Métis' refers to those who are of combined European and Indian or Inuit heritages and who associate themselves with a Métis community and culture. See *Report* 4: 199–208. Although the *Report of the Royal Commission on Aboriginal Peoples* restricts 'First Nations' to Indian people and although, in some Aboriginal communities, 'Native' and 'Métis' are mutually exclu-sive terms, I use both 'First Nations' and 'Native' more broadly for both Indian and Métis.

21 See, for example, Jeannette Armstrong: 'If I were being fully truthful, honest, I would say I'm Okanagan. I'm not Indian. I'm not Native' ('What' [116]). My designations of tribal identity in the book – for example, Anish-inaabe, Ojibway – reflect, when possible, the individuals' preferences, though not always the variations in spelling.

22 A number of the First Nations critics or writers I cite have as well Euro-pean ancestry that can be elided in abbreviated references to their tribal affiliation only. Given the effects of racism and asymmetrical race relations, First Nations people with white ancestry often identify primarily as Na-tive. Still, mixed-race heritage (for those who do not identify as Métis, as well as for those who do) introduces its own complexities and specificities. Some of those I cite, such as Louis Owens or Gerald Vizenor, emphatically identify as 'mixed-bloods' or 'cross-bloods.'

23 With Butler and Epstein, we have a concomitant phenomenon, in which the sexual orientations of uncloseted lesbian/gay/bisexual/transgendered critics figure within their writing, and, for others, a heterosexual norm is simultaneously implied and implicitly dismissed as immaterial.

24 When my nine-year-old daughter's friend insisted on using my presence to verify Elizabeth's Native identity, I concluded that the child's perplexity arose from a radical incompatibility, even at that early age, between the imaginative construct, 'Indian,' and the particular, inevitably richer enactments of that identity. In her response ('Are you Indian, Elizabeth?' 'Yes, I am; thank you for asking'), my daughter reduced a challenge, an incredulity, to a ritual politeness, disarming its assumptions.

25 See, too, the discussion of feminism from Native perspectives, by Kim Anderson (Cree-Métis) and Bonita Lawrence (Mi'kmaq), in Anderson's *A Recognition of Being* (274–7).

26 While noting failures of white feminism to address racial and cultural difference, Patricia Monture-Angus argues that 'To separate Aboriginal history from feminist history is to re-write the past. In particular, early American feminists were influenced by the political power and ownership of property maintained by the women of the Haudenosaunee. To fully reject feminism, means to reject part of my own Mohawk history and the influence of my grandmothers' (*Thunder* 231). While identifying her work as necessarily woman-centred, in *Journeying Forward*, she goes on to challenge the idea of Aboriginal feminism, suggesting that the 'reference point for feminism is the power and privilege held by white men of which I aspire to neither' (156n22).

27 Haudenosaunee or People of the Longhouse, sometimes used interchangeably with the Six Nations or Iroquois Confederacy (Monture-Angus, *Journeying* 36–7), can refer to the People of the Longhouse in a narrower and more specifically political/spiritual sense.

28 In addition, under the 1857 *Act for the Gradual Civilization of the Indian Tribes of the Canadas*, Indian wives with their children were automatically enfranchised (losing their Indian status though not acquiring the share of reserve land that usually accompanied enfranchisement), when an Indian man chose enfranchisement. From the 1869 *Gradual Enfranchisement Act* until 1951, Indian women could not vote in band elections (*Report* 4:26; 2: 275).

29 See, for example, Tobique Women's Group.

30 Organizations of Native women in Canada include the Native Women's Association of Canada (1974–), Pauktuutit (Inuit women; 1984–), and the Métis National Council of Women (1992–), as well as innumerable provincial and local organizations (*Report* 4: 68–9).

31 Other Native women taking early legal action against *Indian Act* discrimination included Mary Two Axe Early (Mohawk) and Sandra Lovelace (Maliseet). Lovelace's 1981 United Nations case led to Canada's being found in contravention of Article 27 of the *International Covenant on Civil and Political Rights* (*Report* 4: 32–3, 69).

32 As Patricia Monture-Angus points out, bills before the Canadian Parliament exist only until turned into law, so that 'Bill C-31' had only temporary existence (*Thunder* 188n31).

33 The amendment also continued the discrimination, as an Indian woman married to a non-Indian, unlike her brother in the same situation, is unable to pass on Indian status beyond her children to her grandchildren. Reinstated Indian women may also receive status without band membership or entitlement to reserve residency, housing, or other band services. For more elaboration on the history of Bill C-31, see Jamieson; Emberley 87–91; Weaver; Monture-Angus, *Thunder* 181–8 and *Journeying* 141–5; and *Report* 1: 303–7; 4: 33–53.

34 The Native Women's Association of Canada legally, and ultimately unsuccessfully, challenged its inequitable standing, by comparison with the Assembly of First Nations, the Métis National Council, the Native Council of Canada, and the Inuit Tapirisat of Canada, at the constitutional talks. For information on Native women and the constitutional process, see *Report* 4: 69–70, Weaver 129, and Monture-Angus, *Thunder* 152–68.

35 For 1999, Anderson indicates that 87 of the 633 chiefs in Canada were women (218).

36 In connection with NWAC's court challenge, Monture-Angus raises questions about the appropriateness of the legal forum and of Charter protection, and about the representativeness of the various Native organizations involved, in *Journeying* 147–52, 155–7 and *Thunder* 145–47.

37 Patricia Monture-Angus mocks the *Report of the Royal Commission on Aboriginal Peoples* for focusing primarily, in its disproportionately brief section on women, on Bill C-31 and on violence. What gender really means in her community, she insists, is that being a woman is a fundamental structure of government, that women are self-government ('Journeying').

38 For early discussion of 'woman' as fiction, see, for example, Kristeva, 'Woman' 137; Flax 627; Alcoff, 'Cultural' 420; de Lauretis, 'Upping' 267; and Butler, *Gender* 15; for identity as strategy, see Alcoff, 'Cultural' 433 and de Lauretis, 'Feminist' 9.

39 Kim Anderson, drawing also on Emma LaRocque and Bea Medicine (Lakota), explores how 'tradition' and 'culture' can be used negatively in a First Nations context to exclude and shame women (34–9).

40 Reflecting on the 'Native American Native renaissance,' especially in fiction, Craig Womack raises a related concern. Recognizing the positive contributions of this burgeoning, he asks simultaneously, 'Why haven't Native-written histories, or political analyses, for example, experienced a renaissance of the same magnitude?' (11).

41 Historically in Canada, Indian status and Canadian citizenship were incompatible, with enfranchisement (under the 1857 *Gradual Civilization Act* or the 1869 *Enfranchisement Act*, for example) entailing loss of some treaty benefits and the right to be classed as Indian. (Briefly after 1920 and again, with qualifications, from 1933 to 1951, enfranchisement could even be imposed without consent.) Residency outside Canada for more than five years (1927–51) and university education or professional standing (1867–1920) could also entail enfranchisement and lost status. The right to vote, without loss of status, was not extended to all Native people until 1960 (Dickason 251, 259, 327, 400; *Report* 1: 286–8; 4: 39).

42 For First Nations history in Canada, see Olive Dickason (Métis), *Canada's First Nations*, and Jeannette Armstrong et al., eds, *We Get Our Living like Milk from the Land*, especially chapters two ('Manifest Destiny') and seven ('Recent Legal Cases').

43 Jeanne Perreault, responding to an earlier version of chapter two in her own, thoughtful analysis of Campbell and Griffiths's text, reads as my conclusion what is rather the first of three (different) possible 'takes' or hypotheses regarding *The Book of Jessica* (15).

44 This is not to say that I set out straw figures, spurious readings to assail subsequently. Each reading has its own plausibility but may remain incomplete or somehow problematic. 'Which of your three "takes" on *The Book of Jessica* are you persuaded by?' asked a colleague. 'Each one, while I was arguing it,' I had to answer (to which her resigned 'How postmodern' was not complimentary). This is not so much the endlessly proliferated possibilities of a playful postmodernism, though, as an attempt to account for multiple effects of the texts. One colleague finds the second part of chapter four, problematizing a poststructuralist reading of Culleton, superfluous, while another considers it the heart, the essential move, of the argument.

45 *How Should I Read These? Let Me Count the Ways* was the title proposed by Greg Staats (Mohawk) as we were jokingly discussing possible postmodern directions of this book and Greg Sarris's related position as a 'pomo' Pomo critic.

46 Anishinaabe (variously spelled; plural Anishinaabeg) is today the tribal name often preferred by the Ojibway (in Canada) and Chippewa (in the United States). Slipperjack herself uses 'Ojibway.'

1: 'Reading from the Inside Out': Jeannette Armstrong's *Slash*

1 The initial version of this chapter was delivered at the Canadian Women's Studies Association, Queen's University, Kingston, Ontario, May 1991. For an earlier published version of this chapter, an article in two voices with Barbara Hodne, that interrogates some of my assumptions here, see *World Literature in English* 32.1 (Spring 1992): 66–87.

Armstrong's other works include poetry – *Breath Tracks* (1991) – and a novel, *Whispering in Shadows* (2000).

2 Barbara Findlay, addressing other whites working against racism, has come up with the term 'white flight' to describe 'the self righteous distancing from any white person we do not consider to be "as advanced" as we on the issue of racism' (13). Melanie Kaye/Kantrowitz disparagingly designates as the 'good white knight,' 'a white woman whose schtik is being the *only* white woman in a given community or institution who is fighting racism,' who attacks rather than working with other antiracist whites, and who ultimately needs racism to maintain power (30).

3 Barbara Godard has explored *Slash*'s 'open challenge to the Canadian feminist movement which has invested so heavily in representations of Native women,' discussing the novel's avoidance of the 'powerful Mother-Goddess' figure ('Politics' 206).

4 In the Hartmut Lutz interview that appeared after these classes, Armstrong noted complaints about her character development and concluded that she couldn't have created character as she had learned in creative writing courses and still have written for her people. Slash she sees as part of other things, his connections – to family, friends, community, and the outer world – more important than his presence as an individual: 'The character development of the people around him, the pieces of character that come in and out, are all part of *his* character development ...' ('Jeannette' 16).

5 One concern Armstrong *has* expressed retrospectively about her characterization in the book involves her sense that, for one unnamed, secondary character, she reproduced rather than critiquing a familiar stereotype of Nativeness (Isernhagen 158).

6 Armstrong herself discusses the absence in English of the Okanagan language, N'silxchn's 'music-based sensitivity in the creation of meaning,' its perception of reality as 'easily changeable and transformative with each speaker,' and its melding of times, places, and things ('Land' 188, 190–1).

7 In a chapter entitled 'Soft Power' in *The Native Creative Process*, Douglas Cardinal (Métis) elaborates on soft power or 'woman power, female

power' (caring and commitment as opposed to adversarial power) within the individual or group, in discussion with Armstrong (96, 100).

8 Kim Anderson looks at traditions of women's political power, indirect as well as direct, in a variety of First Nations (65–8).

9 While noting that women used their heads as men didn't, to make things run smoothly on the caravan to Ottawa, Slash adds, 'We worked together though. Nobody worried too much about role hang-ups. People just did what they were best at' (152). This echoes Armstrong's emphasis on the role of functionality rather than gender divisions in traditional Okanagan families, with manual labour, household work, thinking, and leadership shared equally across genders and allocated to those most capable ('What' 12–13).

10 Dee Horne discusses another aspect of this undertaking: Armstrong's incorporation of Okanagan ideals of gender integration (balancing masculine and feminine) as an alternative for First Nations men pulled between role and ego (*Contemporary* 98–9).

11 'More overtly imperializing project' might be a better way of phrasing this, since no approach from outside, I fear, can hope to avoid imperializing, and subtler forms of colonizing may well be more insidious.

12 *We Get Our Living like Milk from the Land*, edited by Armstrong and others, elaborates on Okanagan values, including the importance of community harmony and sharing (15).

13 Noel Elizabeth Currie analyses in some detail the alternatives and stages in Slash's ultimate arrival at an 'Indian way,' in her article 'Jeannette Armstrong and the Colonial Legacy.'

14 In *The Native Creative Process*, with Douglas Cardinal, Armstrong concludes, 'We know our lives to be the tools of the vast human dream mind which is continuing on into the future' (111).

15 The panel on 'Women in the Universities' at the May 1991 Association of Canadian University Teachers of English conference pointed to the fact that there were then no Native faculty or graduate students in Canadian English departments. Although this was based on an incomplete survey that overlooked at least one Native graduate student and possibly one or two faculty, and although a few faculty and students have since been hired or admitted, the facts are damning.

2: 'When You Admit You're a Thief': Maria Campbell and Linda Griffiths's *The Book of Jessica*

1 See, for example, Cameron, 'Operative'; Godard, 'Politics'; Keeshig-Tobias, 'Magic'; Maracle, 'Moving'; Philip 269–86; Scheier, 'Phrase'; and 'Whose Voice Is It Anyway?'

The initial version of this chapter was delivered at the Canadian Association for Commonwealth Literature and Language Studies, University of Prince Edward Island, Charlottetown, Prince Edward Island, May 1992.

Campbell's publications include her autobiographical *Halfbreed* (1973) and *Stories of the Road Allowance People* (1995).

2 National Symposium on Aboriginal Women of Canada: Past, Present and Future, University of Lethbridge, Alberta, October 1989 and Imag(in)ing Women, University of Edmonton, Alberta, April 1990.

3 Shortly after this conference, in 1992, the association expanded its name to the Association of Canadian *College and* University Teachers of English, from ACUTE to ACCUTE. Across this book, I use whichever name was in use at the time.

4 In her interview with Hartmut Lutz, Campbell concludes, less positively, about the collaboration: 'I worked with a non-Native writer, and I'll never do it again' ('Maria' 57).

5 Reviewers demonstrate a particular propensity for this costume imagery. See, for example, the comment that '[Thomas] King breaks down stereotypes about Indians as rhythmically as the drumbeat at a ceremonial gathering' (Bencivenga 13).

6 Susanna Egan points out, additionally, that 'For Campbell, this "blank receptor" is not blank at all but comes, indeed, culturally endowed with abject guilt, with loss of history, and with the limitations of a rational straitjacket' (15–16).

7 Consider Julie Cruikshank's argument, in *The Social Life of Stories*, for a parallel necessity in the work of dominant-culture academics: 'unless we put ourselves in interactive situations where we are exposed and vulnerable, where these norms are interrupted and challenged, we can never recognize the limitations of our own descriptions' (165).

8 Intriguingly, nine years later I can remember neither the incident nor the friend involved, evidence of how failures to record such moments can help produce an unconsciously edited and sanitized history of academic experience.

3: 'Listen to the Silence': Ruby Slipperjack's *Honour the Sun*

1 The initial version of this chapter was delivered at the Challenging Post-Colonial Models: Gender/Colonialism/Post-Colonialism conference,

fourth Commonwealth in Canada conference, University of Guelph, Guelph, Ontario, November 1992.

Slipperjack's other publications include the novels *Silent Words* (1992) and *Weesquachak and the Lost Ones* (2000).

2 This is a written story that I am anxious to attribute but have been unable as yet to locate again.

3 Further to the issue of naming: to refer to Owl's mother as Delia (rather than Mom), as I do throughout, in itself pulls against the ways of naming, of knowing, that the text establishes, even though her given name is provided, once, in the text.

4 Brant's conclusions are based on work particularly with the Iroquois of southern Ontario and Quebec, the Ojibway of southern Ontario, and the Swampy Cree of James Bay and Hudson Bay (534).

5 In a conversation with me at the 'Distinct Voices' symposium, Slipperjack indicated the existence of a third ending for *Silent Words* as well, in addition to the ambivalent reunion with Danny's father of the manuscript version and the published ending with its precipitous shooting. Although it struck her as the natural development of what she had been depicting and although one can see the graves all around one, she said, that ending might have seemed to condone suicide.

6 Her poetry writing, though, is apparently for her own enlightenment solely (Slipperjack, 'Ruby' 210).

7 Compare the Scollons's argument, '[O]ne does not "teach" a child or a learner. This amount of intervention in the child's autonomy would risk forever destroying the child's ability to observe and learn for his own motives. The child is encouraged only to seek out knowledge of human experience and skills by being present in the practice or their telling' (*Narrative* 101).

8 I am indebted to Barbara Hodne for this reference.

9 In her interview, Slipperjack expressed interest in how the non-Native teacher of the novel might construe it, while adverting, too, to differences between Native readers that would distinguish their readings one from another ('Ruby' 215).

10 'What are you doing?' asked my then ten-year-old daughter as I sat sideways at my desk, staring off, working on the conclusion to this book. 'Trying to think of a sentence,' I said, to her mild amusement. *Plus ça change ...*

11 When I delivered a version of this paper at Queen's University in Kingston (January 1994), a member of the audience questioned whether this meta-

phor (and judgment), like my metaphor of fissures as violence, wasn't itself a manifestation of my cultural perspective.

4: 'Nothing but the Truth': Beatrice Culleton's *In Search of April Raintree*

1 See, for example, 'understated tragedy and relentless honesty' (Norrie 63), 'a novel of documentary realism' (Sand 22), 'written in a raw, unsentimental style ... a powerful story which has been welling up inside of her for quite some time' (Sigurdson 43), 'honest, poignant account' (Turner 266), 'one of the rawest, most tragedy-laden, saddest, most violent books' (Krotz 64), 'a raw, honest portrayal of the experience, not shaped by any particular political viewpoint' (Wiebe 50–1), 'almost artlessly told' (Wilson 30), and 'a book that comes from the heart and from the guts ... full of honesty, commitment, and love' (Cameron, 'Métis' 165, 166). Margaret Clarke, in her 1986 review of the revised edition, has noted a similar tendency among reviewers: 'The book was considered the product of an unsophisticated artistic talent, an author who knows her subject matter, and often instinctively makes good stylistic choices, but who generally is unaware of the subtleties of literary technique' (136).

   The initial version of this chapter was delivered to the Modern Language Association Conference, Toronto, Ontario, December 1993.

   Since the two editions of *In Search of April Raintree*, along with the new, revised critical edition (Mosionier, *In Search of April Raintree*), Culleton has published a second novel, *In the Shadow of Evil* (2000).

2 Unless specified, references are to the original, unrevised edition, *In Search of April Raintree*.

3 Some of my students experienced the insistence on invention and the denial of literalness (in the editorial disclaimer), directly after Cheryl's urgent injunction 'Be proud of what you are' (227), as an abjuration of the story and a diminution of its impact. (To further confound questions of reality and honest response, though, I should add that these student comments emerged as part of a dramatized – playacted – debate on the literary merits of the text.)

   In noting the literary impact of apparently casual editorial decisions such as the making of room for textual apparatus, I do not want to downplay the conditions of funding and production for resource-poor small and/or Native presses, conditions that entail less- 'professional' products and complicate textual reception (for good and ill). To argue that the effects of such details are real is not to minimize the political significance of their origins.

In the revised edition, the biographical note has its own page, the sentence distinguishing Culleton's foster-home experience from April's is deleted, and the disclaimer is moved to the copyright page. The disclaimer is completely absent in the 1999 critical edition, and the biographical note is included at the end, along with those of the authors of the critical essays.

4 Ferguson is reviewing *April Raintree*, in fact, but the point holds.

5 In an article subsequent to the initial version of this chapter and independent of it, Dawn Thompson also analyses critical response to the novel, its autobiographical truth claims, the authorial signature, and the effects of revisions. She argues that, as 'a complex interchange between two cultural and semiotic systems' drawing on an oral epistemology, the novel needs to be read differently, as performance (101).

6 Complaints about Culleton's literary deficiencies and lack of subtlety pepper the reviews: 'rough carpentry' (Engel G8), 'stock characters' (Holman 11), 'caricatures' (Krotz 64), 'One cannot, in all fairness, review *April Raintree* for literary style' (Russell 192), 'blunt moralizing, black and white situations' (Ferguson 42), 'a bit of clumsiness that lacks all pretension of doing anything more than saying something that needs to be said ... nasty characters seem like "boogeymen" ... problems of quite stilted dialogue' (Morris 113), 'harsh and blunt, with little artist style' (Keeshig-Tobias 58), and 'the work of a person who has much to learn of her chosen craft' (Cameron, 'Métis' 165). (The latter five reviews, incidentally, are of the revised edition.) Clarke, by contrast, confounds the dichotomy of documentary power and stylistic skill, referring positively, for instance, to Culleton's employment of 'a typical and *useful* stereotype' (138; emphasis added).

7 See, for example, 'notions of identity are clearly at the heart of *In Search of April Raintree*' (Garrod 85). Moher's review is subtitled 'Beatrice Culleton's Disturbing Tale of a Native Search for Identity' (50). Joyce Carlson's foreword to the revised edition begins, 'The theme of *April Raintree*, simply stated, is a young woman's search for her identity' and adds, 'A strong sense of self-identity is a prerequisite to self-determination' (vii).

8 See also the letter from Maria Campbell, appended to the text: 'How many of those papers [on fostering and adopting Native children] were written by people who have lived through such an experience?' (viii). For references to the autobiographical (or 'highly autobiographical') nature of the book, see Barton 14, Ferguson 41, Grant, 'Contemporary' 128, Krotz 63, Moher 50, Morris 113, Petrone 140, Purcell 35, Sigurdson 43, and Turner 266.

9 Rape is another narrative component rooted in Culleton's own life (Garrod 90), but since it was not included in the biography appended to the text, reviewers do not allude to it in their authenticating of the text.

10 Janice Acoose would, I presume, challenge this characterization of Métis culture as simply an inheritance from two separate peoples, rather than a culture in its own right. Concerned that readers may leave the novel with 'mis-informed notions about the Métis,' she points specifically to passages on the Raintree parents as part white and part Indian ('Problem' 235).

11 A third, musical meaning of 'partial,' denoting the higher notes heard more faintly than the main note produced by an instrument, or one tone in a complex forming an ordinary tone, provides a useful trope for the narrative, with Cheryl's interpolated narrative the overtone or harmonic.

12 Speaking of the principles of his Anishinaabe (or Anishinaubae) nation, Basil Johnston illuminates an alternative both to absolutist notions of truth and to poststructuralist scepticism: 'The person abiding by the principles of addressing only those matters within his knowledge and describing as accurately as his vocabulary enabled him or her was said to have spoken as far as he or she could cast his or her knowledge by means of words ... Of such a person, people said "*w'daebawae*": "he or she speaks the truth"' ('How' 51; page 47 elaborates on this concept).

13 In the original edition, this follows from April's involuntary retching over forced urination into her mouth. In the revised edition, the retching is feigned and strategic throughout, and spares April the renewed assault by the driver, as well as securing the licence number.

14 Of her own rape, Culleton has only indicated in the public forum that she wanted to convey the brutality of rape and her recognition that the raped woman has not somehow asked for it. Writing about rape was, for her, not therapeutic but something to be endured (Garrod 90).

15 Since a younger April would have smelled 'medicine' on the assailant's breath, even this, like any 'raw' evidence, is not unmediated. The passage ironically anticipates reviewer Russell's disparagement when Culleton purportedly deviates from direct experience (193).

16 Again, Janice Acoose might challenge this formulation, arguing that, for April as Métis, Native is not the alternative to white ('Problem' 235).

17 Heather Zwicker argues that the juxtaposition of the powwow with the court hearing undermines the adequacy of Cheryl's way of being Native, given her racist context: 'The symmetry is telling: the character who will survive has to be able to mediate both ceremonies' (151).

18 Emberley would probably insist that it is specifically Indianness as difference, not Nativeness, that remains unrepresented (Cheryl is asked what being *Indian* is like) and that is finally effaced in the novel, with the sacrifice of Cheryl (Emberley 162). Though often positioned as Indian by others and sometimes conflating Indian and Métis politically and culturally,

however, Cheryl repeatedly situates herself as Métis in history and identification.

19 I am not trying here to invoke the intentional fallacy to erase the relevance of biographical context. Clearly perceptions of authorial biography are constituent elements in reader response (see, for example, the controversy around the 'authenticity' of Forrest Carter's *The Education of Little Tree*), as they are in my selection of and approach to this text, and in this chapter's original appearance in a special 'Native' issue of *Ariel*. These perceptions, however, are themselves artefacts, in a symbiotic relationship with the text, artefacts whose construction and implications themselves require investigation.

20 The 1999 publication of yet a third (critical) edition of the text, with corrections 'to improve legibility and style,' further complicates this issue (Mosionier, *In Search* 10).

21 Details of the mother's nakedness and the masturbating man disappear from an early scene, for example (*Search* 13, *April* 4). Instances of non-marital sexual activity, Cheryl's prostitution, and substantial portions of the rape remain. In the latter instance, specifics of breast, crotch, and penis disappear; 'As he prepared to actually rape me' replaces more explicit details; the anal rape becomes implicit only, with the deletion of April's being turned over; and feigned vomiting precludes the forced oral sex and urination (*Search* 141–4, *April* 112–14). Clarke has analysed the unfortunate diminution entailed in the deletion of misogynist invective and of the anal and oral assaults from this scene (Clarke 140–2). In other cases, the sanitizing seems more *pro forma*, as in the substitution of 'scumbags' for 'bastards' (*Search* 180, *April* 145). April's internalized racism is not expurgated, with the exception of one reference to 'bloodthirsty savages' – and that deletion seems to be more a matter of fine-tuning (*Search* 78, *April* 57). Other passages, though, with the potential to hurt children, such as April's shame that her clothes make her look 'worse than a Hutterite,' are deleted (*Search* 71–2, *April* 52). For a strong critique of the bowdlerizing of the revised version, see Peter Cumming.

22 In conversation with me (8 March 1994), Culleton indicated that she stood behind the revised edition, because in it she had been able to make editorial changes that she wanted.

23 Nairn Bridge is changed to Disraeli Bridge (*Search* 202, *April* 162).

24 '[C]uld' becomes 'kood,' and 'wuz' becomes 'was,' for instance (*Search* 33, *April* 21).

25 As random examples, 'I was very grateful for their acceptance' becomes 'I was grateful to be one of them'; April's detached comment on her self-pity

at the prospect of seven more years with the DeRosiers becomes the more immediate 'I wondered how I was going to ride them out'; and her gratitude for the ban on trial publicity becomes the more implicit 'I would still have my privacy' (*Search* 25, *April* 14; *Search* 53, *April* 37; *Search* 166, *April* 133).

26 Examples of such deletions include the dropping of 'I suppose the speech would have been okay if I had been guilty of any wrongdoing' and 'I knew that she had liked them [the MacAdams] a lot and that they were real nice people' (*Search* 79, *April* 58; *Search* 55, *April* 39). An exception is the addition of commentary on the paternalism greeting Cheryl at the Radcliff New Year party: 'it was the fact that they felt they had to say something accommodating, that was the most annoying' (*Search* 117, *April* 91).

27 Cheryl's 'two cents worth' about April's lifestyle becomes 'You like associating with these rich snobs?' (*Search* 117, *April* 92). The lighter tone with which April is said to ask Cheryl for help after snapping at her following the rape finds expression with the addition of 'You available?' (*Search* 149, *April* 118).

28 The exception here is the addition of his comment that Cheryl had an understanding, related to their self-images, to offer April (*Search* 205, *April* 165).

29 April is forthright about her own interest in Roger, for instance, rather than simply speculating about his implied attraction to her without the 'gumption' to inquire (*Search* 154, *April* 123). Her more successful intervention during the rape is the most salient example of such revisions.

30 Both Clarke and Cameron note evidence that Culleton has attended to matters of craft in making her revisions, Clarke examining specifically the deletions following Cheryl's oratorical address to the White Man (Clarke 136, Cameron 165).

31 I am drawing here on Homi Bhabha: 'The problem of *representing difference* as a problem of narrative can only be seen, within this kind of [traditional Nationalist] critical discourse, as the demand for *different representations*' ('Representation' 106).

32 Conversation with Agnes Grant, 14 March 1985. Jo-Ann Thom (Métis) reports a different reaction, of Native readers feeling betrayed by Cheryl's defeat, especially given her early pride in her heritage (298–9).

33 Lutz, too, describes students crying or becoming outraged while reading the novel (Culleton, 'Beatrice' 103).

34 Dee Horne elaborates on the romantic limitations of Cheryl's narratives of Native identity and history (*Contemporary* 79–82).

35 Butler is speaking specifically of gender. Though I have focused on race here, Cheryl's claim to the category 'woman,' as well as to the category 'Canadian,' implies that both have been constituted inconsistently in ways

that exclude her, at the same time as 'Métis' has functioned as a constrictive regulatory category.

36 Clarke recognizes these possibilities, analysing the novel as 'somewhere between the moral fable and the serious fairy-tale' (139).

37 One reason for Culleton's immediacy, for the simultaneous identification and aesthetic reservations she inspires in readers, is her familiar, low-key narrative voice with its reliance on exposition, sequential unfolding, and editorializing: 'That summer and the following summer, we all went to a Catholic camp at Albert Beach on Lake Winnipeg' or 'If I'd had such a grandmother when I was growing up, maybe I wouldn't have been so mixed up' (35, 175).

38 Culleton's appreciation of Margaret Laurence's skill in revealing how others think, *despite* Laurence's omission of the big climaxes or epiphanies of soap operas, suggests an inversion of the conventional aesthetic hierarchy (Garrod 95). Like Culleton's desire to exalt Cheryl so as to make her death more tragic (Garrod 95; Culleton, 'Beatrice' 102; Mosionier, 'Special' 248–9), her regard for soap operas reveals a valuing of the strong effects her critics tend to deplore.

39 Pemmican Publications estimate sales of the novel to 1992 at 80,000 copies (phone conversations with Sue MacLean, managing editor, 31 August and 1 November 1993). Since Peguis took over publication in January of 1992, sales of both editions have averaged over 6,000 copies annually, with *In Search of April Raintree* outselling *April Raintree* by a ratio of three to two (phone conversation with Annalee Greenberg, managing editor, 26 October 1993).

40 Sixteen years after the book's publication, Culleton still thinks in terms of its potential within the community: 'Unfortunately, I still know of people who might have benefited by reading this book and others like it, but didn't' (Mosionier, 'Special' 248).

41 Yet the creation of this voice was quite self-conscious. 'The style of *In Search of April Raintree* was supposed to be somewhat clumsy,' Culleton indicated in conversation with me, 8 March 1994. 'It wasn't supposed to be the style of a writer.'

5: 'And Use the Words That Were Hers': Beverly Hungry Wolf's *The Ways of My Grandmothers*

1 Hungry Wolf is from the Blood people, a division of the Blackfoot Nation. Beverly Hungry Wolf has also published *Daughters of the Buffalo Women: Maintaining the Tribal Faith* (1996). For other co-authored publications, see

discussion in the chapter and bibliographic listings under Adolf and Beverly Hungry Wolf.

2 As with any 'bicultural composite composition' (Krupat, *For Those* 31), one must watch for the hand of the white ethnographer in structuring the narrative – for the influence of the 'Chronological Imperative' (Brumble 76), for example. Cruikshank maintains that her editing employs the chronology dictated by each narrator (*Life* 18).

3 In a fashion similar to Hungry Wolf, Josie also includes, in her 'news,' abbreviated mythic or etiological tales – of why the muskrats populate Crow Flat or how birch and dry willow disputed their merits as firewood. It is these accounts that she specifies will be 'interesting news for the people all over Canada' or 'a nice news for the States and cities' (128, 132).

4 In a related discussion, Julie Cairnie analyses Maria Campbell's reconciliation, in *Halfbreed*, of the concerns of the autobiography and the *testimonio*, of the personal and the communal or social (100–5).

5 Although I am aware of the distinction between the 'self' as a coherent, unitary, ontological reality (a notion challenged by poststructuralism) and the 'subject' as culturally constructed (P. Smith xxvii, S. Smith 189, Neuman 213–15), I choose to invoke the 'self' at times here, precisely because its deployment in un-Western terms plays up the contingent nature of the concept.

6 Other passages of metanarrative are more ambivalent about her medium, noting that household traditions are best transmitted through daily contact rather than through classrooms or books.

7 I am using the self-definition of Ignatia Broker (Ojibway): 'I am a link in a chain to the past' (3).

8 Of course, as poststructuralists point out, we are all interpellated into extant discourses rather than self-generated. Writing such as Hungry Wolf's simply reverses foreground and background, abandoning the Western autobiography's obsession with the differentness whereby the individual distinguishes himself (the model is male) from his cultural matrix.

9 An earlier use of this Edward Curtis photograph in Adolf Hungry Wolf's *The Blood People* does not include this personal connection when identifying the subject of the photograph (117).

10 Timothy Findley, incidentally, in *Not Wanted on the Voyage*, provides caustic commentary on the strategic limitation of focusing on *voices*, on widening the range of perspectives represented, in the absence of systemic shifts in power. The patriarchal Noah willingly deigns to hear the supplications of the ewes for the lives of their lambs: 'Though, of course, there was never

any chance of the lambs being spared, it had still been interesting to hear the cases put by the sheep, some of them very eloquent. Sincere' (47–8).

11 Brumble speaks of Adolf Hungry Wolf's 'characteristic emphasis on the homely and the sacred' (200), a description applicable in general terms to Beverly Hungry Wolf as well, with the significant proviso that for the latter the sacred is more integrally part of the homely.

12 *Children of the Sun* contains Hungry Wolf's description of being estranged from her culture when it was derided at boarding school (167–70); she also comments that, 'Until boarding-school influence distracted her from it, she thought that every important thing in life was explained in the stories these elders told' (*Children* 181).

13 Ironically, the name 'Hungry Wolf,' given to Adolf 'by an earlier Indian friend' from another Nation and eagerly adopted in place of Gutöhrlein, translates infelicitously into Blackfoot, suggesting something closer to randy wolf (Hungry Wolf and Hungry Wolf, *Shadows* 65, 73).

14 *Shadows of the Buffalo* (with its skewed subtitle, *A Family Odyssey among the Indians*) purports to be a collaboration between Adolf and Beverly but, after ten pages from Beverly's perspective in the introduction, Adolf takes over the narrative, ostensibly for simplicity's sake. The limited degree of narrative mutuality can be deduced from speculative passages such as this: '*Beverly may have known* things would not go so smoothly, but she said nothing to dampen my enthusiasm' (135, emphasis added). Here, in 'A 1950s Child of the Sun' from *Children of the Sun*, and in *Daughters of the Buffalo Women*, Beverly provides a more extended personal history than in *The Ways of My Grandmothers*, although her emphasis still falls on shared experience (*Shadows* 8–17; *Children* 148–50, 167–75; *Daughters* throughout).

15 For an emphatic contrast with Adolf's attitude, see the novel *Keeper 'n Me* by Richard Wagamese (Ojibway): 'Us we see power in everythin' except ourselves. Them trees an' rocks an' things are all blessed with power comin' in. Us we gotta look for it. So we go to the land an' see where the real power is' (182).

16 The seven are *Good Medicine in Glacier National Park, Good Medicine: Traditional Dress Issue, Blackfoot People, Indian Summer, Teachings of Nature, Blackfoot Craftworker Book,* and *The Blood People.* Passages from *Blackfoot Craftworker Book*, in particular, resurface in *The Ways of My Grandmothers.* They are often repeated verbatim. The few changes that have been made are of a personal nature: the addition of Hungry Wolf's own experiences with a craft, the incorporation of a comment by her mother, the alteration of the general to the specific ('Blackfoot traditions' becoming 'my grandmothers'), and the replacement of passive constructions with a first-person voice (compare, for example, *Blackfoot Craftworker* 6–7, 79, 42–3 with *Ways*

220–7, 240–2, 227–31). Pictures from other Hungry Wolf books are also cropped, both literally and figuratively, to highlight the female experience of tribal life (see *Blood People* 312 and *Ways* 101, for a literal instance).

17 Some stories, such as the account of Mrs Rides-at-the-Door's being offended by a museum display of a Natoas bundle, appear repeatedly (*Indian Summer* 102, *Ways* 46, *Shadows* 160). Standard copyright warnings do appear in those works published by established presses, though, and even the Good Medicine Books contain cautions such as this, from the copyright page of *Blackfoot People*: 'All Rights Reserved. No part of this book may be reproduced in Any Way except Actual Life.'

18 Arnold Krupat cites the instance of Yellow Wolf (Nez Perce), accompanied by band members to witness or correct his coup stories, as a Native model for the move away from 'monologic presentation and univocal authority' and towards the 'collectivization of autobiography' (*For Those* 120–1).

19 The complexity of Hungry Wolf's positioning is compounded by the influence of a patriarchal Euro-American husband who presumes to attribute female docility to her culture, despite Hungry Wolf's inclusion here of a mythic narrative giving the power of final decision to women, her accounts of Blood women determined to take on warrior roles against all opposition, and the voices of indomitable, living female elders (for Adolf's views, see Hungry Wolf and Hungry Wolf, *Shadows* 28, 116). In *Daughters of the Buffalo Women*, Beverly does describe Blackfoot society as 'traditionally very male-dominated' (85).

20 I am instructed by Kate Shanley's caution against importing ideological terms like 'transvestite' from outside the culture ('Crossing the Genres' discussion period, Modern Language Association, Toronto, 30 December 1993). Hungry Wolf does, however, seem situated within early feminist discourse.

21 This argument needs to be qualified by an awareness that Adolf pressured Beverly to adopt 'the strict old ways' more quickly than she felt comfortable with and urged long skirts and dresses upon her (Hungry Wolf and Hungry Wolf, *Shadows* 256, 116).

6: 'Because You Aren't Indian': Lee Maracle's *Ravensong*

1 The initial version of this chapter was delivered to the Association of Canadian College and University Teachers of English, Université de Québec à Montréal, Montreal, Quebec, June 1995.

Maracle's other works include her autobiographical *Bobbi Lee: Indian Rebel* (1975), non-fiction *I Am Woman* (1988), short-story collection

Sojourner's Truth and Other Stories (1990), novel *Sundogs* (1992), and poetry collection *Bent Box* (2000).

2 Maracle, whose mother is Métis and who has increasingly stressed her connections with her father's Sto:lo or Coast Salish culture, herself embodies the multiplicity of identities that the novel addresses.

3 In some ways Maracle's *Sundogs*, with its attention to pan-Indian solidarity and sovereignty struggles with the Canadian government, might seem the more obvious text through which to explore these questions. I would argue, though, that the internal focus of *Ravensong*'s look at the functioning of a people represents more fully Maracle's sense of Native sovereignty.

4 Reading about nationalism, I have just discovered that my propensity to identify as Irish, four and five generations after emigration, may be in part '"census artifact" ethnicity,' produced by ethnic groups' success in having the Canadian census, until lately, list not language ('English') or ethnic self-identification ('Canadian') but patrilineal ethnic origin (Hobsbawm 161). Other factors – my father's upbringing in a spot of southern Ontario so homogeneous it knew itself as 'little Ireland' and the school and church festivities revolving around 17 March in our Sudbury parish of St Patrick's – played their part, too.

5 Dee Horne catalogues the deficiencies of settler society that Stacey articulates in her process of cultural differentiation (*Contemporary* 118–19).

6 Not to be confused with Métis-Cree writer Maria Campbell.

7 Reviewer Maggie Dwyer also includes 'broadbrush statements about white society' among the weaknesses of the novel (D18).

8 What sense of male entitlement, I had to ask myself, led me to associate this deprivation primarily with my grandfather and not my grandmother, who, after all, had been born (and died) on the very farm they together never owned? And then, of course, how could I think of *their* entitlement or dispossession when it was their immediate forebears who were able to purchase, for three dollars an acre, two-hundred-acre parcels of what was probably 'Crown land,' the land from which Ongwehónwe and Anishinaabe tribes had been displaced.

9 When I was six and standing on the steps of St Patrick's church in Sudbury, Ontario, a fellow parishioner said to my mother, 'You can see the Irish in her.' I had always been warmed by that comment, while believing profoundly, then and since, in its utter mistakenness.

10 Even more than the shifts to focalizations other than Stacey's (Raven's, Cedar's, Celia's), these apparently free-floating interventions underscore the text's multiplication of layers of time and perspective.

11 In a 23 November 1993 address, 'Native Women and Sovereignty,' at the University of Toronto, Maracle defined herself politically as a radical-sovereignty advocate, more interested in working within Native communities to reapply fundamental First Nations laws from the past than in negotiating with Ottawa. Just as the village represents in microcosm a larger tribal or Native entity, so its governing structures model the political strategies Maracle advocates. The Speaker, elders, and community members focus on issues central to the strength and survival of the community, leaving to the chief the less important interactions with outside authorities (*Ravensong* 156). Kim Anderson notes how the organization of the Barrie Native Friendship Centre in Ontario, where Maracle works, reflects Maracle's description of a traditional economic system, with its balanced gender responsibilities. Maracle works as internal-affairs director along with a female finance director, while the male external-affairs director handles relations with government, funding bodies, and outside groups (216).

12 Pratt defines a contact zone as 'the space of colonial encounters, the space in which peoples geographically and historically separated come into contact with each other and establish ongoing relations, usually involving conditions of coercion, radical inequality, and intractable conflict' (6).

13 One further tension in the text arises structurally from the ideological discrepancy between its temporal setting primarily in the fifties and its retrospective contemporary frame. The more radical and hopeful spirit of the present is superimposed on the internalized oppression of the past, creating a logical contradiction between current political imperatives of cross-cultural transformation – 'it must be done' – and the political realities of the period – 'it can't be done.' This may account for some of the apparent anticlimax of the ending.

14 Susan Berry Brill de Ramírez argues that, as with her school principal and even Raven, Stacey's reaction to Steve displays understandable, but unfortunate, oppositional and objectifying rather than connective and intersubjective tendencies (185).

15 *Ravensong* is situated so firmly within the culture that the village's tribal identity as Salish need only be noted once and belatedly: 'He had acquired the unalterable Salish male practice ...' (108).

16 Glaspell's play *Trifles*, produced in 1916, was adapted as a short story in 1917. It is the latter version I will be discussing because its exposition makes it somewhat fuller for my purposes.

17 In a related vein, Jodi Lundgren discusses the solidarity with other people of colour, produced by shared exposure to racism, in writing by Maracle and other Métis writers (66–7).

18 When I presented a shorter version of this chapter to the Association of Canadian College and University Teachers of English in Montreal in 1995, I made a slip of the tongue that exposed some of the anxieties at least of my experience of the novel: I delivered the white characters 'across the bridge into the *river*.'

19 Maracle herself is making something of a leap across temporal and cultural divides in conjuring up the world of a people separate in time from and less transculturated than her own.

20 The question of whether to designate the United States as 'here' or 'there' in this sentence was intensified by my literal boundary crossings, writing the sentence in Montreal for presentation to fellow Canadians, revising it in St Paul shortly before my move back to Canada. But it reflects a larger perceptual instability during my sojourn in the United States. I would find myself wondering why the authorities had to transport a suspect in the Oklahoma bombing back from Europe *through* the United States (assuming somehow that 'here' was Canada and the crisis a Canadian one) or noting approvingly the strong Canadian content of *This Magazine* (assuming that the periodical I was reading must be American).

21 'We believe the proof of a thing or idea is in the doing. Doing requires some form of social interaction and thus, *story* is the most persuasive and sensible way to present the accumulated thoughts and values of a people' (*Oratory* 3).

7: 'How Should I Eat These?': Eden Robinson's *Traplines*

1 This 'Artist's Disclaimer' by Jimmy Durham, mixed-blood Cherokee sculptor, was provoked specifically by the 1990 Indian Arts and Crafts Act (Public Law 101–644) in the United States, which prohibits the display or sale of 'Indian arts and crafts' by anyone not federally recognized as Native American (Churchill 91–2,106–7).

2 The initial version of this chapter was delivered at the Association of Canadian College and University Teachers of English, Memorial University, St John's, Newfoundland, June 1997.

   Robinson's other publications include a novel, *Monkey Beach* (2000).

3 The choice of subject matter may not be entirely at the disposition of the author, as in HarperCollins's selection of only the stories with Native subject matter, from a longer repertoire of short stories, for inclusion in Thomas King's collection *One Good Story, That One*. Robinson has indicated, in conversation with me (16 October 1996), that Knopf editors found 'Terminal Avenue' anomalous, as well as rather short, and urged its replacement.

4 One possible exception is the revelation by Tom's friend, Mike, now living with relatives, that Mike's mother used to put him in the bathtub every night and pour Lysol over him. Such scenes have become *topoi* in autobiographies and fictions by writers of colour, recounting poignant childhood moments of racism turned against the self, of abrasives, cleansers, caustics, and bleaches painfully employed to repudiate a racialized identity, at the literal level of the skin itself.

5 'The middle two stories ... have nothing to do with Indians,' claims Philip Marchand unequivocally, for example ('Steely' G20). 'Robinson ... makes few direct references to any character being Indian – an interesting insistence on the universality of such pain and trouble,' opines Judith Timson (68). 'The characters might be native but the stories aren't necessarily "native" stories,' concludes Derrick Penner (8). Apart from a careless *Echoes Magazine* review, which sets all four stories 'on a Haisla reservation in British Columbia' (in fact, 'Contact Sports' is set in Vancouver, 'Dogs in Winter' in Bended River, Manitoba, in Banff, in Masset, British Columbia, in Vancouver ...), Lynne Van Luven, Millie Knapp, Steve Roe, and Charles Mandel are notable for reading the characters as Native. On a 16 May 1997 CBC *Morningside* radio panel on Canadian literature, Van Luven described the collection as a 'commentary on urban life, and it's really urban Native life but Eden Robinson doesn't bother telling us that.' Speaking equally of Robinson's *Traplines* and her then-forthcoming *Monkey Beach* (which does focus explicitly on Haisla characters), Knapp concludes that 'Her books have identifiable Native elements and her characters are Native people who deal with the immediacy of a situation: death, abuse, hunger' (42). Roe describes *Traplines* as composed of 'four stories that depict aboriginal teenagers struggling with the bleak and often horrific realities of their lives' and, regarding 'Traplines,' refers to 'the social and familial disintegration of reserve life' (192, 193). Mandel similarly places the marten trapping of 'Traplines' 'on the reserve' and reads the collection generally as Robinson's probing of 'the gritty unpleasant aspects of her culture' (C4).

6 In the *Edmonton Journal*, Charles Mandel reaches a similar conclusion: 'The story is meant to mimic the history of encounters between aboriginals and Europeans ... The individuals' mirroring of the cultures is horrifying. Jeremy moves from cajoling, to offering money, to brute force to control Tom' (C4). And Dee Horne suggests that 'Readers may well see a correlation between Jeremy's paternalistic practices and the wardship practices of settlers toward First Nations' (Rev. 161).

7 The typescript submitted to the publishers lacks the published references to Jeremy's military past and rumoured homicide (ts. 102, 107, 178; *Traplines* 77, 83, 147). Robinson reports that, at one point (I presume be-

tween the submitted typescript and the page proofs), she built in longer scenes of Jeremy's history in the military, which editors found too overt, and which she, too, now repudiates.

8 This may reflect the particularities of the Northwest Coast Native economy, where reliance on fisheries, for example, was less immediately subject to the disruptions of European settlement than Plains Indians' hunting or Woodland settlements.

9 The pass system of travel restrictions and permits was applied more to Native tribes on the prairies than to those in British Columbia, but the story's application can be read somewhat broadly.

10 Compare the *Indian Act*, which, as Ron Marken notes, 'proscribed all appearances in "Indian costume," unless countenanced by white society at displays such as parades, rodeos, and fairs, where costumed Natives could be seen as curiosities ...' (165).

11 The apology takes on retroactive irony in light of the 1998 federal Liberal government apology to First Nations for historic wrongs, in the wake of the 1996 *Report of the Royal Commission on Aboriginal Peoples*.

12 'Then I had to find an ending,' Robinson indicated wryly in the Rogers interview. 'I'm thinking a really happy ending, because all the other endings weren't that happy.'

13 As Michigan State football coach Duffy Daugherty declared, 'People call football a contact sport. That's not true. Dancing is a contact sport. Football is a collision sport.'

14 '[P]referably from a horse culture' is the ironic, recurrent phrase running through Sherman Alexie's poem on literary signs of Nativeness, 'How to Write the Great American Indian Novel,' *Summer* 94–5.

15 The 'great *white* mother'? Racial signifiers in 'Dogs in Winter' are ambiguous. Mama's face is 'smooth and pale,' her eyes brown, her 'dark blond hair ... highlighted by streaks that shone in the sunlight,' although in an earlier flashback to her in jail, 'gray streaks showed through the brown' of her hair (53, 45). Alluding to her own lurid heritage from her mother, Lisa imagines Death's handmaiden (her mother/self) as having pale, pale skin and light brown hair with blond streaks. I am perturbed, though, to find myself combing the text for such details, as though racial identity could be reduced to simple measures such as skin colour or genetics. (The presence of my fair-skinned, medium-brown-haired Cherokee-Irish son reminds me, too, that even such external features are not so easily interpreted.)

16 I read Lisa's passion for a Dali-esque painting of a moose giving birth to a human child as a repudiation of the maternal (or allegorically, colonial) connection, Mama represented instead by the minatory woman in the blue

dress holding a drawn bow, projected or discerned ('[i]f you squint your eyes') in the painting's background (59).

17 These readings did not necessarily appear out of the blue but were occasioned, sometimes unexpectedly for me, by the text's location within a course entitled 'Women in Literature,' as I discuss later.

18 Like the earlier postcolonial reading, this gender analysis risks being reductive, constricting the significance of femaleness to a few well-worn figures.

19 The logic of this assumption moves beyond the familiar faulty syllogism, 'If you are Native, then you are alcoholic,' to reveal the even more shockingly sweeping formulation, 'If and only if you are Native, then you are alcoholic.'

20 Robinson's subsequent novel, *Monkey Beach*, includes reference to a predatory legendary ogress T'sonoqua, and a b'gwus or sasquatch mask is similarly used to chase the children (337, 9). Furtive, vengeful, carnivorous 'things' in the trees, who importune the heroine, figure there in psychologically and spiritually suggestive ways.

21 The title *Traplines*, denoting a series of physically separate traps linked socially and conceptually by the supervision and entitlement of an individual or family, supports this idea.

22 One could also argue that the wilful viciousness and gratuitous brutality of the central 'non-Native' stories are placed at the core of the book literally and at the core of the society more generally. Through the collection's structure, then, they are shown leaking into the surrounding stories and Nations. But I am trying here to find alternative readings to the allegorizing of colonization explored above.

23 Robinson is also variously labelled, in reviews, as a young or Generation X or first-time or urban or Vancouver-based or British Columbian or Canadian or female writer. The impulse to view the stories as definitive of a collective identity extends beyond Robinson's Native significance: the U.S.-American reviewer in the *New York Times* credits *Traplines* with dispelling 'the myth that our northern neighbors are any kinder, gentler or saner than we are.' The review itself is entitled 'Canadian Psychos' (Marcus 21).

24 The journal *Aboriginal Voices* plays with this incongruity through a photo of Robinson in colour against a wall of black-and-white photographs of other writers, half of her face grinning out from behind an enlargement of her soulful, shadowed jacket photograph (Knapp 42).

25 As young feminists, we used this insight to good effect in – strategically (I hope) – mobilizing (and so wrenching open) a prescribed gender identity. To the rebuke 'That's not a girl's colour/outfit/ behaviour/posture/job/

talk,' we replied, 'I'm a girl, and I'm wearing/doing/saying it, so it must be a girl's.'

26 I share Marchand's sense that the motivations and needs Robinson creates here are complex; along with all that is obnoxious and insistent and objectifying about Arnold's approaches, wistfulness tinges especially his request to see Adelaine's hair down. For me, however, the complexity intensifies rather than mitigates the problem with Arnold's treating Adelaine as a curiosity.

27 'It is that Third Space, though unrepresentable in itself, which constitutes the discursive conditions of enunciation that ensure that the meaning and symbols of culture have no primordial unity or fixity; that even the same signs can be appropriated, translated, rehistoricized and read anew.' (Bhabha, *Location* 37)

28 Note that, at least in the heterosexual context of the song, Robinson's grandmother anticipates her granddaughter in appropriating a gender as well as a racial location other than the one assigned to her.

In/conclusion

1 Janice Acoose reads this more negatively, expressing concern that 'With its protagonists seduced by popular terms like "Native" and "Halfbreed," and confused by colloquial metaphors such as "mixed-blood" and "part-Indian," the text does not successfully illustrate the Métis cultural identity' ('Problem' 228).

2 'Queen of the North,' with its explicitly Haisla characters and indictment of Native residential schooling, is also the story most loaded with the icons and brand names of mainstream culture: Midol, Bruce Lee, Ichiban, World Wrestling Federation, Visine, Garfield, Elvis, Mr Rogers, Lysol, Abba, Kmart, *Star Trek*, Kraft, Tweety Bird, Extra-Strength Tylenol, Mr Bubble, Jolt Cola, and Ziploc, among others. Uncle Jock's seiner is juxtaposed ironically with a Barbie Doll speedboat.

3 See Thomas King's gloss on the phrase 'all my relations': 'the relationships that Native people see go further, the web of kinship extending to the animals, to the birds, to the fish, to the plants, to all the animate and inanimate forms that can be seen or imagined. More than that, "all my relations" is an encouragement for us to accept the responsibilities we have within this universal family by living our lives in a harmonious and moral manner (a common admonishment is to say of someone that they act as if they have no relations)' (Introduction, *All* ix).

4 Jennifer Andrews identifies various theoretical feminist directions within

and between the playscript *Jessica* and *The Book of Jessica* (299–300). Maureen Slattery argues, about Campbell's writing, that 'While *Half-Breed* [sic] decolonizes her native female legacy, *The Book of Jessica* decolonizes her white female heritage' (140).

5 Renate Eigenbrod connects the narrative's capacity to place the reader in the place of the character, through the absence of analysis, with the ability, in Native spirituality, 'to change oneself into something else,' founded in the 'inherent equality of all life forms' (95, 97).

6 Renée Hulan notes that the ability to produce feelings in readers is one of three criteria for literary value formulated by her Native students ('Some' 223). I wonder, though, whether Hulan may not be overstating, as I tend to do, the divide between Native and non-Native. The aesthetic criteria devised by the students – the other two being to be understood by readers and to teach – are ones I would anticipate from non-Native undergraduates as well.

7 With Native oratory, says Armstrong, 'you're trying to draw on symbols, metaphors, and images to help the understanding of your presentation of internal philosophy' ('Jeannette' 20). Although her use of 'oratory' places it between poetry and prose as a separate genre ('What' 20–1), her comments have something in common with Maracle's.

8 Dee Horne suggests that, in 'Queen of the North,' Robinson less characteristically demonstrates the breaking of the cycle of abuse (Rev. 161).

9 In the cases of Armstrong and to a lesser extent Robinson, my focus on the Native provenance of the texts has ironically produced some neglect of their theoretical substance, so that the specific details of the authors' implicit (or, in Armstrong's case, explicit) analysis remain to be explored more fully.

10 *Little House in Brookfield* was written by Maria D. Wilkes, long after Laura Ingalls Wilder's death.

11 See, for example, Berkhofer; P. Deloria; D. Francis; Goldie, *Fear*; LaRocque, *Defeathering*; Monkman; and Stedman.

12 I don't believe that other non-Native academics or I have nothing useful to say about Native writing. Rather, the difficulty is that these partial readings have the power to establish themselves as authoritative, confirmed and supplemented by other scholars with precisely the same limitations and assumptions. And, as Jeannette Armstrong points out about non-Native creative writers representing Native culture, 'every time a space is taken up in the publishing world and the reading community, it means that a Native person isn't being heard and that has great impact' ('What' 22).

Works Cited

Acoose, Janice/Misko-Kìsikàwihkwè (Red Sky Woman). *Iskwewak – Kah' Ki Yaw Ni Wahkomakanak: Neither Indian Princesses nor Easy Squaws*. Toronto: Women's, 1995.

– 'The Problem of "Searching" for April Raintree.' Mosionier 227–36.

Ahmad, Aijaz. 'Jameson's Rhetoric of Otherness and the "National Allegory."' *Social Text* 17 (Fall 1987): 3–25.

Alarcón, Norma. 'The Theoretical Subject(s) of *This Bridge Called My Back* and Anglo-American Feminism.' Anzaldúa, *Making* 356–69.

Alcoff, Linda. 'Cultural Feminism versus Post-Structuralism: The Identity Crisis in Feminist Theory.' *Signs* 13.3 (1988): 405–36.

– 'The Problem of Speaking for Others.' *Cultural Critique* 20 (Winter 1991–2): 5–32.

Alexie, Sherman. *The Business of Fancydancing: Stories and Poems*. Brooklyn, NY: Hanging Loose, 1992.

– *First Indian on the Moon*. Brooklyn, NY: Hanging Loose, 1993.

– *Indian Killer*. New York: Atlantic, 1996.

– *Old Shirts and New Skins*. Los Angeles: American Indian Studies Center, U of California, Los Angeles, 1993.

– *The Summer of the Black Widows*. Brooklyn, NY: Hanging Loose, 1996.

Allen, Paula Gunn. 'Paula Gunn Allen.' Coltelli 11–39.

– *The Sacred Hoop: Recovering the Feminine in American Indian Traditions*. Boston: Beacon, 1986.

–, ed. *Studies in American Indian Literature: Critical Essays and Course Designs*. New York: MLA, 1983.

Almon, Bert. 'Stories from the Okanagan Perspective.' Rev. of *Neekna and Chemai*, by Jeannette C. Armstrong. *Canadian Children's Literature* 73 (Spring 1994): 82–3.

Althusser, Louis. 'From *Capital* to Marx's Philosophy.' *Reading* Capital. By Louis Althusser and Etienne Balibar. 1968. Trans. Ben Brewster. London: New Left, 1970. 11–70.

Anderson, Benedict. *Imagined Communities: Reflections on the Origin and Spread of Nationalism*. 1983. Rev. ed. London: Verso, 1991.

Anderson, Kim. *A Recognition of Being: Reconstructing Native Womanhood*. Women's Issues Publishing Program. Toronto: Second Story, 2000.

Andrews, Jennifer. 'Framing *The Book of Jessica*: Transformation and the Collaborative Process in Canadian Theatre.' *English Studies in Canada* 22.3 (Sept. 1996): 297–313.

Anzaldúa, Gloria. Foreword to the Second Edition. Moraga and Anzaldúa [iv–v].

–, ed. *Making Face, Making Soul / Haciendo Caras: Creative and Critical Perspectives by Women of Color*. San Francisco: aunt lute, 1990.

Armstrong, Jeannette. *Breath Tracks*. Stratford, ON: Williams-Wallace/Theytus, 1991.

– 'Cultural Robbery: Imperialism. Voices of Native Women.' *Trivia* 14 (1988): 21–3.

– 'Jeannette Armstrong.' Lutz, *Contemporary* 13–32.

– 'Land Speaking.' Ortiz 174–94.

–, ed. *Looking at the Words of Our People: First Nations Analysis of Literature*. Penticton, BC: Theytus, 1993.

– *Neekna and Chemai*. Illus. Barbara Marchand. Kou-Skelowh / We Are the People Ser. Penticton, BC: Theytus, 1984.

– 'Panel One: Audience Discussion.' Telling It Book Collective 43–52.

– 'Rights on Paper.' *Fuse* 11 (Mar.-Apr. 1988): 36–8.

– *Slash*. Penticton, BC: Theytus, 1985.

– 'What I Intended Was to Connect ... and It's Happened.' Williamson 7–26.

– *Whispering in Shadows*. Penticton, BC: Theytus, 2000.

– 'Words.' Telling It Book Collective 23–9.

– 'Writing from a Native Woman's Perspective.' *In the feminine: women and words / Les femmes et les mots: Conference Proceedings 1983*. Ed. Ann Dybikowski et al. Edmonton: Longspoon, 1985. 55–7.

Armstrong, Jeannette C., Delphine Derickson, Lee Maracle, and Greg Young-Ing, eds. *We Get Our Living like Milk from the Land*. Researched and comp. by the Okanagan Rights Committee and the Okanagan Indian Education Resource Society. [Penticton, BC]: Theytus, 1993.

Ashcroft, W.D. 'The Function of Criticism in a Pluralist World.' *New Literature Review* 3 (1978): 3–14.

Atwood, Margaret. *Selected Poems: 1966–1984*. Toronto: Oxford UP, 1990.

Baker, Houston A., Jr. 'Caliban's Triple Play.' Gates, 'Race' 381–95.

Bannerji, Himani, ed. *Returning the Gaze: Essays on Racism, Feminism and Politics*. Toronto: Sister Vision, 1993.

– *Thinking Through: Essays on Feminism, Marxism, and Anti-Racism*. Toronto: Women's, 1995.

Bar On, Bat-Ami. 'Marginality and Epistemic Privilege.' *Feminist Epistemologies*. Ed. Linda Alcoff and Liz Potter. New York: Routledge, 1993. 83–100.

Barton, Marie. 'Write the Wrong.' Rev. of *In Search of April Raintree*, by Beatrice Culleton. *Canadian Author and Bookman* 61.1 (Fall 1985): 14.

Bataille, Gretchen M., and Kathleen Mullen Sands. *American Indian Women: Telling Their Lives*. Lincoln: U of Nebraska P, 1984.

Baym, Nina. *Novels, Readers, and Reviewers*. Ithaca, NY: Cornell UP, 1984.

Bell, Betty Louise. 'American Indian Literature' panel, St Malo Book Fair, France, 19 May 1997.

– *Faces in the Moon*. Norman: U of Oklahoma P, 1994.

Bencivenga, Jim. 'Searching for Home in High-Plains Canada.' Rev. of *Medicine River*, by Thomas King. *Christian Science Monitor* 3 Oct. 1990: 13.

Berkhofer, Robert F. *The Whiteman's Indian: Images of the American Indian from Columbus to the Present*. New York: Vintage, 1979.

Bessai, Diane. 'Collective Theatre and the Playwright: *Jessica*, by Linda Griffiths and Maria Campbell.' *Writing Saskatchewan: 20 Critical Essays*. Ed. Kenneth G. Probert. Regina, SK: CPRC, 1989. 100–10.

Bhabha, Homi K. 'DissemiNation: Time, Narrative, and the Margins of the Modern Nation.' *Nation and Narration*. Ed. Homi K. Bhabha. London: Routledge, 1990. 291–322.

– *The Location of Culture*. London: Routledge, 1994.

– 'The Other Question: Difference, Discrimination and the Discourse of Colonialism.' *Out There: Marginalization and Contemporary Cultures*. Ed. Russell Ferguson et al. New York: New Museum of Contemporary Art, 1990. 71–87.

– 'Representation and the Colonial Text: A Critical Exploration of Some Forms of Mimeticism.' *The Theory of Reading*. Ed. Frank Gloversmith. Brighton: Harvester, 1984. 93–122.

Blaeser, Kimberley. 'Native Literature: Seeking a Critical Center.' Armstrong, *Looking* 51–62.

Brand, Dionne. *Bread out of Stone: Recollections, Sex, Recognitions, Race, Dreaming, Politics*. Toronto: Coach House, 1994.

– 'Interview by Dagmar Novak.' *Other Solitudes: Canadian Multicultural Fictions*. Ed. Linda Hutcheon and Marion Richmond. Toronto: Oxford UP, 1990. 271–7.

– 'Jazz Ritual and Resistance: The Cultural Politics of Drumming,' Guelph Jazz Festival, Guelph, ON, 6 Sept. 1998.

Brant, Clare C. 'Native Ethics and Rules of Behaviour.' *Canadian Journal of Psychiatry* 35 (Aug. 1990): 534–9.

Brill de Ramírez, Susan Berry. *Contemporary American Indian Literatures and the Oral Tradition*. Tucson: U of Arizona P, 1999.

Brodzki, Bella, and Celeste Schenck, eds. *Life/Lines: Theorizing Women's Autobiography*. Ithaca, NY: Cornell UP, 1988.

Broker, Ignatia. *Night Flying Woman: An Ojibway Narrative*. St Paul: Minnesota Historical Society P, 1983.

Brumble, H. David, III. *American Indian Autobiography*. Berkeley: U of California P, 1988.

Butler, Judith. *Gender Trouble: Feminism and the Subversion of Identity*. New York: Routledge, 1990.

– 'Imitation and Gender Insubordination.' *Inside/Out: Lesbian Theories, Gay Theories*. Ed. Diana Fuss. New York: Routledge, 1991. 13–31.

Cahill, Linda, with Peter Giffen. 'Adolescent Fiction Comes of Age.' *Maclean's* 21 Apr. 1986: 62–4.

Cairnie, Julie. 'Writing and Telling Hybridity: Autobiographical and Testimonial Narratives in Maria Campbell's *Halfbreed*.' *World Literature Written in English* 34.2 (1995): 94–108.

Cameron, Anne. 'Métis Heart.' Rev. of *April Raintree* and *Spirit of the White Bison*, by Beatrice Culleton. *Canadian Literature* 108 (Spring 1986): 164–6.

– 'The Operative Principle Is Trust.' Scheier, Sheard, and Wachtel 63–71.

Campbell, Maria. *Halfbreed*. Toronto: McClelland, 1973.

– 'Maria Campbell.' Lutz, *Contemporary* 41–65.

– *Stories of the Road Allowance People*. Penticton, BC: Theytus, 1995.

Campbell, Maria, and Linda Griffiths. *The Book of Jessica: A Theatrical Transformation*. Toronto: Coach House, 1989.

Campbell, Marie. 'In Short.' Rev. of *Ravensong*, by Lee Maracle. *Quill and Quire* 59 (July 1993): 46.

Carby, Hazel. 'The Multicultural Wars.' *Radical History Review* 54 (1992): 7–18.

– 'The Politics of Difference.' *Ms.* 1.2 (Sept.-Oct. 1990): 84–5.

Cardinal, Douglas, and Jeannette Armstrong. *The Native Creative Process*. Penticton, BC: Theytus, 1991.

Carr, Helen. 'In Other Words: Native American Women's Autobiography.' Brodzki and Schenck 131–53.

Chicago Cultural Studies Group. 'Critical Multiculturalism.' *Critical Inquiry* 18 (Spring 1992): 530–55.

Chona, Maria. *The Autobiography of a Papago Woman*. Ed. Ruth Underhill. 1936. New York: Holt, 1979.

Chrystos. 'Askenet–Meaning "Raw" in My Language.' *InVersions: Writing by Dykes, Queers and Lesbians*. Ed. Betsy Warland. Vancouver: Press Gang, 1991. 237–47.

– *Not Vanishing*. Vancouver: Press Gang, 1988.

Churchill, Ward. *Indians Are Us? Culture and Genocide in Native North America*. Toronto: Between the Lines, 1994.

Clarke, Margaret. 'Revisioning April Raintree.' Rev. of *April Raintree*, by Beatrice Culleton. *Prairie Fire* 7.3 (Autumn 1986): 136–42.

Cliff, Michelle. 'Women Warriors: Black Writers Load the Canon.' *Voice Literary Supplement (Village Voice)* May 1990: 20–3.

Clifford, James. *The Predicament of Culture: Twentieth-Century Ethnography, Literature, and Art*. Cambridge, MA: Harvard UP, 1988.

Coke, A.A. Hedge. 'Two Views into Contemporary Native Poetry.' Armstrong, *Looking* 83–92.

Collins, Patricia Hill. *Black Feminist Thought: Knowledge, Consciousness, and the Politics of Empowerment*. New York: Routledge, 1991.

– 'Comment on Hekman's "Truth and Method: Feminist Standpoint Theory Revisited": Where's the Power?' *Signs* 22.2 (Winter 1997): 375–81.

Coltelli, Laura, ed. *Winged Words: American Indian Writers Speak*. Lincoln: U of Nebraska P, 1990.

Corbett, John. 'Tympanum of the Other Frog: Other Music #1.' The Other Side of Nowhere: Jazz, Improvisation, and Cultural Theory. Guelph Jazz Festival, Guelph, ON, 10 Sept. 1998.

Crosby, Marcia. 'Construction of the Imaginary Indian.' *By, For and About: Feminist Cultural Politics*. Ed. Wendy Waring. Toronto: Women's, 1994. 85–113.

Cruikshank, Julie. *The Social Life of Stories: Narrative and Knowledge in the Yukon Territory*. Lincoln: U of Nebraska P, 1998.

Cruikshank, Julie, comp., with Angela Sidney, Kitty Smith, and Annie Ned. *Life Lived like a Story: Life Stories of Three Yukon Native Elders*. Lincoln: U of Nebraska P, 1990.

Culleton [Mosionier], Beatrice. *April Raintree*. 1984. Winnipeg: Peguis, 1992.

– 'Beatrice Culleton.' Lutz, *Contemporary* 97–105.

– 'Images of Native People and Their Effects.' *School Libraries in Canada* Spring 1987: 47–52.

– *In Search of April Raintree*. Winnipeg: Pemmican, 1983.

– 'The Pain and Pleasure of That First Novel.' *Pemmican Journal* Winter 1981: 7–10.

– '"This Was Her Story": An Interview with Beatrice Culleton.' With J.M. Bridgeman. *Prairie Fire* 4.5 (July-Aug. 1983): 42–9.

– [pseud. A Proud Métis Woman]. 'What a Shame!' *Pemmican Journal* (Winter 1981): 22–5.

Cumming, Peter. '"The Only Dirty Book": The Rape of *April Raintree*.' Mosionier 307–22.

Currie, Noel Elizabeth. 'Jeannette Armstrong and the Colonial Legacy.' *Canadian Literature* 124–5 (Spring-Summer 1990): 138–52.

Dauenhauer, Nora Marks. *The Droning Shaman: Poems*. Haines, AK: Black Current, 1988.

de Lauretis, Teresa. 'Feminist Studies / Critical Studies: Issues, Terms and Contexts.' *Feminist Studies / Critical Studies*. Ed. Teresa de Lauretis. Bloomington: Indiana UP, 1986. 1–19.

– 'Upping the Anti (sic) in Feminist Theory.' *Conflicts in Feminism*. Ed. Marianne Hirsch and Evelyn Fox Keller. New York: Routledge, 1990. 255–70.

Deloria, Philip J. *Playing Indian*. New Haven: Yale UP, 1998.

Deloria, Vine, Jr. *Custer Died for Your Sins: An Indian Manifesto*. London: Macmillan, 1969.

Delpit, Lisa. *Other People's Children: Cultural Conflict in the Classroom*. New York: New, 1995.

Dickason, Olive Patricia. *Canada's First Nations: A History of Founding Peoples from Earliest Times*. Norman: U of Oklahoma P, 1992.

Donaldson, Laura. *Decolonizing Feminisms: Race, Gender, and Empire-Building*. Chapel Hill: U of North Carolina P, 1992.

Donovan, Kathleen N. *Feminist Readings of Native American Literature: Coming to Voice*. Tucson: U of Arizona P, 1998.

Dorris, Michael, and Louise Erdrich. *The Crown of Columbus*. New York: Harper, 1991.

duCille, Ann. 'The Occult of True Black Womanhood: Critical Demeanor and Black Feminist Studies.' *Signs* 19.3 (Spring 1994): 591–629.

– 'Postcolonialism and Afrocentricity: Discourse and Dat Course.' *The Black Columbiad: Defining Moments in African American Literature and Culture*. Ed. Werner Sollors and Maria Diedrich. Cambridge, MA: Harvard UP, 1994. 28–41.

Dumont, Marilyn. 'Popular Images of Nativeness.' Armstrong, *Looking* 45–50.

– *A Really Good Brown Girl*. London, ON: Brick, 1996.

Dwyer, Maggie. 'Native Woman Faces Turmoil: Aboriginal Culture Gracefully Explored.' Rev. of *Ravensong*, by Lee Maracle. *Winnipeg Free Press* 28 Nov. 1993: D18.

Eakin, Paul John. Foreword. Krupat, *For Those* xi–xxvi.

Egan, Susanna. '*The Book of Jessica*: The Healing Circle of a Woman's Autobiography.' *Canadian Literature* 144 (Spring 1995): 10–26.

Eigenbrod, Renate. 'The Oral in the Written: A Literature between Two Cultures.' *Canadian Journal of Native Studies* 15.1 (1995): 89–102.

Elam, Diane. *Feminism and Deconstruction: Ms. en abyme.* London: Routledge, 1994.

Emberley, Julia V. *Thresholds of Difference: Feminist Critique, Native Women's Writings, Postcolonial Theory.* Toronto: U of Toronto P, 1993.

Engel, Marian. Rev. of *In Search of April Raintree*, by Beatrice Culleton. *Sunday Star* (Toronto) 3 July 1983: G8.

Epstein, Steven. 'Gay Identity, Ethnic Identity: The Limits of Social Constructionism.' *Socialist Review* 17.3/4 (May–Aug. 1987): 9–54.

Erdrich, Louise. *Tracks.* New York: Holt, 1988.

Ermine, Willie. 'Aboriginal Epistemology.' *First Nations Education in Canada: The Circle Unfolds.* Ed. Marie Battiste and Jean Barman. Vancouver: UBC P, 1995. 101–12.

Essed, Philomena. *Understanding Everyday Racism: An Interdisciplinary Theory.* Newbury Park, CA: Sage, 1991.

Fee, Margery. 'Discourse Conventions in Fourth-World Fiction in English: The Examples of Ruby Slipperjack, Patricia Grace and Witi Ihimaera.' *Cross/Cultures* 23 (1996): 41–51.

– 'Romantic Nationalism and the Image of Native People in Contemporary English-Canadian Literature.' King, Calver, and Hoy 15–33.

– 'Upsetting Fake Ideas: Jeannette Armstrong's *Slash* and Beatrice Culleton's *April Raintree*.' *Canadian Literature* 124–5 (Spring-Summer 1990): 168–80.

Ferguson, Rob. '"Native Girls' Syndrome."' Rev. of *April Raintree*, by Beatrice Culleton. *City Magazine* (Winnipeg) Fall 1985: 41–2.

Findlay, Barbara. *With All of Who We Are: A Discussion of Oppression and Dominance.* Vancouver: Lazara, 1991.

Findley, Timothy. *Not Wanted on the Voyage.* Markham, ON: Viking, 1984.

Flax, Jane. 'Postmodernism and Gender Relations in Feminist Theory.' *Signs* 12.4 (1987): 621–43.

Foucault, Michel. *The Archaeology of Knowledge and The Discourse on Language.* Trans. A.M. Sheridan Smith. New York: Pantheon, 1972.

– 'Nietzsche, Genealogy, History.' *Language, Counter-Memory, Practice: Selected Essays and Interviews.* Ed. Donald Bouchard. Ithaca, NY: Cornell UP, 1977. 139–64.

– *Power/Knowledge: Selected Interviews and Other Writings, 1972–77.* Ed. Colin Gordon. Trans. Colin Gordon et al. New York: Pantheon, 1980.

- 'What Is an Author?' *Textual Strategies*. Ed. Josué V. Harari. Ithaca, NY: Cornell UP, 1979. 141–60.

Francis, Anne. Rev. of *In Search of April Raintree*, by Beatrice Culleton. *Quill and Quire* 49.11 (1983): 20.

Francis, Daniel. *The Imaginary Indian: The Image of the Indian in Canadian Culture*. Vancouver: Arsenal Pulp, 1992.

Frankenberg, Ruth. *White Women, Race Matters: The Social Construction of Whiteness*. Minneapolis: U of Minnesota P, 1993.

Friedman, Susan Stanford. 'Beyond White and Other: Relationality and Narratives of Race in Feminist Discourse.' *Signs* 21.1 (Autumn 1995): 1–49.

Gagnier, Regenia. *Subjectivities: A History of Self-Representation in Britain, 1832–1920*. New York: Oxford UP, 1991.

Garrod, Andrew, ed. 'Beatrice Culleton.' *Speaking for Myself: Canadian Writers in Interview*. St John's, NF: Breakwater, 1986. 79–95.

Gates, Henry Louis, Jr. '"Authenticity," or the Lesson of Little Tree.' *New York Times*, 24 Nov. 1991, sec. 7: 1, 26–30.

–, ed. *'Race,' Writing, and Difference*. Chicago: U of Chicago P, 1986.

Giovanni, Nikki. 'And Now for a Word from Our Sponsor: Civilization.' Joseph Warren Beach Lecture, U of Minnesota, 30 Apr. 1992.

Glaspell, Susan. 'A Jury of Her Peers.' *Modern Drama: Plays/Criticism/Theory*. Ed. W.B. Worthen. Fort Worth, TX: Harcourt, 1995. 212–21.

Godard, Barbara. 'Listening for the Silence: Native Women's Traditional Narratives.' King, Calver, and Hoy 133–58.

- 'The Politics of Representation: Some Native Canadian Women Writers.' *Canadian Literature* 124–5 (Spring-Summer 1990): 183–225.

Goldie, Terry. *Fear and Temptation: The Image of the Indigene in Canadian, Australian, and New Zealand Literature*. Kingston, ON: McGill-Queen's UP, 1989.

- 'The Majority Critic.' *Literature and Opposition*. Ed. Chris Worth, Pauline Nestor, and Marko Pavlyshyn. Clayton, Victoria, Australia: Centre for Comparative Literature and Cultural Studies, Monash U, 1994. 83–96.

Grant, Agnes. 'Contemporary Native Women's Voices in Literature.' *Canadian Literature* 124–5 (Spring-Summer 1990): 124–32.

- Rev. of *Honour the Sun*, by Ruby Slipperjack. *Studies in American Indian Literatures* 2nd Ser. 1.1 (Summer 1989): 34–6.

Halfe, Louise. *Bear Bones and Feathers*. Regina: Coteau, 1994.

Hall, Stuart. 'What Is This "Black" in Black Popular Culture?' *Black Popular Culture*. A Project by Michele Wallace. Ed. Gina Dent. Seattle: Bay, 1992. 21–33.

Harding, Sandra. 'Comment on Hekman's "Truth and Method: Feminist Standpoint Theory Revisited": Whose Standpoint Needs the Regimes of Truth and Reality?' *Signs* 22.2 (Winter 1997): 382–91.

Harjo, Joy. 'In Love and War and Music: An Interview with Joy Harjo.' With
Marilyn Kallet. *Kenyon Review* 15.3 (1993): 57–66.
– 'Q & A.' *Minnesota Daily* 1 Oct. 1992: 14.
Harris, Claire. 'Why Do I Write?' *Grammar of Dissent: Poetry and Prose by Claire
Harris, Marlene Nourbese Philip, Dionne Brand*. Ed. Carol Morrell.
Fredericton, NB: Goose Lane, 1994. 26–33.
Hartsock, Nancy C.M. 'Comment on Hekman's "Truth and Method: Feminist
Standpoint Theory Revisited": Truth or Justice?' *Signs* 22.2 (Winter 1997):
367–74.
Heilbrun, Carolyn G. 'Non-Autobiographies of "Privileged" Women: England
and America.' Brodzki and Schenck 62–76.
– *Writing a Woman's Life*. New York: Norton, 1988.
Hekman, Susan. 'Reply to Hartsock, Collins, Harding, and Smith.' *Signs* 22.2
(Winter 1997): 399–402.
– 'Truth and Method: Feminist Standpoint Theory Revisited.' *Signs* 22.2
(Winter 1997): 341–65.
Hildebrandt, Gloria. Rev. of *Honour the Sun*, by Ruby Slipperjack. *Prairie Fire*
11.3 (Autumn 1990): 94–5.
Hill, Kay. *Glooscap and His Magic: Legends of the Wabanaki Indians*. Toronto:
McClelland, 1963.
Hobsbawm, E.J. *Nations and Nationalism since 1780: Programme, Myth, Reality*.
Cambridge: Cambridge UP, 1990.
Hodne, Barbara, and Helen Hoy. '"Reading from the Inside Out": Jeannette
Armstrong's *Slash*.' *World Literature in English* 32.1 (Spring 1992): 66–87.
Hogan, Linda. 'The Two Lives.' Swann and Krupat, *I Tell* 231–49.
Holman, John. 'An Agonizing Tale of Two Métis Foster Children.' Rev. of *In
Search of April Raintree*, by Beatrice Culleton. *Windspeaker* 6 July 1990: 11.
hooks, bell. *Black Looks: Race and Representation*. Boston: South End, 1992.
– *Yearning: Race, Gender, and Cultural Politics*. Boston: South End, 1990.
Horne, Dee. *Contemporary American Indian Writing: Unsettling Literature*.
American Indian Studies Ser. 6. New York: Peter Lang, 1999.
– 'Listening to Silences in Ruby Slipperjack's *Silent Words*.' *Studies in Canadian
Literature / Etudes en littérature Canadienne* 23.2 (1998): 122–37.
– Rev. of *Traplines*, by Eden Robinson. *Canadian Literature* 156 (Spring 1998):
160–2.
Hoy, Helen. Rev. of *Fear and Temptation*, by Terry Goldie. *Ariel* 21 (Apr. 1990):
98–100.
Hulan, Renée, ed. *Native North America: Critical and Cultural Perspectives*.
Toronto: ECW, 1999.
– 'Some Thoughts on "Integrity and Intent" and Teaching Native Literature.'
Essays on Canadian Writing 63 (Spring 1998): 210–30.

Hungry Wolf, Adolf. *Blackfoot People: A Tribal Handbook.* Good Medicine Ser. 12. Invermere, BC: Good Medicine, 1975.

– *The Blood People, A Division of the Blackfoot Confederacy: An Illustrated Inter-pretation of the Old Ways.* New York: Harper, 1977.

– *Good Medicine in Glacier National Park: Inspirational Photos and Stories from the Days of the Blackfoot People.* Good Medicine Ser. 4. Golden, BC: Good Medicine, 1971.

– *Good Medicine: Life in Harmony with Nature.* Good Medicine Ser. 1. Golden, BC: Good Medicine, 1970.

– *Good Medicine, Traditional Dress Issue: Knowledge and Methods of Old Time Clothings.* Good Medicine Ser. 3. Golden, BC: Good Medicine, 1971.

– *Indian Summer.* Good Medicine Ser. 13. Invermere, BC: Good Medicine, 1975.

– *Teachings of Nature.* Good Medicine Ser. 14. Invermere, BC: Good Medicine, 1975.

Hungry Wolf, Adolf, and Beverly Hungry Wolf, comp. *Blackfoot Craftworker Book.* Good Medicine Ser. 15. 1977; 2nd rev. ed. Skookumchuck, BC: Good Medicine, 1983.

– *Children of the Sun: Stories by and about Indian Kids.* New York: Quill-Morrow, 1987.

–, comp. *Indian Tribes of the Northern Rockies.* Skookumchuck, BC: Good Medicine, 1989.

– *Shadows of the Buffalo: A Family Odyssey among the Indians.* New York: Morrow, 1983.

Hungry Wolf, Beverly. *Daughters of the Buffalo Women: Maintaining the Tribal Faith.* [Skookumchuck, BC]: Canadian Caboose, 1996.

– *The Ways of My Grandmothers.* New York: Morrow, 1980.

Isernhagen, Hartwig, ed. *Momaday, Vizenor, Armstrong: Conversations on American Indian Writing.* American Indian Literature and Critical Studies Ser. Norman: U of Oklahoma P, 1999.

Jacobus, Mary. *Reading Woman: Essays in Feminist Criticism.* New York: Columbia UP, 1986.

Jahner, Elaine. 'Metalanguages.' *Narrative Chance: Postmodern Discourse on Native American Indian Literatures.* Ed. Gerald Vizenor. Albuquerque: U of New Mexico P, 1989. 155–85.

Jamieson, Kathleen. *Indian Women and the Law in Canada: Citizens Minus.* Ottawa: Minister of Supply and Services, 1978.

JanMohamed, Abdul. 'The Economy of Manichean Allegory: The Function of Racial Difference in Colonialist Literature.' *Critical Inquiry* 12.1 (1985): 59–87.

Joe, Rita. *Song of Eskasoni: More Poems of Rita Joe*. Charlottetown, PE: Ragweed, 1988.

Johnston, Basil. 'Basil Johnston.' Lutz, *Contemporary* 229–39.

– 'How Do We Learn Language: What Do We Learn?' Murray and Rice 43–51.

Josie, Edith. *Here Are the News*. Toronto: Clarke, 1966.

Kaye/Kantrowitz, Melanie. 'Anti-Semitism, Homophobia, and the Good White Knight.' *off our backs* May 1982: 30–1.

Keeshig-Tobias, Lenore. 'An Emergent Voice.' Rev. of *Slash*, by Jeannette Armstrong. *Fuse* Mar.-Apr. 1988: 39.

– 'The Magic of Others.' Scheier, Sheard, and Wachtel 173–7.

– Rev. of *April Raintree*, by Beatrice Culleton. *Resources for Feminist Research* 15.1 (Mar. 1986): 58.

– 'White Lies?' *Saturday Night* Oct. 1990: 67–8.

– 'Woman, Native, Other.' Association of Canadian University Teachers of English / Association of Canadian and Quebec Literatures / Canadian Association for Commonwealth Literature and Language Studies panel, Kingston, ON, 28 May 1991.

Kincaid, James R. 'Who Gets to Tell Their Stories?' *New York Times Book Review* 3 May 1992: 1, 24–9.

King, Thomas. 'Godzilla vs. Post-Colonial.' *World Literature Written in English* 30.2 (1990): 10–16.

– *Green Grass, Running Water*. Toronto: Harper, 1993.

– Introduction. *All My Relations: An Anthology of Contemporary Canadian Native Fiction*. Ed. Thomas King. Toronto: McClelland, 1990. ix–xvi.

– Introduction. King, Calver, and Hoy 7–14.

– *Medicine River*. Toronto: Viking, 1989.

King, Thomas, Cheryl Calver, and Helen Hoy, eds. *The Native in Literature: Canadian and Comparative Perspectives*. Downsview, ON: ECW, 1987.

Kinsella, W.P. 'Yellow Scarf.' *Born Indian*. [Ottawa]: Oberon, 1981. 105–16.

Knapp, Millie. Rev. of *Traplines*, by Eden Robinson. *Aboriginal Voices* 4.1 (Jan./ Feb./Mar. 1997): 42.

Kristeva, Julia. *Nations without Nationalism*. Trans. Leon S. Roudiez. New York: Columbia UP, 1993.

– 'Woman Can Never Be Defined.' Trans. Marilyn A. August. *New French Feminisms*. Ed. Elaine Marks and Isabelle de Courtivron. New York: Schocken, 1981. 137–41.

Krotz, Larry. Rev. of *In Search of April Raintree*, by Beatrice Culleton. *United Church Observer* Nov. 1983: 63–4.

Krupat, Arnold. *For Those Who Come After: A Study of Native American Autobiography*. Berkeley: U of California P, 1985.

– *The Voice in the Margin: Native American Literature and the Canon.* Berkeley: U of California P, 1989.

LaRocque, Emma. 'The Colonization of a Native Woman Scholar.' *Women of the First Nations: Power, Wisdom, and Strength.* Ed. Christine Miller and Patricia Chuchryk, with Marie Smallface Marule, Brenda Manyfingers, and Cheryl Deering. Manitoba Studies in Native History IX. Winnipeg: U of Manitoba P, 1996. 11–18.

– *Defeathering the Indian.* Agincourt, ON: Book Society of Canada, 1975.

– 'Emma LaRocque.' Lutz, *Contemporary* 181–202.

– 'The Place of Native Writing in Canadian Intellectual Categories: Native Resistance Literature.' Association of Canadian College and University Teachers of English, Université de Québec à Montréal, 29 May 1995.

– 'Preface or Here Are Our Voices – Who Will Hear?' *Writing the Circle: Native Women of Western Canada.* Ed. Jeanne Perreault and Sylvia Vance. Edmonton: NeWest, 1990. xv–xxx.

– 'When the Other Is Me: Native Writers Confronting Canadian Literature.' *Issues in the North.* Vol. 1. Ed. Jill Oakes and Rick Riewe. Occasional Publication Number 40. Np: Canadian Circumpolar Institute, with U of Alberta and U of Manitoba, 1996. 115–24.

Laurence, Margaret. *The Diviners.* Toronto: McClelland, 1974.

Lauter, Paul. *Canons and Contexts.* New York: Oxford UP, 1991.

Leclair, Carole. 'Métis Wisdom: Learning and Teaching across the Cultures.' *Atlantis* 22.2 (Spring/Summer 1998): 123–6.

Lee, Sky. 'Yelling It: Women and Anger across Cultures.' Telling It Book Collective 177–85.

Lejeune, Philippe. *On Autobiography.* Ed. Paul John Eakin. Trans. Katherine Leary. Minneapolis: U of Minnesota P, 1989.

Lorde, Audre. *Sister Outsider.* Freedom, CA.: Crossing House, 1984.

Lugones, Maria. 'On the Logic of Pluralist Feminism.' *Feminist Ethics.* Ed. Claudia Card. Lawrence, KS: UP of Kansas, 1991. 35–44.

– 'Purity, Impurity, and Separation.' *Signs* 19.2 (Winter 1994): 458–79.

Lundgren, Jodi. '"Being a Half-breed": Discourses of Race and Cultural Syncreticity in the Works of Three Métis Women Writers.' *Canadian Literature* 144 (Spring 1995): 62–77.

Lutz, Hartmut, comp. *Contemporary Challenges: Conversations with Canadian Native Authors.* Saskatoon, SK.: Fifth House, 1991.

– 'Native Literatures in Canada Today: An Introduction.' *Zeitschrift der Gesellschaft für Kanada-Studien* 10.1 (1990): 27–47.

Mandel, Charles. 'Aboriginal Culture Corrupted: Gutsy Writer Probes Bleaker Aspects of Her Culture.' Rev. of *Traplines*, by Eden Robinson. *Edmonton Journal* 16 Mar. 1997: C4.

Maracle, Lee. *Bent Box*. Penticton, BC: Theytus, 2000.

– *Bobbi Lee: Indian Rebel*. 1975. 2nd ed. Toronto: Women's, 1990.

– 'Coming Out of the House: A Conversation with Lee Maracle.' With Jennifer Kelly. *Ariel* 25.1 (Jan. 1994): 73–88.

– 'Fork in the Road: A Story for Native Youth.' Rev. of *Slash*, by Jeannette Armstrong. *Fuse* July 1988: 42.

– *I Am Woman*. North Vancouver: Write-On, 1988.

– 'An Infinite Number of Pathways to the Centre of the Circle.' Williamson 166–78.

– 'Lee Maracle.' Lutz, *Contemporary* 169–79.

– 'Moving Over.' *Trivia* 14 (1988): 9–12.

– 'Native Women and Sovereignty.' University College, U of Toronto, 23 Nov. 1993.

– *Oratory*. North Vancouver: Gallerie, nd.

– *Ravensong*. Vancouver: Press Gang, 1993.

– *Sojourner's Truth and Other Stories*. Vancouver: Press Gang, 1990.

– *Sundogs*. Penticton, BC: Theytus, 1992.

Marchand, Philip. 'In the Steely Jaws of Life.' Rev. of *Traplines*, by Eden Robinson. *Toronto Star* 14 Dec. 1997: G20.

– 'World Turns to Author.' *Toronto Star* 19 Dec. 1997: C6–C7.

Marcus, James. 'Canadian Psychos.' Rev. of *Traplines*, by Eden Robinson. *New York Times* 24 Nov. 1996, sec. 7: 21.

Marken, Ron. '"There Is Nothing but White between the Lines": Parallel Colonial Experiences of the Irish and Aboriginal Canadians.' Hulan, *Native* 156–73.

McClintock, Anne. '"The Very House of Difference": Race, Gender, and the Politics of South African Women's Narrative in *Poppie Nongena*.' *The Bounds of Race: Perspectives on Hegemony and Resistance*. Ed. Dominick LaCapra. Ithaca. NY: Cornell UP, 1991. 196–230.

McGoogan, Ken. 'Fighting Words: Wiebe versus Kinsella Battle Raises Questions about Racism and Censorship in Literature.' *Calgary Herald* 10 Feb. 1990: C1.

Memmi, Albert. *The Colonizer and the Colonized*. Trans. Howard Greenfeld. Boston: Beacon, 1965.

Miller, Christopher L. 'Theories of Africans: The Question of Literary Anthropology.' Gates, *'Race'* 281–300.

Mohanty, Chandra Talpade. 'On Race and Voice: Challenges for Liberal Education for the 1990s.' *Cultural Critique* 14 (Winter 1989–90): 179–208.

Moher, Frank. 'April in the Métis Netherworld.' Rev. of *In Search of April Raintree*, by Beatrice Culleton. *Alberta Report* 10 Oct. 1983: 50.

Momaday, N. Scott. *The Names: A Memoir*. New York: Harper, 1976.

Monkman, Leslie. *A Native Heritage: Images of the Indian in English-Canadian Literature*. Toronto: U of Toronto P, 1981.

Monture-Angus, Patricia. *Journeying Forward: Dreaming First Nations' Independence*. Halifax, NS: Fernwood, 1999.

– 'Journeying Forward: First Nations Women.' University of Guelph, ON, 15 Feb. 2000.

– 'Native America and the Literary Tradition.' Hulan, *Native* 20–46.

– *Thunder in My Soul: A Mohawk Woman Speaks*. Foreword Mary Ellen Turpel. Halifax: Fernwood, 1995.

Moore, David L. 'Myth, History, and Identity in Silko and Young Bear: Postcolonial Praxis.' *New Voices in Native American Literary Criticism*. Ed. Arnold Krupat. Washington: Smithsonian Institution P, 1993. 370–95.

Moraga, Cherríe. Preface. Moraga and Anzaldúa xiii–xix.

Moraga, Cherríe, and Gloria Anzaldúa, eds. *This Bridge Called My Back: Writings by Radical Women of Color*. 1981. 2nd ed. New York: Kitchen Table, 1983.

Morris, Roberta. Rev. of *April Raintree*, by Beatrice Culleton. *Waves* 14.1–2 (Fall 1985): 112–13.

Morrison, Toni. *Playing in the Dark: Whiteness and the Literary Imagination*. Cambridge, MA: Harvard UP, 1992.

Mosionier, Beatrice Culleton. *In Search of April Raintree: Critical Edition*. Ed. Cheryl Suzack. Winnipeg: Portage and Main, 1999.

– *In the Shadow of Evil*. Penticton, BC: Theytus, 2000.

– 'The Special Time.' Mosionier, *In Search* 247–50.

Munro, Alice. *Lives of Girls and Women*. Toronto: McGraw, 1971.

Murray, David. *Forked Tongues*. Bloomington: Indiana UP, 1991.

Murray, Laura J., and Keren Rice, eds. *Talking on the Page: Editing Aboriginal Oral Texts*. Papers Given at the Thirty-Second Annual Conference on Editorial Problems, University of Toronto, 14–16 November 1996. Toronto: U of Toronto P, 1999.

Narayan, Uma. 'Contesting Cultures: "Westernization," Respect for Cultures, and Third-World Feminists.' *The Second Wave: A Reader in Feminist Theory*. Ed. Linda Nicholson. New York: Routledge, 1997. 396–414.

– 'Working across Differences.' *Hypatia* 3.2 (1988): 31–47.

Narogin, Mudrooroo. *Writing from the Fringe: A Study of Modern Aboriginal Literature*. Melbourne: Hyland House, 1990.

Neuman, Shirley. 'Autobiography: From Different Poetics to a Poetics of Difference.' *Essays on Life Writing: From Genre to Critical Practice*. Ed. Marlene Kadar. Toronto: U of Toronto P, 1992. 213–30.

Norrie, Helen. Rev. of *April Raintree*, by Beatrice Culleton. *Winnipeg Free Press* 11 May 1985: 63.

Opekokew, Delia, and Alan Pratt. 'The Treaty Right to Education in
  Saskatchewan.' *Windsor Yearbook of Access to Justice* 12 (1992): 3–51.
Ortiz, Simon J., ed. *Speaking for the Generations: Native Writers on Writing.*
  SunTracks, American Indian Literary Ser. 35. Tucson: U of Arizona P, 1998.
Osennontion [Marlyn Kane] and Skonaganleh:rá [Sylvia Maracle]. 'Our
  World.' *Canadian Woman Studies / Les cahiers de la femme* 10.2/3 (Summer/
  Fall 1989): 6–19.
Owens, Louis. 'Acts of Recovery: The American Indian Novel in the '80s.'
  Western American Literature 22.1 (Spring 1987): 53–7.
– 'American Indian Literature' panel, St Malo Book Fair, France, 19 May 1997.
– *Mixedblood Messages: Literature, Film, Family, Place.* American Indian Litera-
  ture and Critical Studies Ser. Norman: U of Oklahoma P, 1998.
– *Other Destinies: Understanding the American Indian Novel.* American Indian
  Literature and Critical Studies Ser. Norman: U of Oklahoma P, 1992.
Parker, Pat. *Movement in Black: The Collected Poetry of Pat Parker, 1961–1978.*
  1978. Foreword Audre Lorde. Intro. Judy Grahn. Ithaca, NY: Firebrand,
  1989.
P[aul]-D[ene], S[imon]. Rev. of *Traplines*, by Eden Robinson. *Aboriginal Voices*
  5.4 (Oct.-Dec. 1996): 58.
Penner, Derrick. 'Author Snares Rocket to First Success.' *Northern Sentinel*
  5 June 1996: 8.
Perreault, Jeanne. 'Writing Whiteness: Linda Griffiths' Race Subjectivity in *The
  Book of Jessica.*' *Essays on Canadian Writing* 60 (Dec. 1996 – Mar. 1997): 14–31.
Petrone, Penny. *Native Literature in Canada: From the Oral Tradition to the
  Present.* Toronto: Oxford UP, 1990.
Philip, Marlene Nourbese. *Frontiers: Essays and Writings on Racism and Culture.*
  Stratford, ON: Mercury, 1992.
Pratt, Mary Louise. *Imperial Eyes: Travel Writing and Transculturation.* London:
  Routledge, 1992.
Pratt, Minnie Bruce. 'Identity: Skin Blood Heart.' *Yours in Struggle: Three
  Feminist Perspectives on Anti-Semitism and Racism.* By Elly Bulkin, Minnie
  Bruce Pratt, and Barbara Smith. Brooklyn, NY: Long Haul, 1984. 11–63.
Purcell, Jeanne. Rev. of *April Raintree*, by Beatrice Culleton. *Humanist in
  Canada* 18.3 (Fall 1985): 35–6.
Rabinowitz, Paula. *Labor and Desire: Women's Revolutionary Fiction in Depres-
  sion America.* Chapel Hill: U of North Carolina P, 1991.
Razack, Sherene H. *Looking White People in the Eye: Gender, Race, and Culture in
  Courtrooms and Classrooms.* Toronto: U of Toronto P, 1998.
Report of the Royal Commission on Aboriginal Peoples. Ottawa: Minister of
  Supply and Services, 1996. 5 vols.

Revard, Carter. 'Traditional Osage Naming Ceremonies: Entering the Circle of Being.' Swann and Krupat, *Recovering* 446–66.

Robinson, Eden. *Monkey Beach*. Toronto: Knopf, 2000.

– 'Terminal Avenue.' *Aboriginal Voices* 4.5 (July-Sept. 1997): 36–9.

– *Traplines*. Toronto: Knopf, 1996.

Robinson, Gordon. *Tales of Kitimaat*. Illus. Vincent Haddelsey. Kitimat, BC: Sentinel, 1956.

Roe, Steve. Rev. of *Traplines*, by Eden Robinson. *Northern Review* 17 (1996): 192–4.

Rogers, Shelagh. 'Interview with Eden Robinson.' *Morningside*. CBC Radio. Toronto. 2 Oct. 1996.

Rosaldo, Renato. *Culture and Truth*. Boston: Beacon, 1989.

Rose, Wendy. 'Just What's All This Fuss about Whiteshamanism Anyway?' Schöler 13–24.

– 'Neon Scars.' Swann and Krupat, *I Tell* 251–61.

Rowse, Tim. *Australian Liberalism and National Character*. Malmsbury, Australia: Kibble, 1978.

Ruppert, James. *Mediation in Contemporary Native American Fiction*. Norman: U of Oklahoma P, 1995.

Rushin, Kate. *The Black Back-Ups*. Ithaca, NY: Firebrand, 1993.

Russell, Judith. Rev. of *April Raintree*, by Beatrice Culleton. *Queen's Quarterly* 94.1 (Spring 1987): 191–3.

Salat, M.F. 'Other Words, Other Worlds: Of Ruby Slipperjack.' Vevaina and Godard 74–89.

Sand, Cy-Thea. Rev. of *In Search of April Raintree*, by Beatrice Culleton. *Kinesis* Dec. 1983: 22.

Sangari, Kumkum. 'The Politics of the Possible.' *Cultural Critique* 7 (Fall 1987): 157–86.

Sarris, Greg. *Keeping Slug Woman Alive: A Holistic Approach to American Indian Texts*. Berkeley: U of California P, 1993.

Scheier, Libby. 'Phrase Fraud?' *Saturday Night* Nov. 1989: 89–92.

Scheier, Libby, Sarah Sheard, and Eleanor Wachtel, eds. *Language in Her Eye*. Toronto: Coach House, 1990.

Schöler, Bo, ed. *Coyote Was Here: Essays on Contemporary Native American Literary and Political Mobilization*. Aarhus, Denmark: Seklos, 1984.

Scollon, Ronald. *The Context of the Informant Narrative Performance: From Sociolinguistics to Ethnolinguistics at Fort Chipewyan, Alberta*. National Museum of Man Mercury Ser. Canadian Ethnology Service Paper No. 52. Ottawa: NMC, 1979.

Scollon, Ronald, and Suzanne B.K. Scollon. *Narrative, Literacy and Face in Interethnic Communication*. Norwood, NJ: Ablex, 1981.

Scott, Joan W. 'The Evidence of Experience.' *Critical Inquiry* 17 (Summer 1991): 773–97.

Shanley, Kate. 'Thoughts on Indian Feminism.' *A Gathering of Spirit*. Ed. Beth Brant. Toronto: Women's, 1988. 213–15.

Sigurdson, Norman. 'Métis Novel Overwhelming.' Rev. of *In Search of April Raintree*, by Beatrice Culleton. *Winnipeg Free Press* 30 July 1983: 43.

Silko, Leslie Marmon. 'Landscape, History, and the Pueblo Imagination.' *Women's Voices: Visions and Perspectives*. Ed. Pat C. Hoy, II, Esther H. Schor, and Robert DiYanni. New York: McGraw, 1990. 677–88.

Slapin, Beverly. *The Basic Skills Caucasian Americans Workbook*. Illus. Annie Esposito. Foreword Doris Seale. Berkeley: Oyate: 1994.

Slattery, Maureen. 'Border-Crossings: Connecting with the Colonized Mother in Maria Campbell's Life-Writings.' *Canadian Woman Studies / Les cahiers de la femme* 18.2/3 (Summer/Fall 1998): 139–44.

Slemon, Stephen. 'Unsettling the Empire: Resistance Theory for the Second World.' *World Literature Written in English* 30.2 (1990): 30–41.

Slipperjack, Ruby. *Honour the Sun*. Winnipeg: Pemmican, 1987.

– 'Ruby Slipperjack.' Lutz, *Contemporary* 203–15.

– *Silent Words*. Saskatoon, SK: Fifth House, 1992.

– *Weesquachak and the Lost Ones*. Penticton, BC: Theytus, 2000.

Smith, Barbara. 'Racism and Women's Studies.' Anzaldúa, *Making* 25–8.

Smith, Dorothy. 'Comment on Hekman's "Truth and Method: Feminist Standpoint Theory Revisited."' *Signs* 22.2 (Winter 1997): 392–8.

Smith, Paul. *Discerning the Subject*. Minneapolis: U of Minnesota P, 1988.

Smith, Sidonie. *Subjectivity, Identity, and the Body: Women's Autobiographical Practices in the Twentieth Century*. Bloomington: Indiana UP, 1993.

Sommer, Doris. '"Not Just a Personal Story": Women's *Testimonios* and the Plural Self.' Brodzki and Schenck 107–30.

Spacks, Patricia Meyer. 'Female Rhetorics.' *The Private Self: Theory and Practice of Women's Autobiographical Writings*. Ed. Shari Benstock. Chapel Hill: U of North Carolina P, 1988. 177–91.

Spears, Heather. *Poems Selected and New*. Toronto: Wolsak, 1998.

Spelman, Elizabeth. *Fruits of Sorrow: Framing Our Attention to Suffering*. Boston: Beacon, 1997.

– *Inessential Woman: Problems of Exclusion in Feminist Thought*. Boston: Beacon, 1988.

Spelman, Elizabeth, and Maria Lugones. 'Have We Got a Theory for You! Feminist Theory, Cultural Imperialism and the Demand for "The Woman's Voice."' *Women's Studies International Forum* 6.6 (1983): 573–81.

Spivak, Gayatri Chakravorty. *In Other Worlds: Essays in Cultural Politics*. New York: Routledge, 1988.

- 'Three Women's Texts and a Critique of Imperialism.' Gates, *'Race'* 262–80.
Srivastava, Aruna. 'Re-Imaging Racism: South Asian Canadian Women Writers.' Bannerji, *Returning* 103–21.
- 'Stealing Stories Still? Teaching "Native Literature."' Association of Canadian University Teachers of English, Kingston, ON, 27 May 1991.
Stedman, Raymond William. *Shadows of the Indian: Stereotypes in American Culture.* Norman: U of Oklahoma P, 1982.
Steed, Judy. 'A Double Odyssey, Full of Conflict and Drama.' Rev. of *The Book of Jessica*, by Maria Campbell and Linda Griffiths. *Toronto Star* 4 Nov. 1989: M3.
Suleri, Sara. *Meatless Days.* Chicago: U of Chicago P, 1989.
- 'Woman Skin Deep: Feminism and the Postcolonial Condition.' *Critical Inquiry* 18.4 (Summer 1992): 756–69.
Swann, Brian, and Arnold Krupat, eds. *I Tell You Now: Autobiographical Essays by Native American Writers.* Lincoln: U of Nebraska P, 1987.
–, eds. *Recovering the Word: Essays on Native American Literature.* Berkeley: U of California P, 1987.
Taylor, Drew Hayden. *Funny, You Don't Look Like One: Observations from a Blue-Eyed Ojibway.* Penticton, BC: Theytus, 1996.
Telling It Book Collective, ed. *Telling It: Women and Language across Cultures.* Vancouver: Press Gang, 1990.
Thom, Jo-Ann. 'The Effect of Readers' Responses on the Development of Aboriginal Literature in Canada: A Study of Maria Campbell's *Halfbreed*, Beatrice Culleton's *In Search of April Raintree*, and Richard Wagamese's *Keeper 'n Me*.' Mosionier 295–305.
Thompson, Dawn. 'Typewriter as Trickster: Revisions of Beatrice Culleton's *In Search of April Raintree*.' Vevaina and Godard 90–105.
Timson, Judith. 'Bad Boys and Indians: An Impressive Newcomer Writes on the Wild Side.' Rev. of *Traplines*, by Eden Robinson. *Maclean's* 9 Dec. 1996: 68.
Tobique Women's Group. *Enough Is Enough: Aboriginal Women Speak Out.* Ed. Janet Silman. Toronto: Women's, 1987.
Travis, Molly. '*Beloved* and *Middle Passage*: Race, Narrative and the Critic's Essentialism.' *Narrative* 2.3 (Oct. 1994): 179–200.
Trilling, Lionel. *Sincerity and Authenticity.* Cambridge, MA: Harvard UP, 1972.
Trinh, Minh-ha T. *Woman, Native, Other: Writing Postcoloniality and Feminism.* Bloomington: Indiana UP, 1989.
Trinh, Minh-ha T., with Annamaria Morelli. 'The Undone Interval.' *The Post-Colonial Question: Common Skies, Divided Horizons.* Ed. Iain Chambers and Lidia Curti. London: Routledge, 1996. 3–16.
Turner, Lillian M. Rev. of *April Raintree*, by Beatrice Culleton. *Canadian Materials for Schools and Libraries* 13.6 (Nov. 1985): 266–7.

Uttal, Lynet. 'Inclusion without Influence: The Continuing Tokenism of Women of Color.' Anzaldúa, *Making* 42–5.

Vangen, Kate Shanley. 'The Devil's Domain: Leslie Silko's *Storyteller*.' Schöler 116–23.

Van Luven, Lynne. 'Startling Promise.' Rev. of *Traplines*, by Eden Robinson. *Quill and Quire* Oct. 1996: 41.

Vevaina, Coomi S., and Barbara Godard, ed. *Intersexions: Issues of Race and Gender in Canadian Women's Writing*. New Delhi: Creative, 1996.

Vizenor, Gerald. *Bearheart: The Heirship Chronicles*. 1978. Minneapolis: U of Minnesota P, 1990.

– *Dead Voices: Natural Agonies in the New World*. Norman: U of Oklahoma P, 1992.

– 'Gerald Vizenor.' Coltelli 154–82.

– *Manifest Manners: Postindian Warriors of Survivance*. Hanover, NH: Wesleyan UP, 1994.

Wagamese, Richard. *Keeper 'n Me*. Toronto: Doubleday, 1994.

Warland, Betsy. '*Slash*/reflection.' *Proper Deafinitions*. Vancouver: Press Gang, 1990. 67–73.

Warley, Linda. 'National Subjects in Post-Colonial Australia: The Case of Sally Morgan's *My Place*,' U of Guelph, ON, 11 Nov. 1996.

Warrior, Robert Allen. *Tribal Secrets: Recovering American Indian Intellectual Traditions*. Minneapolis: U of Minnesota P, 1995.

Weaver, Sally. 'First Nations Women and Government Policy, 1970–92: Discrimination and Conflict.' *Changing Patterns: Women in Canada*. 2nd ed. Ed. Sandra Burt, Lorraine Code, and Lindsay Dorney. Toronto: McClelland, 1993. 92–150.

White, Leslie. 'Autobiography of an Acoma Indian.' *New Material from Acoma. Bureau of American Ethnology* 136 (1943): 326–37.

'Whose Voice Is It Anyway?' *Books in Canada* Jan.-Feb. 1991: 11–20.

Wiebe, Armin. Rev. of *In Search of April Raintree*, by Beatrice Culleton. *Prairie Fire* 4.5 (July-Aug. 1983): 49–51.

Wilkes, Maria D. *Little House in Brookfield*. Illus. Dan Andreasen. New York: Harper, 1996.

Williamson, Janice, ed. *Sounding Differences: Conversations with Seventeen Canadian Women Writers*. Toronto: U of Toronto P, 1993.

Wilson, Paul. Rev. of *In Search of April Raintree*, by Beatrice Culleton. *Books in Canada* 13 (Feb. 1984): 30.

Wissler, Clark. *A Blackfoot Source Book. Papers by Clark Wissler*. 1910–18. Ed. David Hurst Thomas. New York: Garland, 1986.

Womack, Craig S. *Red on Red: Native American Literary Separatism*. Minneapolis: U of Minnesota P, 1999.

Wong, Hertha Dawn. *Sending My Heart Back across the Years: Tradition and Innovation in Native American Autobiography*. New York: Oxford UP, 1992.

Yee, May. 'Finding the Way Home through Issues of Gender, Race, Class.' Bannerji, *Returning* 3–44.

Young-Ing, Greg, ed. *IndigeCrit: Aboriginal Perspectives on Aboriginal Literature and Art*. Penticton, BC: Theytus, forthcoming.

Zwicker, Heather. 'Canadian Women of Color in the New World Order: Marlene Nourbese Philip, Joy Kogawa, and Beatrice Culleton Fight Their Way Home.' *Canadian Women Writing Fiction*. Ed. Mickey Pearlman. Jackson: UP of Mississippi, 1993. 142–54.

Index